THE PRAGMATIC WHITMAN

REIMAGINING AMERICAN DEMOCRACY

STEPHEN JOHN MACK

In this surprisingly timely book, Stephen Mack examines Whitman's particular and fascinating brand of patriotism: his far-reaching vision of democracy. For Whitman, loyalty to America was loyalty to democracy. Since the idea that democracy is not just a political process but a social and cultural process as well is associated with American pragmatism, Mack relies on the pragmatic tradition of Emerson, James, Dewey, Mead, and Rorty to demonstrate the ways in which Whitman resides in this tradition.

Mack analyzes Whitman's democratic vision both in its parts and as a whole; he also describes the ways in which Whitman's vision evolved throughout his career. He argues that Whitman initially viewed democratic values such as individual liberty and democratic processes such as collective decision-making as fundamental, organic principles, free and unregulated. But throughout the 1860s and 1870s Whitman came to realize that democracy entailed processes of human agency that are

STEPHEN MACK received his Ph.D. in English and American literature from the University of Southern California, where he currently teaches advanced writing.

THE IOWA

WHITMAN

SERIES

Ed Folsom,
series editor

The
Pragmatic
Whitman

Reimagining American Democracy

STEPHEN JOHN MACK

UNIVERSITY OF IOWA PRESS Ψ Iowa City

University of Iowa Press, Iowa City 52242

Copyright © 2002 by the University of Iowa Press
Printed in the United States of America

Design by Richard Hendel

http://www.uiowa.edu/uiowapress

The publication of this book was generously supported by
the University of Iowa Foundation.

Printed on acid-free paper

Library of Congress Cataloging-in-Publication Data
Mack, Stephen John, 1952–
The pragmatic Whitman: reimagining American democracy /
by Stephen John Mack.
p.   cm.—(The Iowa Whitman series)
Includes bibliographical references (p.   ) and index.
ISBN 0-87745-822-7 (cloth)
1. Whitman, Walt, 1819–1892—Political and social views.
2. Whitman, Walt, 1819–1892—Knowledge—United States.
3. Political poetry, American—History and criticism.   4. Patriotic
poetry, American—History and criticism.   5. United States—In
literature.   6. Democracy in literature.   I. Title.   II. Series.

PS3242.P64 M33 2002
811'.3—dc21   2002021137

02   03   04   05   06   C   5   4   3   2   1

For June and J. J.,
with whom I am privileged to
share life's adventure and
"travel by maps yet unmade"

Our future may lie beyond our vision, but it is not completely beyond our control. It is the shaping impulse of America that neither fate nor nature nor the irresistible tides of history, but the work of our own hands, matched to reason and principle, will determine destiny. There is pride in that, even arrogance, but there is also experience and truth. In any event, it is the only way to live.

Robert F. Kennedy
To Seek a Newer World

Contents

Acknowledgments

Befitting a work about democracy and the poet who "contains multitudes," this book would not be possible but for the kind and thoughtful contributions of many people. First, I am enormously grateful to Jay Martin at the University of Southern California. Jay's help with the scope and design of this study was invaluable. As a scholar of extraordinary depth in a variety of fields from psychoanalysis to literature to theory, he helped me sharpen the connections I attempt to make among the many seemingly disparate elements I discuss in these pages. His constant friendship and support have been more valuable still; he has been an inexhaustible source of inspiration, and whenever I felt the need of some permission to explore unfamiliar terrain, he has been there to grant it. I was also fortunate to have the guidance and encouragement of three other fine professors. Ron Gottesman's keen eye and unsparing criticism helped rid the initial manuscript of much of its imprecise prose; in the process, he also taught me much about the responsibilities of membership in the academic community. Tim Gustafson's encyclopedic knowledge of rhetorical history, and especially his deep appreciation for the ideals intoned in American political rhetoric, was both a rich source of instruction and an important moral guidepost. And Howard Gillman's insights on American political history and pragmatic philosophy were instrumental in helping me deepen my understanding of those two subjects.

The project was considerably improved as it moved through the review process at the University of Iowa Press. I am especially grateful to Ed Folsom for pointing out many of the arguments that were either unproductive or underdeveloped, as well as suggesting a number of very useful connections to the critical literature. I owe him a considerable debt for his help in bringing this book into focus, and I am honored that he has chosen it for inclusion in his series on Walt Whitman. I am thankful as well for Mark Bauerlein's sound and meticulous advice on matters of style and concept. Throughout this process, I have also imposed on a number of friends and colleagues to read (and sometimes reread) specific chapters or sections. My heartfelt thanks to Jim Kincaid, Ryan Stark, Spence Olin, and Wayne Faber — people who bore the burden of friendship with remarkable grace while offering a countless number of important suggestions. Charlotte Wright and Robert Burchfield worked tirelessly to save me from embarrassment and put the manuscript in its final form. And finally, I am deeply appreciative of Holly Carver, who, as a wise and energetic leader of the University of Iowa Press, transformed these words into a book.

Abbreviations

CRE
> Walt Whitman, *Leaves of Grass: Comprehensive Reader's Edition*, ed. Harold W. Blodgett and Scully Bradley. New York: New York University Press, 1965.

EN
> John Dewey, *Experience and Nature*. 1929. La Salle: Open Court, 1989.

LV
> Walt Whitman, *Leaves of Grass: A Textual Variorum of the Printed Poems*, ed. Scully Bradley, Harold W. Blodgett, Arthur Golden, and William White. 3 vols. New York: New York University Press, 1980.

PW
> Walt Whitman, *Prose Works 1892*, ed. Floyd Stovall. 2 vols. New York: New York University Press, 1963.

QC
> John Dewey, *The Quest for Certainty*. New York: Holt, 1922.

Introduction

The Evolution of Whitman's Democratic Vision

Walt Whitman has always been our most embarrassing poet. Our perceptions of his offenses change from generation to generation, but at no time have the words of America's "representative poet" failed to provoke some degree of displeasure, squeamishness, or disgust. Some of his earliest critics were simply confused by the stylistic innovations of his barbaric yawp or put off by the immodesty.[1] Other, more perceptive readers — readers able either to understand or appreciate these elements — sometimes objected to the poet's sexual frankness. When Emerson famously implored Whitman not to publish his explicit "Children of Adam" poems celebrating heterosexual love, he was representing not only his own sense of decency but that of much of American culture, then as well as now. And there has always been the problem of Whitman's homoerotic poetry — an embarrassment deep enough, it seems, to motivate an otherwise credible biographer, Emory Holloway, to redeem the poet by attempting to authenticate Whitman's own spurious account of a mistress and illegitimate children.[2] In every generation there are at least some Whitman partisans who seem to wish that his "offence," as W. D. Howells put it, "will some day [be] remove[d] for him" by "the judicious pencil of the editor."[3]

I believe that a wiser appraisal of Whitman's offenses, however, suggests that they are not so much his but our own. The history of hostile responses to Whitman tracks, in many ways, the history of our own moral, political, and cultural failures — failure to take full advantage of a new and liberating literary language, failure to give an honest accounting of our own sexuality, failure to recognize the humanity of gay and lesbian people or to appreciate the moral significance of that humanity. Likewise, the history of critical rereadings of Whitman is in part the history of our own moral maturation. To say that American culture is in many ways "catching up to Whitman" is to pay ourselves a significant compliment. It is in this context that I believe we would do well to reexamine Whitman's latest offense — patriotism. What we now tend to think of as Whitman's jingoism or chauvinism was not likely to worry his nineteenth-century contemporaries. He was, after all, right in the mainstream on that issue. The same can probably be said for readers in the first half of the twentieth century. In post-Vietnam, post-Watergate America, however, Whitman's seemingly mawkish celebrations of the United States become one of those problematic features of his works that teachers and critics read past or explain away. This is even true for critics who are interested in Whitman precisely because they find aspects of his political vision so compelling. In his sensitive reading of Whitman's depiction of democratic individualism, for example, the political philosopher George Kateb makes a point of distancing himself— and even Whitman— from the poet's nationalism: "For me," he writes, "Whitman's greatness does not lie in his pursuit of an image of a democratic nationality. . . . Nationhood is too close to a conception of group identity: a shared pride in tribal attributes rather than in adherence to a distinctive and principled human self-conceptualization that may one day be available to persons everywhere in the world."[4] For Kateb, as for many other critics, Whitman's virtues as a political visionary make forgiving his nationalism worth the effort.

The notions that national pride is an evil and that its presence in Whitman's work is an embarrassment are not convictions shared by all critics. Charles Altieri, for instance, asserts that "the primary social reason we need concepts of a nation is that no other social unit can impose the kinds of responsibilities that enable us to address the needs and sufferings of large classes of people." In that light, he argues that Whitman's particular kind of nationalism is attractive because it focuses on "forms of responsibility to other persons" while also emphasizing "significant ways of pursuing selves we can become."[5] In *Achieving Our Country*, Richard Rorty also argues for Whitman's form of nationalism. Rorty acknowledges that excessive and uncritical patriotism may lead to "bellicosity" or, more dangerous, a taste for "imperialism"; nevertheless, he asserts that national pride plays the same role that self-respect plays for individuals. It is, he writes, "a necessary condition for self-improvement. . . . Emotional involvement with one's country— feelings of intense shame or of glowing pride aroused by various parts of its history, and by various present-day national policies— is necessary if political deliberation is to be imaginative and productive." For Rorty, American patriotism means identifying oneself emotionally and intellectually with classic American democratic values and ideals. Loyalty to America, in this sense, is loyalty to a utopian democratic creed—a "civic religion," as writers such as William James, Herbert Croly, John Dewey, and, of course, Walt Whitman viewed it. In practice, such patriotism means permitting oneself genuine pride in those moments in history when Americans were able to translate their ideals into successful public policy. But even more important, it means laying legitimate claim to those democratic values and ideals—both as a resource for imagining new policy goals and as a powerful rhetorical tool to aid in achieving them. In a sense, Rorty urges Americans to accept what Martin Luther King Jr. might have called ownership of their country and its heritage; Rorty does not cite King, but it was just such a view of American ideals that permitted the civil rights leader to proclaim that "when the architects of our republic wrote the magnificent words of the Constitution and the Declaration of Independence, they were signing a promissory note to which every American was to fall heir." Only by seeing America as a magnificent promise was he able to march in 1963 to the American capital to demand its fulfillment.[6]

In recent years, the kind of idealism and patriotism that King represented has fallen largely out of fashion, especially among progressive writers and academics. As a result, much of the intellectual talent that might be used to envision an America worth making is unused or misspent. Indeed, by rejecting faith in America and the promise of its ideals, Rorty argues, social critics on the Left have given up their traditional role as agents for change in order to become "spectator[s] and to leave the fate of the United States to the operation of nonhuman forces." As spectators, "[t]he academic Left has no projects to propose to America, no vision of a country to be achieved by building a consensus on the need for specific reforms. Its members no longer feel the force of James's and Croly's rhetoric. The civic religion seems to them narrow-minded and obsolete nationalism."[7] Our best hope for reinvigorating progressive thought in America, Rorty maintains, is in returning to that civic religion. Or, to put it another way, we need to look once again at Whitman's patriotism and the civic religion that inspires it. Then, perhaps, we might treat our embarrassment over Whitman's patriotism in the same way we might have urged earlier generations to treat the source of their embarrassment: not as evidence of some shortcoming of the poet's but rather as a symptom of their profound and debilitating failure of vision.

In this book, I intend to make just such an examination of the civic religion behind Whitman's patriotism. The essence of that civic religion, the real object of his patriotism, is his own far-reaching vision of democracy. For Whitman, loyalty to America was loyalty to democracy—or as the poet himself put it in *Democratic Vistas*, he uses "the words America and democracy as convertible terms" (*PW* 363). My primary arguments concerning Whitman's democracy will proceed along two basic lines. First, I attempt to explicate the many parts of Whitman's democratic vision and describe how those parts fit together as a whole; second, I attempt to explain the processes that shaped and reshaped that vision through the course of Whitman's poetic career. I argue that Whitman viewed democracy as a comprehensive description of human society and culture, analogous (at least) to the fundamental forces of nature. He believed that democratic values such as individual liberty and self-governance and democratic processes such as collective decision-making are not just aspects of political life but also manifestations of principles that operate throughout the cosmos. I then argue that his vision of democracy did not come to him whole, fully formed, but developed in stages, each one forged in struggle and complicating the one that came before it. The theme of that development can be quickly summarized as a movement from freedom to governance; that is, when Whitman first articulates his vision of democracy in 1855, he is essentially concerned with describing and celebrating a free, unregulated cosmos. But through the 1860s and 1870s, as biographical events trigger changes in his poetic style and historical events force him to reevaluate American social realities, his vision turns decidedly prescriptive, evolving into a complex primer on democratic self-government.[8]

One of the consequences of this shift is that when Whitman's early and late works are viewed together, the word "democracy" winds up naming a number of different and even contradictory ideas. It is all material and at the same time all spiritual. Democracy is the warrant nature gives for human freedom as well as the protocol it establishes for disciplined living. It both describes the universe as it actually is and prescribes the process that can make it so. Democracy is the very way we imagine our relations to one another and to the material and spiritual world in which we live. It is not a single aspect of a larger organic vision: it is the organism itself and the quality of relations that binds it together.[9] But in a sense, the two lines of argumentation converge on this point, for in the final analysis, the substance of Whitman's vision and the processes by which it develops are inextricable. I argue that the vision that finally crystallizes by the time he writes *Democratic Vistas* (1871) is more complex and dynamic than its original counterpart because it is grounded in a necessity to reconcile the tensions it incorporates. If on one level democracy implies antithetical ideas (say, an individual's complete freedom to think and decide for oneself and the right of the community to bind that individual to majoritarian will), then on a deeper level democracy must mean the process by which its many contradictions are adjudicated.

The notion that democracy is more than a political process, that it is a social and cultural process as well, is an idea often associated with American pragmatic thinkers, and so throughout this exegesis of Whitman's democratic poetry, I will lean heavily on the philosophical tradition of American pragmatism, especially such pragmatists as Ralph Waldo Emerson, William James, John Dewey, George Herbert Mead, and Richard Rorty. One of my intentions in this study is to demonstrate, more thoroughly than other authors have previously tried, how Whitman participates in that tradition and how the insights of other pragmatist thinkers can help to produce worthwhile readings of his poetry and, by extension, his democratic poetics.[10] There are three reasons that pragmatic philosophy offers an especially useful tool for the study of Whitman. First, like Whitman, pragmatism's major thinkers have been particularly interested in reconciling the material discoveries of science (however relative and contingent we understand those discoveries to be) with the deepest cultural— that is, political and moral— problems of the day. Second, again like Whitman, many of pragmatism's leading thinkers have sought a more expansive meaning for democracy, attempting to justify it as a metaphysical system that illuminates the various consequences that follow from the choices we make while organizing and living our lives. And third, both Whitman and pragmatism are quintessentially American; pragmatic philosophy shares with the Whitmanian vision an intimate awareness of the unique ways that cultural and material relationships have patterned themselves in American society— and, more important, both use their knowledge of these "realities" to ground prescriptions for American life that are ultimately prophetic and redemptive.

In form, my discussion of Whitman's democracy is a story: I describe the evolution of his vision of democracy from its 1855 articulation of the metaphysical conditions that privilege human freedom to his ultimate understanding in the 1870s that, paradoxically, those same metaphysical conditions necessitate, even entail, a principle of governance. I organize this narrative into three stages. In part I, I lay out the metaphysical foundations of Whitman's democracy as they are found in the first two editions of *Leaves of Grass*, 1855 and 1856. In part II, I examine how the two most significant events of Whitman's midlife, his 1859 and 1860 sexual crisis and the Civil War, transformed his democratic poetics in "Sea-Drift," "Calamus," *Drum-Taps*, and *Sequel to Drum-Taps*. And in part III, I explore Whitman's mature vision in *Democratic Vistas* and conclude with some observations on its moral and political implications for contemporary America.

The elaboration of Whitman's metaphysics in part I begins in chapter 1 with a discussion of how Whitman uses "pragmatic" language to construct his democratic mythology. Focusing on particular sections of the poem he eventually named "Song of Myself," I demonstrate how Whitman's explicit appropriation of ancient mythological constructs actually functions to set the rules for verifying the truth claims of his own vision.[11] In chapter 2, I take up the issue of Whitman's democratic conception of selfhood. I explain why, contrary to common critical assumption, Whitman's philosophy of identity is not dualistic in the classical sense. As poems such as "Song of Myself" and "There Was a Child Went Forth" make clear, Whitman understood the self as fundamentally material and social. In chapter 3, I explicate the elements of Whitman's open universe, his democratic "Kosmos." Continuing the discussion of "Song of Myself" while drawing additional evidence from such works as "Crossing Brooklyn Ferry," I argue that by imagining a universe that is both material and infinitely expanding, Whitman constructs a cosmological warrant for democratic freedom. But as I show in chapter 4, it is also a laissez-faire universe. Whitman's cosmos is only free because he has rid it of all material danger — what John Dewey called the precariousness of life. There, corporal death is merely one more material change in an endless and benign continuum of change; freedom is guaranteed by existential conditions; and human choice-making is irrelevant. Whitman's universe moves inexorably toward some ill-defined good as if guided by an invisible hand.

In part II, I explore the way two events — Whitman's sexual crisis of 1859 and 1860 and the Civil War — transformed his poetics and his vision of democracy. As we see in the discussion of his "Sea-Drift" and "Calamus" poems in chapter 5, Whitman discovered that the poetics that made the depiction of laissez-faire possible were completely inadequate to the task of managing his own personal crisis. The poet needed a language of agency. Whitman develops agency in the "Calamus" poems by using his verse to restructure, in pragmatic fashion, a textualized model of his own identity. The importance of this development transcends whatever therapeutic value it held for Whitman himself, for, in so doing, he incorporated into his democratic vision the dynamics of individual choice-making essential to democratic practice. This development bears fruit when Whitman confronts the second crisis, the Civil War. Implicit in a poetics of human agency is an understanding that human behavior is neither determined by nor perfectly analogous to natural events — as laissez-faire theories suggest. This becomes poignantly clear when the poet confronts the calamity of the Civil War, a calamity that could not be reconciled with the security of a laissez-faire universe. Then, as will be seen in the discussion of *Drum-Taps* and *Sequel to Drum-Taps* in chapter 6, the poet's democratic vision subsumes a new awareness: that the successes and failures that attend the struggle to manage human destiny are not reducible to natural processes but belong to the hybrid category *history*. This is a germinal insight for Whitman. To recognize human history as a distinct category is to confront what Sidney Hook calls the tragic sense of life, the recognition that all human choice-making necessarily entails difficult choices, choices against some good in favor of another.

Whitman's mature reflections, the focus of part III, pivot on the recognition that human destiny is largely the product of human effort— that a truly humane society can only be shaped by intelligent human efforts to govern the forces that would otherwise govern them. Whitman's challenge was to discover how that truth might be reconciled with the affirmations of freedom that originally informed his poetry. Looking backward, he had to repossess all that he could of the democratic vision that had enlivened the 1855 edition of *Leaves of Grass*. But looking forward, he had to reimagine the fundamental dynamic of that vision and build in the mechanism by which a fuller democracy might be achieved absent the workings of laissez-faire nature's invisible hand. In *Democratic Vistas*, the focus of chapter 7, Whitman responds to this dilemma by articulating a theory of democratic culture, one that envisions the creation of a new kind of democratic individual nurtured by a cultural and spiritual democracy. It is here that Whitman finally brings together all the strands of his democratic thought: the social and material self, the cosmically sponsored freedom, the imperative of human agency, the consequences of human history. In Whitman's mature conception of democracy, all of these elements become organically interconnected as the poet defines democracy as a cultural— and ultimately, a religious — practice by which the everyday experience of subjectivity can be transcended so as to indulge in an imaginative experience of human sociality.

The importance of Whitman's democracy— of any such sweeping conception of human organization— is to be found in the moral quality of whatever demands it makes upon those who take its principles to heart. In this book's conclusion, I suggest what those demands are. To understand the moral and political demands that Whitman's vision entails we need to look to the forces that shaped its growth. Whitman's visionary development both parallels and anticipates much in the political evolution of the nation whose song he would sing. As the dominant political ideology in the United States moved from the laissez-faire doctrine of freedom prevalent in Jacksonian America to the philosophical assumptions that underpinned the growing regulative functions of activist government, so, too, did Whitman's democratic vision move from one assuming uncritical faith in laissez-faire to one increasingly reliant upon the enlightened work of a democratic nation.[12] The forces that animated these parallel developments in the nation's governing ideology and the poet's prophetic vision were, of course, different. For Whitman, visionary development came in response to dislocations that were not only social and political but highly personal as well, while for the nation, ideological development came largely as a response to the dislocations triggered by industrialization. Still, for both Whitman and American political thought generally, the ideological elements of development are essentially the same: faith in radical, individualist freedom and belief in the possibilities of active, centralized governance.

The idea of individual freedom did not die as a political ideal, supplanted by notions of the regulated state. To be sure, both live on as the great antinomies of the American democratic tradition. The particular virtue of Whitman's vision is that it strives to bring these philosophical antagonists into relation.[13] Whitman does not propose a political morality that demonizes either individual freedom or collective self-governance; he presents them instead as the polar points of an enduring political and spiritual tension — antithetical but mutually dependent abstractions. As Whitman sees it, all public debate in a democratic society is necessarily structured by the opposing ideals of liberty and governance. It is when these dynamic ideals are seen to authorize competing policy choices within the public debate that their meanings are redefined and relative values reformulated. Thus, he teaches, we continuously imagine new possibilities for human freedom while thinking through the concrete means to achieve them.

The Metaphysics of Democracy
Leaves of Grass, 1855 and 1856

*[I]f to construct democratic institutions is our aim,
how then shall we construe and interpret the natural
environment and natural history of humanity in order
to get an intellectual warrant for our endeavors[?] . . .
Is the world as an object of knowledge at odds with
our purposes and efforts? Is it merely neutral and
indifferent? . . . Or is its nature such that it is at least
willing to cooperate, that it not only does not say us nay,
but gives us an encouraging nod?*
— *John Dewey, "Philosophy and Democracy"*

1

"My Voice Goes after What
My Eyes Cannot Reach"
*Pragmatic Language and the
Making of a Democratic Mythology*

Any credible discussion of Walt Whitman's democratic vision — indeed, of any political philosophy cast in poetry — must necessarily begin with an examination of that thinker's approach to language. It is one of the great truisms of Whitman criticism that his revolutionary language style and his revolutionary politics are inextricably linked. Whitman's poetics and politics are connected symbiotically.[1] We first see this mutual dependence of language and democracy in the extraordinarily comprehensive way that Whitman conceptualizes democracy. Because the poet regards democracy as the central organizing principle of nature — including all things humanly natural, such as culture — his theory of language is but an extension of his vision of natural democracy. That is, democracy grounds his theory of language. Conversely, his democracy depends upon language in that his comprehensive vision of democracy is so unique that it could not even be articulated, it seems, were it not for the special features of Whitman's poetic theory, which, in turn, they justify.

Not only is language a central concern of Whitman's democracy, it is also a concern of any conception of liberal democracy. Democracy engages a number of linguistically oriented issues. For example, its foundation in such verbal instruments as contracts and constitutions inevitably begs a host of questions about what interpretative theories should govern the reading of these documents. Even more deeply, democracy would seem to privilege a certain theoretical assumption about language: as it is commonly conceived, democracy asserts the primacy of natural and human (in other words, secular) authority. It implicitly yet unavoidably stands as a challenge to all claims to authority rooted in mystical and supernatural representations — especially the positivist view of language that permits "literal" interpretations of sacred texts while also inoculating those texts from criticism. (This same challenge requires scrutiny of Whitman's own political vision and its reliance on a special kind of language — a critical burden intensified, moreover, by the most commonplace assumptions of modern critical theory, which not only reject the possibility of unmediated, positive language but the possibility of politically disinterested language as well.) For the critic, then, as for the poet, to examine the meaning of democracy is to consider the unique grammar that would govern the construction of that meaning.

At first blush, Whitman's language theory may strike the contemporary critical reader as highly problematic, especially when it is viewed as a mere elaboration of theories prevalent in the nineteenth century. For example, in 1855, when Whitman wrote in the first preface to *Leaves of Grass* that the "greatest poet has less a marked style and is more the channel of thoughts and things without increase or diminution, and is the free channel of himself," he was hardly challenging his generation's basic assumptions about the unmediated nature of language; to the contrary, he was attempting to wrench new insights from those beliefs, attempting to advance some of the deepest thinking of his time (*CRE* 719). After all, Emerson, in the vanguard of American romanticism, had already taught that "words are signs of natural facts."[2] All that was left to Whitman, it seems, was to specify the American cast of those natural facts that the poet utters. To the modern reader, such innocent faith in the possibility of unmediated speech is more likely to look like elegant naïveté. The envelope of language theory has been pushed in the exact opposite direction. Richard Rorty argues that "the notion of knowledge as accurate representation, made possible by special mental processes, and intelligible through a general theory of representation, needs to be abandoned."[3] Rorty's argument now reads more like a description of current epistemological assumptions than the bold claim it was only a few years ago. In this context, Whitman's "language experiment" may read more like an ironic demonstration in the futility of trying to accurately represent the real. Inevitably, this sharp contrast between nineteenth- and twentieth-century beliefs about language requires, at the very least, that modern critics approach Whitman with an extremely high degree of skepticism.

But when we push beyond Whitman's theoretical formulations to his actual poetic practice, a far savvier poetics may come into view. His poetics may constitute a pragmatically viable democratic metaphysics and an eminently useful political vision as well. Still, to appreciate the significance of Whitman's democracy, does one need to play the scofflaw of contemporary theoretical assumptions concerning the contingency of language or the problems of representation? I do not believe so, and in this chapter I will explore the possibility that Whitman's metaphysics are in fact convincing for the very reason that they do not conform to the explicit dictates of his own poetic theory.

Rather, Whitman's poetry implicitly seems to demonstrate an awareness of the arbitrary nature of linguistic communication, of the futility of attempting to verify the truthfulness of words by how accurately they correspond to non-linguistic fact. In Whitman's verse, words appear to function pragmatically, as tools for the construction of a "reality" that is not bound by the constraints of correspondence theory. Such an awareness of the constructed nature of all representation would clearly afford Whitman enormous freedom; it would allow him to invent a democratic mythology, a metanarrative that functions as a paradigmatic expression of his larger democratic theory while simultaneously appropriating and subordinating the mythological narratives of competing power arrangements. Ultimately, such a pragmatic language would necessarily reveal itself in an equally pragmatic verification regime. And so, mindful of William James's great pragmatic insight that "truth happens to an idea," I will test the proposition that, in effect, Whitman argues that the validity of his democratic vision rests not on its correspondence to known fact or in its ability to explain the present but on its capacity to produce a worthwhile future.

Whitman's Language Experiment

If Whitman did adopt a pragmatic mode of poetic expression, it was probably necessitated by his reluctant conclusion that, ultimately, words really cannot refer to objects in any immediate or pristine sense. His direct statements on language, of course, suggest a much more positivist theory. But his attempts to put that theory into practice seem to have undermined his confidence in the positive power of language. If so, the seeds of doubt were probably latent in Whitman's poetics from the start. In piecing together Whitman's poetic theory from the many comments on language scattered throughout his corpus, Mark Bauerlein has detected "a curious bifurcation" in the poet's opinions on language. At times, Bauerlein notes, his comments reflect the exalted view of language so predominant in the 1855 preface. At other times "he also condemns language for its wanton artificiality," its susceptibility to corruption. Bauerlein does not see this as a contradiction. He maintains that Whitman's poetics stage a competition between conventional language, understood as inherently false because it "involve[s] some supplementation that veils . . . [its] emotive origin," and his own invention of a mode of pure expression that is authentic because it is transparent. Still, while Whitman attempts to "expurgate the artificial sign from human relations" through the perfection of a natural idiom, he may not have been convinced it was possible. Bauerlein argues persuasively "that Whitman knew very well the contradictions his theory led him into, but he clung to it nevertheless and welcomed those contradictions as the material of great poetry." Bauerlain sees this tension within Whitman's language theory as the force that animates the early editions of *Leaves of Grass*. Thus, a poem such as "Song of Myself," for example, can be read as a "modernist" work, "a self-reflexive poem relentlessly challenging the possibilities of its creation and openly presaging its incompletion."[4]

Bauerlein is surely correct to identify Whitman's struggle against arbitrary language as a central concern of his poetics. But we miss much by locating the primary significance of Whitman's poetry in the way it acquiesces to that problematic. However "modernist" "Song of Myself" may be, it is also a poem that reaches beyond itself to organize new forms of meaning by exploiting the very same linguistic indeterminacy it would otherwise try to stabilize. This is clearly illustrated in section 25 of "Song of Myself," the passage that Bauerlein describes as "the most sustained and far-reaching instance" of the poet's "obsession" with the problem of "*writing* a natural language."[5]

> Dazzling and tremendous how quick the sunrise would kill me,
> If I could not now and always send sunrise out of me.
>
> We also ascend dazzling and tremendous as the sun,
> We found our own my soul in the calm and cool of the daybreak.
>
> My voice goes after what my eyes cannot reach,
> With the twirl of my tongue I encompass worlds and volumes of worlds.
>
> Speech is the twin of my vision . . . . it is unequal to measure itself.
> It provokes me forever,
> It says sarcastically, Walt, you understand enough . . . . why don't you let
>   it out then?
>
> Come now I will not be tantalized . . . . you conceive too much of
>   articulation,
>
> Do you not know how the buds beneath are folded?
> Waiting in gloom protected by frost,
> The dirt receding before my prophetical screams,
> I underlying causes to balance them at last,
> My knowledge my live parts . . . . it keeping tally with the meaning of
>   things,
> Happiness . . . . which whoever hears me let him or her set out in search
>   of this day.
>
> My final merit I refuse you . . . . I refuse putting from me the best I am.

6 : The Metaphysics of Democracy

Encompass worlds but never try to encompass me,
I crowd your noisiest talk by looking toward you.

Writing and talk do not prove me,
I carry the plenum of proof and everything else in my face,
With the hush of my lips I confound the topmost skeptic. (*LV* 35–36)

The immediate problem in this section is the tension established between the differing capabilities of speech and visual cognition, as the poet makes clear in the opening monologue he addresses to his own soul. On the one hand, it would seem that speech is omnipotent, for it preserves the poet's own life, and perhaps life itself, through the continuation (or duplication) of natural processes, the perpetual sending of "sunrise out of me." On the other hand, such power and the ambition it seems to breed inevitably separate it from whatever might be verified by the senses: when he boasts that his "Voice goes after what" even his own "eyes" cannot confirm, he seems to employ eyesight as a "mastersense," symbolically representing the cognitive functions of his other senses and their inability to keep pace with the omnipotent voice. Thus his speech cannot only encompass worlds but "volumes of worlds" because it is infinite, exceeding even the possibility of empirical measurement. Being beyond restraint, it becomes incorrigible as well, taunting the poet to hasty expression: "Walt, you understand enough," it says "sarcastically," indifferent to its own failure to stay within sensory limits, "why don't you let it out then?"

The rejoinder to this challenge reveals that the omnipotence of language is, paradoxically, a manifestation of a corresponding impotence. The poet sternly rebukes his speech: he will not be "tantalized," he fumes; moreover, the problem, he tells language, is that "you conceive too much of articulation." Language is not omniscient; it cannot know — and thus cannot express — all that the senses *sense*, such as the magnificent confluence of natural processes concealed within the folds of the bud they produce. Whitman insists on a romantic conception of subsensory intuitive knowledge, an immediate apprehension of "underlying causes" which are the poet's responsibility to "balance" in a way that renders his "live parts," those natural processes folded budlike within himself, sensible as meaning. Yet, ironically, the only intuition he succeeds in making explicit is his nagging awareness that such knowledge is too elusive to be pinned down by words, too vast to be contained by language. "My final merit I refuse you," he says in mock obstinacy, as if his failure to achieve a language of perfect correspondence were planned from the start. "I refuse putting from me the best I am." What section 25 dramatizes is perhaps best described as a standoff — not a failure of language per se but a failure of correspondence. On the one side stands the infinite potential of language, the measureless capacity of words to combine and re-combine in endless permutations of meaning, indifferent, as it were, to the constraints of worldly human experience. "With the twirl of my tongue," it boasts, "I encompass worlds and volumes of worlds." On the other side stands the infinite human experience of self and things to which language can only imperfectly refer — the fathomless, inarticulate depths of sensory life only a fraction of which even rises to consciousness. Each is characterized by a superfluidity that renders it incapable of synchronizing with the other. They are mutually transcendent. The section ends with the unutterable getting the last word, so to speak; "writing and talk do not prove," the poet asserts, for he carries the "plenum of proof" within him.[6]

But this conclusion does not resolve the impasse. In the couplet that pre-cedes the concluding stanza, just after the poet refuses to put from him the best that he is, he seems to strike a flippant but significant one-line bargain: "Encompass worlds but never try to encompass me." There is in this line an unmistakable note of comic exasperation. The poet seems to play the role of a beleaguered parent who must chase the loud, exuberant, irrepressible, childlike voice from the house in order to gain a bit of self-sustaining silence. "Go!" he seems to say, "encompass worlds, play wherever you wish — just stay out of the house, you're crowding me!" The only way the poet can pre-serve his authentic sense of self against the manipulations of his own intrusive, overbearing voice is to exile voice to the exterior, to the worlds that lie beyond the self. But (as every child knows) there is freedom in exile. By commanding voice to "encompass worlds," the poet has, in effect, granted language a li-cense for unrestricted play — linguistic play that need not be collared by the stiff expectations of correspondence theory.

To be sure, the poet had no choice. He did not emancipate language; in-deed, the failure of his own poetic theory to produce a perfect mode of repre-sentation pushed him to recognize that language was always already free. In a sense, Whitman pursues the paradoxical implications of our own critical meta-phors. We typically describe the discontinuity between words and things — their noncorrespondence — in metaphors of encumbrance. Bauerlein, for example, observes that words "bear supplemental properties" alien to experi-ence.[7] Inverted, however, the metaphor reminds us that the objects of expe-rience do not tightly control our words. The failure of correspondence may have forced the poet to confront the inevitability of metaphoric language, but in so doing, it liberated him to exploit its rich potential.

Pragmatic Mythology

Whitman is not generally regarded as an especially metaphoric poet, even though metaphors abound in his poetry. Indeed, if George Lakoff and Mark Johnson are correct in claiming that metaphor is fundamental to language itself, it would be impossible for Whitman's poetry to be anything but metaphoric.[8] Still, the critical consensus has been that his poetry does not rely on elaborate metaphors or finely developed conceits. At least one reason for this view is the recognition that his poetry is performative, a verse style that, however defined, is thought by many critics to be antithetical to metaphoric expression. C. Carroll Hollis, for example, points out the essentially oratorical nature of Whitman's early verse; relying heavily on J. L. Austin's speech-act theory, he argues convincingly that Whitman's desire to touch and change the lives of his readers led him to develop poetic lines of "illocutionary" power. Thus, drawing on Roman Jakobson's well-known distinction between metaphoric and metonymic language, Hollis asserts that Whitman was predisposed to write metonymically because of that style's association with the sensual, the physical, the concrete, the particular, and the real — rather than in the intellectualized abstractions of metaphor.[9] Bauerlien, too, treats Whitman's verse as performative, albeit of a much different kind. In his interpretation of Whitman's ambition, language is not simply a more energetic and demanding mode of communication but one in which "the word must function as a cooperative participant in or an instantaneous manifestation" of experience. He reads Whitman as struggling to develop (or recover) a paradoxical kind of natural language, one that is "vitally metaphoric yet corresponding uniformly with things." The problem, the critic points out, is deciding "[w]hich metaphors are the least metaphoric."[10]

There is, however, one sequence in "Song of Myself" in which the poet quite successfully puts a highly performative poetic style to work within an elaborate metaphoric construction. In sections 41 through 43, the poet, in effect, takes up his own challenge to "encompass worlds" by encompassing — indeed, subordinating — the totality of world religious, mythical, and cosmological tradition within his own democratic mythology. In brief, Whitman begins these passages by constructing a metaphorical marketplace in which both democracy and religion, figured here as mere rhetorical enterprises, must compete. Predictably, democracy, as personified by the poet, easily "outbids" his competitors. The scaffolding of the commercial metaphor then recedes into the background, whereupon the divine democratic poet exercises his prerogative to appropriate the narratives of his competitors. He reads himself into these narratives, inhabiting them in a way that effectively usurps the mythological grounds upon which they base their claims to authority. This sequence of sections is important, not simply because Whitman has managed to unite two seemingly antithetical literary modes, but rather in doing so, he has created a powerful synecdoche for his entire democratic vision. In other words, even though the whole Whitman canon may usefully be read as a complex democratic mythology, one that is implicitly aware of its own metaphorical foundations and specifically designed to supplant competing systems through a process of appropriation, here the poet makes both this process and its purpose explicit. He provides a kind of narrative blueprint for that mythological construction — including a protocol for appropriating alternative or competing systems.

He inaugurates the commercial metaphor in section 41, where he summons the whole tradition of religious cosmology to account by inviting comparisons with his own assertions:

> I heard what was said of the universe,
> Heard it and heard of several thousand years;
> It is middling well as far as it goes . . . . but is that all?

> Magnifying and applying come I,
> Outbidding at the start the old cautious hucksters,
> The most they offer for mankind and eternity less than a spirt of my own
> seminal wet, (*LV* 63–64)

The immediate function of the commercial metaphor is ideological or doctrinal, initially having little to do with performance; the metaphor is simply a useful device for making a few important points. First, it permits him to equate democracy and religion by bringing them into the same metaphysical realm in a manner that underscores their status as competitors. He taunts and condescends to "the old cautious hucksters" — yet he also expresses limited credulity: "It is middling well as far as it goes. . . ." This provisional credulity is strategic. He does not want to discredit the pantheon of unnamed generic gods he evokes but seeks to assert his rightful place in it. More important is the way the metaphor allows him to redefine that realm. The pantheon he would join is no hilltop temple elevated high above the traffic of common experience. It is quite the opposite. By identifying all theological assertions, including his own, with the noise and chaos of the marketplace, he avails himself of the huckster's real commercial power — the sales pitch, the banter, the line: rhetoric. The product is power and the power is rhetoric; product and pitch are barely distinguishable. When read in the context of Jacksonian laissez-faire, the metaphor gains in force as the poet's power seems an extension of that era's hyperactive petit bourgeoisie and its explosion of small-time entrepreneurs, ubiquitous shopkeepers, barking street vendors, and traveling snake-oil salesmen who collectively outbid the "old cautious hucksters" of entrenched wealth for economic dominance in antebellum America. In any event, the commercial metaphor pays off: Whitman effectively democratizes all conceptions of spiritual and political hierarchy by shifting their grounds from the supposed authority of their cosmological representations to the material and egalitarian market. Thus he can proceed to catalog the traditions he has outbid as though he were a merchant taking inventory — while ruefully reminding readers that all metaphysical authority is ultimately dependent upon one's willingness to buy a little rhetoric.

> Taking myself the exact dimensions of Jehovah and laying them away,
> Lithographing Kronos and Zeus his son, and Hercules his grandson,
> Buying drafts of Osiris and Isis and Belus and Brahma and Adonai,
> In my portfolio placing Manito loose, and Allah on a leaf, and the crucifix
>   engraved,
> With Odin, and the hideous-faced Mexitle, and all idols and images,
> Honestly taking them all for what they are worth, and not a cent more,
> Admitting they were alive and did the work of their day,
> Admitting they bore mites as for unfledged birds who have now to rise
>   and fly and sing for themselves, (*LV* 64)

Another important point the commercial metaphor permits the poet to make concerns the problem of "value." The poet asserts that he takes all theological metaphors "for what they are worth, and not a cent more." Significantly, Whitman underscores his indifference to correspondence theory by declining to recognize accuracy of representation as a legitimate test of value. Rather, he calculates the worth of theological metaphors pragmatically, according to their function. Judged in their historical context, he admits, their value was high; they were "alive" in that they functioned effectively, doing "the work of their day" — which is only to say that they provided persuasive and socially useful descriptions of experience, although he is quick to qualify that acknowledgment by observing that they also bore ideological "mites" that are antithetical to freedom. The pragmatic determination of truth and value is one of the logical cornerstones of Whitman's democratic vision and will be developed in detail in subsequent discussions. It is worth noting, however, that by commodifying religious myth and reducing it to rhetoric, Whitman has neatly anticipated William James's pragmatic conception of truth as that which has "cash value."

The commercial metaphor is also a demonstration of literary appropriation. In one sense, the appropriation is obvious. Whitman has imported the gods of traditional religion into his own fictive construction to serve as foils: as personified ideas, privileged by custom, his own democratic mythology can vanquish them (through rhetorical force) as a way of allegorizing the legitimacy of democracy's claim to power. But in another sense, the commercial metaphor also functions as a paradigm for the function of appropriation in Whitman's entire democratic mythology. By identifying the "old cautious hucksters," his mythological competitors, with their rhetorical or literary assertions, the poet has utilized the logic of his metaphor to transform those agents he would "outbid" into products he might acquire. He buys "drafts of Osiris and Isis and Belus" and puts others in his portfolio. Their immediate value to the poet is as models of form, a special class of exceptionally powerful metaphors:

> Accepting the rough deific sketches to fill out better in myself . . . .
>   bestowing them freely on each man and woman I see,
> Discovering as much or more in a framer framing a house,
> Putting higher claims for him there with his rolled-up sleeves, driving the
>   mallet and chisel;
> Not objecting to special revelations . . . . considering a curl of smoke or a
>   hair on the back of my hand as curious as any revelation; (LV 64)

Mythological gods then become important not simply as antagonists within the poet's fiction but as literary conventions, elaborate metaphorical arrangements with enormous residual cultural power. They serve Whitman's democratic purposes as mythological prototypes, "rough deific sketches" he may appropriate for use in the construction of a far grander democratic vision. In "The Poet," Emerson refers to the mythological gods Whitman would appropriate as "a sort of tomb of the muses." [11] But he also makes clear that once liberated from their visionary architecture, they are capable of a chameleon-like resiliency. He writes in one of the more famous passages from "The Poet":

> The religions of the world are the ejaculations of a few imaginative men.
>   But the quality of the imagination is to flow, and not to freeze. . . . Here
> is the difference betwixt the poet and the mystic, that the last nails a symbol to one sense, which was a true sense for a moment, but soon becomes
> old and false. For all symbols are fluxional; all language is vehicular and
> transitive, and is good, as ferries and horses are, for conveyance, not as
> farms and houses are, for homestead. [12]

Emerson may be as much or more concerned with the way all poetic language works (perhaps all language) and the art of reading poetry as he is with establishing a particular poetic methodology. In his discussion of "Circles" in *Pragmatism and Poetry*, Richard Poirier argues convincingly that Emerson is troubled with the way all writing, his own and others', "the very efforts at nonconformity that result in his tropings of previous truths," amounts inevitably to a kind of entrapment of "creative energy" within the circle of a "discursive formation." [13] Hence the poets who would understand and use the past as material for the construction of their own art would be wise to find a way "by which the creative efforts inferable from the productions of the past are, by a hermeneutical leap of faith, replicated and changed within the different linguistic and historical conditions of the present." The past, understood "as a series of monuments," is in a sense discarded in favor of an identification with "those in the past whose energies brought those monuments into existence." [14]

Whitman would appear to understand Emerson's apprehension concerning the residual ideological content of mythology but chooses instead to try to gut that ideology to render the myths more usable. To do so, his narrative takes on the aspect of a ritual performance, and literary appropriation now becomes a strategy for achieving deep cultural transformation. In the lines quoted above, the poet attempts an act of apotheosis: to put "higher claims" for the framer "with his rolled-up sleeves" is to deify the democratic self. Or perhaps more accurately, it is to acknowledge the always already divine status of democratic being and ground democratic authority in the common experience of human labor, such as the framing of a house. Here the poet travels beyond the scope of his commercial metaphor. The logic of the marketplace allowed him to equalize all ideologies by reducing them to the status of rhetorical competitors. By extension, it permitted him to justify democratic power by virtue of its "superior" (more persuasive) rhetoric. But democracy, as Whitman and others conceive it, has a special claim to legitimacy based on the primacy of common human sensuous experience. I will develop the argument for that claim in subsequent discussions throughout the book; for now, it is important to note that the commercial metaphor does not (indeed, cannot) even suggest such an argument. And the commercial metaphor especially does not put the argument for democracy in the form of a compelling narrative alternative to traditional religious belief. One possible solution would be simply to propound an explicitly democratic mythology, to cast the entire complex of democratic arguments in mythological terms. Whitman's more ambitious strategy is to read himself, as the emblem of common experience and democratic selfhood, into the very narratives he would subordinate. He appropriates — and attempts to reorient — not particular myths or religions but mythology itself and the mode of thinking it structures. In effect, he rereads mythology to uncover the latent democratic aspect at its core.

The poet begins his mythological performance at the conclusion of section 41 in an explicit assertion of his own divinity.

> The supernatural of no account . . . . myself waiting my time to be one of
>   the supremes,
> The day getting ready for me when I shall do as much good as the best,
>   and be as prodigious,
> Guessing when I am it will not tickle me much to receive puffs out of
>   pulpit or print;
> By my life-lumps! becoming already a creator!
> Putting myself here and now to the ambushed womb of the shadows!
>
>   (*LV* 65)

Of course, he also restricts the meaning of that divinity by playing with the classic definition of poet as maker or creator. As he makes the poet (and the people he would represent) into a god — he is "already a creator" — he simultaneously reveals that the gods are, in fact, poets. And since "The supernatural [is] of no account," all claims to authority that are grounded in supernatural representations are equally of no account. All such metaphysical constructions are the work of creator-poets who are certainly not supernatural in the sense of being outside or above nature but who may be considered superior to nature in the limited sense of being able to expropriate the terms of past creations and thereby originate new symbolic versions of nature out of themselves.

Having thus laid claim to divine status — while simultaneously restricting what the notion of divinity may mean — he proceeds in section 42 to root his own divinity in his identification with common people. Momentarily adopting the position of an objective narrator to locate himself among the people, he then gathers them to himself in a song of ritual unification:

> . . . . A call in the midst of the crowd,
> My own voice, orotund sweeping and final.
>
> Come my children,
> Come my boys and girls, and my women and household and intimates,
> Now the performer launches his nerve . . . . He has passed his prelude on
>   the reeds within. (*LV* 65 – 66)

"Music rolls," he says, "but not from the organ. . . . Folks are around me" (*LV* 66). Indeed, the song the "performer" sings would unite people by articulating the common rhythm of living, sensuous experience. For example, he reduces them to fundamental acts of consumption and then contextualizes them within the natural cycles of solar orbit and oscillating tides. "Ever the eaters and drinkers. . . . ever the upward and downward sun. . . . Ever the air and the ceaseless tides" (*LV* 66). Likewise, he sings of labor as though it were rhythmic physical experience, a continuous, often oppressive, dance: "Many sweating and ploughing and thrashing, and then the chaff for payment receiving" (*LV* 67). Still, for the poet, the images do not dramatize the brutality of precultural life but the vitality and authenticity of sensuous experience. He asserts that the people are "refreshing, wicked and real," a conjunction of adjectives suggesting that the immediacy of experience that distinguishes the people as "real" is not just opposed to fossilized moral ideas but the agency by which the moral tradition might be "refreshed." Throughout this section, the poet makes it clear that the people are the sum total of their sensuous experience. He also makes it clear that he is one of them: "This is the City. . . . And I am one of the citizens," he proclaims (*LV* 67). As section 42 concludes, the primacy of sensuous experience is reaffirmed in a sequence of questions, each presenting a choice between the artificial and the real: "printed book" versus "printer and printing-office boy"; the "marriage estate" versus the "body and mind" of bridegroom and bride; the painting of the sea versus "the sea itself"; and so on, until finally,

"The saints and sages in history. . . . but you yourself? / Sermons and creeds and theology. . . . but the human brain, and what is called reason, and what is called love, and what is called life?" (*LV* 68).

Having thus made himself the "divine" emblem of "divine" human sensuous *democratic* experience, the poet stands ready to commandeer the narratives of the "cautious old hucksters," the "saints and sages in history" and their lifeless "creeds and theology." Hence in section 43 he mythologizes a return through time to the zenith of each religion's reign:

I do not despise you priests;
My faith is the greatest of faiths and the least of faiths,
Enclosing all worship ancient and modern, and all between ancient and
    modern,
Believing I shall come again upon the earth after five thousand years,
Waiting responses from oracles . . . . honoring the gods . . . . saluting
    the sun,

> Making a fetish of the first rock or stump . . . . powowing with sticks in
> the circle of obis, (*LV* 68)

The poet can enclose "all worship ancient and modern" not simply because, as the emblem of the democratic people, he has assumed the role of a superior god. More pointedly, as the representative of sensuous experience, material consciousness, he can testify to the irrational origins of the religious imagination: he himself made "a fetish of the first rock or stump." As such, he was from the outset both initiator of those myths and a participant in their ritual practices:

> Helping the lama or brahmin as he trims the lamps of the idols,
> Dancing yet through the streets in a phallic procession . . . . rapt and
> austere in the woods, a gymnosophist,
> Drinking mead from the skull-cup . . . . to shasta and vedas admirant . . . .
> minding the koran,
> Walking the teokallis, spotted with gore from the stone and knife —
> beating the serpent-skin drum;
> Accepting the gospels, accepting him that was crucified, knowing
> assuredly that he is divine,
> To the mass kneeling — to the puritan's prayer rising — sitting patiently
> in a pew,
> Ranting and frothing in my insane crisis — waiting dead-like till my spirit
> arouses me;
> Looking forth on pavement and land, and outside of pavement and land,
> Belonging to the winders of the circuit of circuits. (*LV* 69)

In his commercial metaphor, he had figured belief systems as rhetorical competitors; now he depicts them as physical experiences. The first physical experiences take on the aspect of highly ordered ritual expressions, as he helps the lama trim the lamps. They quickly descend into the elemental or primitive: he dances through the streets, a "gymnosophist"; he drinks from the "skull-cup"; he walks the teokallis beating a drum; he kneels in mass, rises in prayer, and sits in the pew. Eventually, formal ritual disintegrates completely, and he rants and froths, consumed by nothing more than the explosion of his own inchoate senses. Of course, he "encloses all worship ancient and modern," is "one of the supremes," "already a creator," for he is pure sense, pure physicality. Thus critics who assert that Whitman presents a religion without God surely miss the point. The real and acknowledged god at the heart of every religion, he seems to say, is the sensuous self — the "framer framing a house," indeed, all the "eaters and drinkers" who sweat, plough, and thrash. His "faith," then, "is the greatest of faiths and the least of faiths" because he can see that at the core of the supernatural narratives by which hierarchies justify their usurpation of power there is a very natural, experiential, democratic god that belies their claims. In effect, the poet thus delineates the proper function of religious thought in a secular democratic society. He asserts democracy's prerogative to embrace whatever moral ideas a people choose to venerate by establishing democracy's prior claim of ownership over these ideas. At the same time, he denies authority to the clergy (or any entity) who might interpret these ideas as a rationale for their own exercise of power.

The significance of these three sections to Whitman's practical poetics is manifold. As an example of Whitman's poetic practice, particularly his reliance on metaphoric constructions, his acknowledgment of the value of rhetoric, and his radical style of appropriation, these sections reveal him to be far more pragmatic than his positivist theoretical assertions would suggest. As performative poetry, they dramatize Whitman's particularly aggressive style of textual reinterpretation — characteristic of his approach to other texts generally — while also modeling a strategy for cultural reform. As a mythological expression of his democratic vision, they function paradigmatically, signaling the comprehensive scope of that vision while organizing many of its key elements. The common thread linking all of these manifestations of Whitman's poetics, however, is that they are all antithetical to correspondence theories of truth. In one way or another they each exploit the undecidability of words and the inescapably problematic notion of truth. Yet they are all true — at least in the context of the pragmatic theory of truth Whitman develops in *Leaves of Grass*.

Truth and Verification

The pragmatic theory of truth, intended as a challenge to the notion of simple correspondence, received its first full articulation in William James's *Pragmatism*. Even if one were to accept the findings of a correspondence theory and "grant an idea or belief to be true," he writes, the pragmatist is still left with the primary question of "what concrete difference will its being true make in any one's actual life? What experiences will be different from those which would obtain if the belief were false?" [15] This is not, as it has often been accused of being, an anti-intellectual bias against speculation in favor of simple utility; rather, it is a recognition that the "truth of an idea is not a stagnant property inherent in it. Truth *happens* to an idea" through the very process of its validation. [16] In other words, truthful ideas are fruitful ideas, ideas that produce new insights or successfully open up new lines of inquiry. By shifting the concern for truth away from an idea's ability to "copy" nature and onto an ongoing experimental process of verification, James introduces the element of time; to be sure, as John Dewey points out, so long as humankind continues to live, work, and think, the results of any experimental process are always open to revision. Empirical thinkers who properly conceive their role "are not concerned with framing a general theory of reality, knowledge and value once and for all, but with finding how authentic beliefs about existence as they currently exist can operate fruitfully and efficaciously in connection with the practical problems that are urgent in actual life."(*QC* 45). Full realization of this condition means an empiricism that understands itself to be "prophetic rather than descriptive. It can offer hypotheses rather than report of facts adequately in existence. . . . It is speculative in that it deals with 'futures.'" (*QC* 77–78).

One consequence of such a conception of truth is that it acknowledges no sharp distinction between scientific inquiry and moral or poetic speculation — between our ideas about nature and our ideals about how to live as part of it. When we think of ideas as instruments whose truth value resides in their capacity to direct a course of experimentation toward desired consequences, we open ourselves up to the consideration of all possible consequences of those ideas, not just the narrowly conceived results of a particular scientific procedure but any way that a potential action latent in an idea might affect the course of human life. But if our empirical investigations, subject as they are to future validation, are in that sense subordinated to our ideals about what we want that future to be, the converse is also true. Our ideals about the future are the projections of what is good about the present. Thus our ideals are dependent on our understanding of the real world in that they represent what Dewey calls in *Reconstruction in Philosophy* "intelligently thought out possibilities *of* the existent world which may be used as methods for making over and improving it." [17] For Dewey, as for James, truth-making is the process by which we test the efficacy of our ideals, a "prophetic" act of the imagination that reads one version of the present into the future so that that future may exert a corrective influence on the present.

The logic of the pragmatic conception of truth is so prevalent in *Leaves of Grass* that it seems that Whitman actually anticipates James and Dewey. More to the point, it adds a pragmatic dimension to his poetics and conditions the way we should read his democratic mythology and prophetic vision. This is particularly evident in his treatment of futurity. "The greatest poet," he writes in the 1855 preface, "forms the consistence of what is to be from what has been and is . . . he places himself where the future becomes present" (*CRE* 718).

This is the poet in his role of pragmatic prophet. Though the consistence of his imagined future is formed from past and present, it is still an edited and reconstructed version, for "[i]f he does not expose superior models and prove himself by every step he is not what is wanted" (*CRE* 715). Vision and verification, in other words, go hand in hand. But recall that pragmatic verification is a two-way street — a kind of continuous dialogue between the constructed present and the imagined future: as our constructions of the real and present must be validated by their ability to anticipate the way phenomena will behave in the future, so, too, must our ideals, which are but selected projections of our constructed present, be subjected to verification based on the desirability of the concrete behaviors that they generate in the here and now. While the former involves the verification of the present by the future, the latter is a verification of the future by the present. Both, as Whitman will make clear, involve the kind of manipulation of time that will necessitate a poet who "places himself where the future becomes present." When the poet asserts that he must "prove himself by every step," it is the latter, the validation of ideals, to which he refers — a point I will take up shortly. But it is because our ideals are intimately linked to our ability to construct nature adequately — the real in the here and now — that the job of judging these constructions must be one of his poetic functions. "Still the final test of poems *or any character or work* remains," he writes in the preface (*CRE* 728, emphasis added). "The prescient poet projects himself centuries ahead and judges performer or performance after the changes of time" (*CRE* 728). By these lights, his claim that he is "no arguer" but rather "is judgment" itself becomes more clear. It is an existential kind of "process" judgment, one that requires no criteria, or even a final decision, for "he judges not as the judge judges but as the sun falling around a helpless thing" might simply shed light on phenomena in a way that enables continued examination (*CRE* 715).

Like William James's pragmatic theory of truth, Whitman's conception of judgment endlessly defers any final determination of value, thereby laying special stress on the notion of usability as a criterion for judgment. "Of all nations the United States with veins full of poetical stuff most need poets," he claims. And he is confident that the need will be met, for the United States "doubtless will have the greatest and use them the greatest" (*CRE* 714). The clear implication is that the poet is to be judged according to his *usability*. But, this only begs the question: how are we to judge usefulness? Whitman raises the question and then struggles to answer with a sexual metaphor: "Will it help breed one goodshaped and wellhung man and a woman to be his perfect mate?" (*CRE* 730). He develops the metaphor later in his letter to

Emerson that prefaced the 1856 edition. "Submit to the most robust bard till he remedy your barrenness," he wrote. "Then you will not need to adopt the heirs of others; you will have true heirs, begotten of yourself, blooded with your own blood" (*CRE* 734).

These and other similar sexual metaphors are typical of Whitman's descriptions of his poetry, and they serve a variety of purposes in his work. In this context, they would deflect the impulse to assess the efficacy of his vision, its usability, in terms of its ability to shape specific policies or produce concrete initiatives. For many, this generalized procreative energy may seem to be no criterion at all. The poet recognizes this in section 40 of "Song of Myself": "Earth! you seem to look for something at my hands, / Say old topknot! . . . what do you want?" (*LV* 61–62). But rather than responding with some tangible demonstration of the poet's powers, the poet curiously asserts that he is dumb:

> Man or woman! I might tell how I like you, but cannot,
> And might tell what it is in me and what it is in you, but cannot,
> And might tell the pinings I have . . . . the pulse of my nights and days.
>
> Behold I do not give lectures or a little charity,
> What I give I give out of myself. (*LV* 62)

The poet would have us believe that the value of his poetry is to be found not so much in its ability to shape inchoate emotion or structure the kind of intellectualized meanings conveyable through lectures but rather in its ability to reproduce in others something vital within himself. But he cannot articulate the idea without also qualifying it. That is, he cannot tell us of his inability to reduce to mere words the full experience of his affection for us — to "tell how I like you" or to tell us his "pinings" — without at least pointing to the fact that such feeling exists and is central to his purpose. Neither can that affection be dissociated from the rest of his democratic vision, for it is one of its defining features. Thus, as he completes section 40, making it clear that the poetic procreative energy must be understood as a functional, creative, even mystical force, we see that it is also implicitly but inescapably concrete in that it suggests the entirety of his more programmatic, goal-oriented, democratic philosophy:

> You there, impotent, loose in the knees, open your scarfed chops till I
>   blow grit within you,
> Spread your palms and lift the flaps of your pockets,
> I am not to be denied . . . . I compel . . . . I have stores plenty and to spare,

And anything I have I bestow.

I do not ask who you are . . . . that is not important to me,
You can do nothing and be nothing but what I will infold you.
To a drudge of the cottonfields or emptier of privies I lean . . . . on his
    right cheek I put the family kiss,
And in my soul I swear I never will deny him.

On women fit for conception I start bigger and nimbler babies,
This day I am jetting the stuff of far more arrogant republics.

To any one dying . . . . thither I speed and twist the knob of the door,
Turn the bedclothes toward the foot of the bed,
Let the physician and the priest go home.

I seize the descending man . . . . I raise him with resistless will.

O despairer, here is my neck,
By God! you shall not go down! Hang your whole weight upon me.

I dilate you with tremendous breath . . . . I buoy you up;
Every room of the house do I fill with an armed force . . . . lovers of me,
    bafflers of graves:
Sleep! I and they keep guard all night;
Not doubt, not decrease shall dare to lay finger upon you,
I have embraced you, and henceforth possess you to myself,
And when you rise in the morning you will find what I tell you is so.

(LV 62–63)

On the one hand, if we are looking for a specific policy prescription by
which to verify the Whitman vision, we shall not find it here. The ultimate test
of the of the poet's oration, he asserts, is in the sheer force of the "blow[n]
grit," the "tremendous breath" that dilates all indiscriminately with an invig-
orating, "jetting," seminal power. Rather than action we have activation — a
form of pure power that can enable action but not control or specify it. On the
other hand, this seminal poetic power is not totally devoid of ideological content. For example, in his insistence that the power be disseminated indiscriminately ("I do not ask who you are") and most especially in his identification with the powerless, particularly the laboring class (in the cotton fields
or emptying privies), the poet has linked his notion of an enabling, "procreative" poetic force to the larger complex of democratic ideas of his vision. The
poet would not have us judge his work according to its ability to specify the

material means by which a humane democracy might be realized but rather in its ability to generate the spiritual, cultural, and emotive energy each new generation needs to reinvent for themselves the meaning of a humane democracy — and then to use whatever historically contingent means are at their disposal to make it a reality. The validity of Whitman's prophetic democracy is in its capacity to inspire the continuous re-creation of democracy.

The vision of democracy Whitman advances in *Leaves of Grass* is an explicitly constructed vision. Its mythology, as well as the whole range of psychological, cosmological, historical, cultural, and political ideas that that mythology symbolizes, must be read in the light of his distinctly modern recognition of the undecidability of language. But it is a construction that takes into account the many implications of being constructed. Whitman exploits these implications — sifting the past for usable mythological or linguistic forms from which he might construct a vision to guide the continuous process of social reconstruction in an ever-receding future. In that sense it is also prophecy but of a special kind: a pragmatic prophecy, a vision that understands that the future it names is a contingent one and that also builds in the mechanism to test and realize that future. William James famously claimed that pragmatism is not a philosophy but a methodology only, not a closed set of representations but an ongoing process by which we continuously construct, test, and reconstruct our representations. Whitman would claim that democracy is more than just a methodology — but the burden of deciding precisely how much more he leaves to us and to those who follow.

"What Is Less or More Than a Touch?"
Sensory Experience and the Democratic Self

The pragmatic nature of Whitman's language — particularly the purely utilitarian way he pillages the world's warehouse of religious ideas to cobble together a democratic mythology — certainly suggests that Whitman did not feel bound by literal readings of the ancient texts he appropriated. We would especially expect that he would be hostile to the various mystical and spiritual conceptions of selfhood codified by those texts, for they are clearly at odds with his affirmation of the democratic implications of material and experiential conceptions of self. By extension, we should find in Whitman a poet who is indifferent to one of the most fundamental truth claims of nearly every religion from which he would borrow: "dualism," or the ontological distinction between body and mind or spirit. Still, dualism seems to be everywhere in Whitman's poetry; paradoxically, it even appears to be central to his entire architectural vision of democratic selfhood. For example, the dramatic premise of "Song of Myself" is that a separation between the poet's body and soul has somehow occurred and must now be healed — a point that has led critics such as Malcolm Cowley and James E. Miller Jr. to see Whitman as a mystic who seeks a reunion of antinomies.[1] Whitman opens the great poem by proclaiming:

> I celebrate myself,
> And what I assume you shall assume,
> For every atom belonging to me as good belongs to you.
>
> I loafe and invite my soul,
> I lean and loafe at my ease . . . . observing a spear of summer grass. (*LV* 1)

Clearly, the poet assumes a kind of objectified aspect of himself, a soul, which is distinguishable from the physical (speaking) subject that is loafing on the summer grass.

All that is distinguishable, however, is not necessarily ontologically separable. And a literal interpretation here is a mistake. Whitman's soul is nothing like an ethereal entity at all; it is a naturalistic conception of consciousness. It is, in fact, an elaboration of his conception of natural, democratic selfhood. The particular role it plays in Whitman's poetry may dramatize its fundamentally social — and democratic — origins. George Herbert Mead, John Dewey's younger colleague at the University of Chicago, claimed in his posthumously published lectures, "Mind, Self and Society," that objectifications of the self (such as we find in references to the human soul) are wholly consistent with naturalistic theory, even though they form the basis of so much mystical, religious, or superstitious thought.[2] The natural origin of the objectified self — or *self*-consciousness — was one of Mead's most fruitful preoccupations. A brief sketch here of Mead's insights will be useful in explaining Whitman's invitation to his soul — especially in its social context, its reliance on immediate experience as a vehicle of realization, and the passive pose he takes in extending his invitation.

The solution to the dilemma of selfhood, Mead believed — as well as the source of enormous confusion about it — was located in our commonsense experience of the self as both object and subject. "It is the characteristic of the self as an object to itself that I want to bring out," Mead wrote. "This characteristic is represented in the word 'self,' which is a reflexive, and indicates that which can be both subject and object."[3] On the one hand, we sense ourselves living in and responding to our environment spontaneously, from the position of an immediate subjectivity. On the other hand, there are times when we think about the nature of that spontaneous being, our "self," objectively, as though it were distinguishable from the subjectivity that at any given moment might bring the self into consciousness. But the fact that making such a distinction seems to be an inescapable habit of human thought does not mean that the distinction has metaphysical standing. Mead thought the distinction is *functional* — reflective of the different aspects of the mind's operations within the ever-present social environment in which it lives. He expressed these different functions in terms of a contrast between the subjective "I" and the objective "me." Effective social life, Mead argued, required of every human that they internalize the attitudes, codes, and standards of the group they belong to — the "rules of the game" that regulate conduct and organize relationships among individuals. The vehicle of this internalization is language, and the very necessity of this internalization, Mead believed, accounted for the natural evolution of the linguistic capability in humans. Language, then, and the very cognition that language makes possible (the "internalized conversation of gestures," as he put it), amounts to a "generalized other" that every individual imports into the self. Within the matrix of the generalized other, people can witness themselves acting; they can imagine the responses of others to their actions and, in turn, imagine their own reactions to those imagined responses of others in a seemingly infinite circuit of social interplay. The imaginative being we each construct from this interplay of subjective responses to the internalized social material is what Mead calls the "me." When people think of their own selves, they are thinking of entities that only manifest themselves as an objective "presentation" to consciousness through their behavior within the web of social relationships. When we conjure up an image of a self, in other words, what we see is a being defining itself through a process of social interactions: "That which we have acquired as self-conscious persons makes us such members of society and gives us selves. No hard-and-fast line can be drawn between our own selves and the selves of others, since our own selves exist and enter as such into our experience only in so far as the selves of others exist and enter as such into our experience also. The individual possesses a self only in relation to the selves of the other members of his social group."[4]

The function of this "me," the objectified and socially implicated aspect of the self, is to mediate the individual's responses to his or her environment by organizing and internalizing socially governed perceptions of that environment. But this is not to say that the entire self consists of an organization of social attitudes. To the contrary, it exists in tension with the subjective "I," the bare, impulsive, immediate, reacting function of the self. In an "active" sense, the "I" contributes to selfhood through the novelty of its responses to the environment — including the internalized environment that comprises the "me." Since every new situation in which we act is to some degree unique, unprecedented, so, too, must each response the "I" makes contain some element of novelty. But at the instant of completion, the action of the "I" becomes a memory, which is to say an object to consciousness, an aspect of the "me" to be reconciled with the rest of the "me." In a more "reflective" sense, the "I" contributes to selfhood through introspection. It is "the 'I' which is aware of the social 'me,'" Mead writes; put another way, it is the consciousness upon which self-consciousness is predicated.[5] One point must be underscored: the "I" is not directly apprehensible — it is a presumption, derived from our awareness of the "me":

> The "I" does not get into the limelight; we talk to ourselves, but do not see ourselves. The "I" reacts to the self which arises through the taking of the attitudes of others. . . .
> The simplest way of handling the problem would be in terms of mem-

ory. I talk to myself, and I remember what I said and perhaps the emotional content that went with it. The "I" of this moment is present in the "me" of the next moment. There again I cannot turn around quick enough to catch myself. I become a "me" in so far as I remember what I said. The "I" can be given, however, this functional relationship. It is because of the "I" that we say that we are never fully aware of what we are, that we surprise ourselves by our own action.[6]

If Mead's conception of a dialogic structure to consciousness that is irreducible to human physicality places him outside the school of mechanical materialism, he is, nevertheless, no dualist; while primary, sensuous experience cannot alone account for the workings of the mind, it still plays a key role in Mead's understanding of the process of selfhood. And to the degree that sensuous experience is significant to the development of the self (and much sensuous experience is so habitual, Mead asserts, that it is not), it becomes significant only when processed by the sociolinguistic agency of the mind. This same dynamic is clearly at work in Whitman's poetry. In the 1855 version of "There Was a Child Went Forth," Whitman explicitly and dramatically links the process of identity formation to the individual's internalization of socially entwined responses to physical stimuli. The psycho-dynamics informing the poem are sketched in its first stanza, whose titular first line begins with a self so objectified as an artifact of memory that the subject "I" — the speaking subject — is concealed and must be assumed:

There was a child went forth every day,
And the first object he looked upon and received with wonder or pity or
     love or dread, that object he became,
And that object became part of him for the day or a certain part of
     the day . . . . or for many years or stretching cycles of years. (*LV* 149)

By asserting in line 2 that "he became" the "first object" encountered and then modifying the formula in line 3 so that subsequent objects "became part of him," assimilated into the existing self, the speaker opens up the intriguing prospect that no subjective self exists to organize sensory data prior to the emergence of an objectified self, or Mead's "me," the self of introspection. Just as significant is the pivotal part played by emotion in the transaction. It is not simple sensory perception that makes the difference; the "me" can only emerge as an object to itself when sensory experience is conditioned by wonder, pity, love, or dread. Central here is Dewey's definition of emotions, which Mead drew upon, as "attitudes" abstracted from formerly useful primordial behavior that are aroused as a means for realizing ends. As Andrew

Feffer further explains Dewey's conception, "emotions are 'truncated acts,' acts which do not achieve their full purpose because they are inhibited either by circumstances or by the actor. Emotions signify the inhibition of the act, and spur the actor to find a solution to the problem."[7] The suggestion of passivity conveyed by the poet's encountered objects "received" with emotion conceals the active manipulations of a consciousness becoming a "self-consciousness"; that is, what the poet imports into consciousness is not a set of objects that he, in some simplistic sense, becomes but a set of latent acts regarding those objects, which, through the reconstructive work of the imagination, becomes a kind of architecture of relations defining the self. What he becomes is the totality of those relations — manifested to the self objectively as the things that induce the self to act.

As the poem continues in the third stanza — following the stages, we now realize, of a child's development — the poet chronicles all types of sensory data that provide material for the self's reconstruction. But that the truly significant objects in the process of self-consciousness are human and social becomes clear as soon as we read beyond the catalog of "early lilacs," "morningglories," "white and red clover," "noisy brood of the barnyard," pond fish, and other natural objects that also "all became part of him," to the third stanza's "old drunkard staggering home from the outhouse of the tavern whence he had lately risen" (*LV* 150).

> And the schoolmistress that passed on her way to the school . . and the
>   friendly boys that passed . . and the quarrelsome boys . . and the tidy
>   and freshcheeked girls . . and the barefoot negro boy and girl,
> And all the changes of the city and country wherever he went.
>
> His own parents . . he that had propelled the fatherstuff at night, and
>   fathered him . . and she that conceived him in her womb and birthed
>   him . . . . they gave this child more of themselves than that,
> They gave him afterward every day . . . . they and of them became part
>   of him.
>
> The mother at home quietly placing the dishes on the suppertable,
> The mother with mild words . . . . clean her cap and gown . . . . a
>   wholesome odor falling off her person and clothes as she walks by:
> The father, strong, selfsufficient, manly, mean, angered, unjust,
> The blow, the quick loud word, the tight bargain, the crafty lure,
> The family usages, the language, the company, the furniture . . . . the
>   yearning and swelling heart, (*LV* 150–151)

When we recall at this point that the poet is not simply recounting childhood experiences but enumerating those "objects" that were to become part of the growing child's actual self, the last quoted line becomes particularly remarkable. By linking the objectivity of the relevant social group, the family, its customs, its language, and even its collectively owned furniture, together with the subjectivity of the individual's emotional responses within the group, "the yearning and swelling heart," the poet has blurred the boundary between externally perceived objects and internally experienced emotions. He has effectively erased all subject-object distinctions. Though the individual organism may "feel," the mediation of those feelings is understood as a social fact. The organizing of those feelings into recognizable objects requires, then, the imaginative reconstruction of "others" (in this case a mild-speaking mother or an angered father) who are differentiated from each other by their particular responses to the subject; as others become differentiated, so may the poet differentiate himself as an object available for introspection and translation into poetry.

But such insight comes at a cost to the poet, as the next few lines indicate. In recognizing just how blurred the separation between object and subject is, the poet appears to become anxious about what within that matrix may truly be called essential. Though he would feel confident of his possession of the "Affection that will not be gainsayed," that confidence is unavoidably undermined by "The sense of what is real . . . the thought if after all it should prove unreal." And, "The doubts of daytime and the doubts of nighttime . . . the curious whether and how, / Whether that which appears so is so. . . . Or is it all flashes and specks?" (*LV* 151). The profound specter of doubt and anxiety captured in these lines catches the adventuresome spirit of the remaining eleven lines of the poem in an undercurrent of uncertainty about the exact boundaries of the self. So as the poem's child moves in a centripetal fashion, out and away from the family and village and toward the "horizon's edge," he is also moving centrifugally, *in* from the objectified sense of the self that is entangled in social fact and toward the "Shadows . . aureola and mist" of pure subjectivity, unmediated by other human beings — toward, in other words, the immediate, organic, impulsive presumption of essence we might usefully call the soul (*LV* 152).

To say that the soul is not an entity but an intimation, a reified function of self-consciousness, is not to say that "inviting" it to the center of one's attention — deliberately heightening one's sensitivity to the workings of the self it designates — makes no sense. As "Song of Myself" makes clear, such an invitation — or, more precisely, such a retreat to a (sometimes meditative) state wherein sensory experience seems more immediate, more "authentic," and less controlled by the already socially restricted self of introspection — is a very logical choice of tools for the job of personal liberation. To subordinate the directives of the social "me" by living, if only momentarily, on the level of pure impulse, one, in effect, alters or expands the "me" through an increased level of "novel" behavior — behavior once outside the self's known boundaries but which now becomes new information to be assimilated into the new, reorganized, "me." Since the "soul-function" is concerned with a particular body's unique responsiveness to physical stimuli, what better way to focus one's attention on such an internal abstraction than by leaning and loafing at ease, while the mind, perhaps a little numbed by the summer heat, allows the eyes to fix themselves on "a spear of summer grass"?

So prevalent in Whitman is this retreat to the senses — and so closely associated are sensations with his conception of his essential self — that references often seem like comic postures. When he announces himself in section 24 of "Song of Myself," for instance, as "Walt Whitman, an American, one of the roughs, a kosmos," he immediately adds that he is "Disorderly fleshy and sensual . . . . eating drinking and breeding," (*LV* 31), a point about himself he will amplify a few lines later by saying, "I believe in the flesh and the appetites, / Seeing hearing and feeling are miracles, and each part and tag of me is a miracle" (*LV* 32–33).

But what is truly miraculous about the visual, auditory, and tactile senses is not simply that they are inexplicable organic marvels that enable the body to operate; it is more that, as contact points with the environment, they provide the machinery for the self's reorganization. Section 26 of "Song of Myself" begins with the poet saying explicitly that "I think I will do nothing for a long time but listen, / And accrue what I hear into myself . . . . and let sounds contribute toward me" (*LV* 36). If the poet of "There Was a Child Went Forth" was sufficiently insightful to recognize that the objectified self is a socially implicated being, a product of the process whereby external material is imported through the senses into consciousness, here the poet has taken the next step of attempting to regulate that process by choosing the particular moment and type of sensory stimulation. He then proceeds to rapidly catalog the wealth of sounds around him, such as the "bravuras of birds," the bustle of wheat, the clack of flames, and all other manner of city and country sounds, but he slows to concentrate on those types of sounds that seem to move and mark him in particular ways:

I hear the trained soprano . . . . she convulses me like the climax of my
  love-grip;
The orchestra whirls me wider than Uranus flies,
It wrenches unnamable ardors from my breast,
It throbs me to gulps of the farthest down horror,
It sails me . . . . I dab with bare feet . . . . they are licked by the indolent
  waves,
I am exposed . . . . cut by bitter and poisoned hail,
Steeped amid honeyed morphine . . . . my windpipe squeezed in the
  fakes of death,
Let up again to feel the puzzle of puzzles,
And that we call Being. (*LV* 38)

Though the only sense engaged here is auditory, the stimulation is so intense
that the poet seems to have lost all volition, all ability to act; his responses appear to be completely involuntary, completely beyond conscious direction or
control. As he is brought to the "fakes of death," the "puzzle of puzzles" that
"we call Being" becomes not a matter to be pondered, thought about, or reasoned through. It is a puzzle to be felt. By engineering an experience of such
intensity, the poet has attempted to bypass the manipulations of what Mead
calls the "me" so that he might apprehend directly the subjective "I," the most
intimate aspect of "Being."

Still, however close the poet may have come to a direct apprehension of
subjectivity while sitting paralyzed in his seat in the opera house, the very act
of translating that moment into the verbal machinery of poetry is at once the
act of bringing the moment into cognition and making it a matter for reflection
and analysis. Thus he begins section 27 with the question the experience has
raised: "To be in any form, what is that? / If nothing lay more developed the
quahaug and its callous shell were enough" (*LV* 38). The poet's own rhetorical question prompts him to shift his attention away from what Mead and others have called the "distance" class of sensory experience (for example, the visual, olfactory, and auditory senses) to the "contact" senses (for example,
touch and taste). While even the hard-shelled quahaug has a being to be democratically affirmed, what seems to set it apart from the more "developed" human being is primarily the latter's responsiveness to tactile experience. Thus
the poet immediately declares:

Mine is no callous shell,
I have instant conductors all over me whether I pass or stop,

They seize every object and lead it harmlessly through me.

I merely stir, press, feel with my fingers, and am happy,
To touch any person to someone else's is about as much as I can stand.

(LV 38)

In the very next line, the first of section 28, the poet makes it explicit that the significance of immediate, tactile experience is in the role it plays in the reformulation of the self. "Is this then a touch?" he asks, ". . . . quivering me to a new identity" (*LV* 39). But the reader might easily lose track of the question, for the twenty-eight lines that follow, comprising all of sections 28 and 29, are a riveting and dramatic rendition of a highly charged autoerotic fantasy:

Flames and ether making a rush for my veins,
Treacherous tip of me reaching and crowding to help them,
My flesh and blood playing out lightning, to strike what is hardly different
    from myself,
On all sides prurient provokers stiffening my limbs,
Straining the udder of my heart for its withheld drip,
Behaving licentious toward me, taking no denial,
Depriving me of my best as for a purpose,

Unbuttoning my clothes and holding me by the bare waist,
Deluding my confusion with the calm of the sunlight and pasture fields,
Immodestly sliding the fellow senses away,
They bribe to swap off with touch, and go and graze at the edges of me,
No consideration, no regard for my draining strength or my anger,
Fetching the rest of the herd to enjoy them awhile,
Then all uniting to stand on a headland and worry me.

The sentries desert every other part of me,
They have left me helpless to a red marauder,
They all come to the headland to witness and assist against me.

I am given up by traitors;
I talk wildly . . . . I have lost my wits . . . . I and nobody else am the
    greatest traitor,
I went myself first to the headland . . . . my own hands carried me there.

You villain touch! what are you doing? . . . . my breath is tight in its
    throat;
Unclench your floodgates! you are too much for me.

29

Blind loving wrestling touch! Sheathed hooded sharptoothed touch!
Did it make you ache so leaving me?

Parting tracked by arriving . . . . perpetual payment of the perpetual loan,
Rich showering rain, and recompense richer afterward.

Sprouts take and accumulate . . . . stand by the curb prolific and vital,
Landscapes projected masculine full-sized and golden. (*LV* 39 – 40)

What must not be lost in the fury of this fantasy is that even though the poet is
addressing an objectified "villain touch," it is his own subjective capacity for
response to tactile stimulation — especially sexual stimulation — that is at issue. Much can and will be said about Whitman's very interesting use of both
sexual energy and imagery, but as it relates to the particular dynamics of self-
organization I am discussing, it is especially important to point out that the
sexual nature of the poet's experience differs only by degree — not kind —
from other tactile experience. All tactile experience is to some extent immediate; as such, the generic "touch" is always potential material for the self's
"quivering" reorganization into "a new identity." But the intense, consuming
quality of Whitman's sexual trance makes the difference of degree nearly one
of kind: the obvious totality of the poet's state of arousal and the infinite modes
of its potential expression make recourse to sexual reverie a highly productive
(and favorite) means by which the poet accesses his "soul."

In effect, Whitman has dramatized in poetry the same relationship between
sense and mind that Dewey articulated in "The Reflex Arc Concept in Psychology," the essay that provided the foundation for Mead's theory of socialized identity.[8] There Dewey argued for an organic conception of experience
and consciousness. Challenging the simplistic formulations of his contemporary psychologists who assumed that actions were always a response to some
external stimulus, Dewey asserted that both stimulus and response should be
viewed as mutually modifying acts within a coordinated behavioral circuit.
Borrowing from William James, Dewey offered the example of a child reaching for a burning candle. The naive assumption would have it that the burning flame was stimulus to the child's act of reaching, but upon closer reflection
it should be clear that the sensory-motor coordination of the eye focusing on
the candle (a movement) preceded the sensory stimulation of light. That is, an
action preceded the stimulus. Once the sensory data are deciphered, the hand
and eye must work together, in effect mutually stimulating and responding to
each other in order to coordinate the act of reaching. As hand and eye com-

municate with each other, guiding each other in the focusing and reaching, each performs simultaneously functions of stimulus and response. In Dewey's analysis, stimulus and response were not ontological distinctions but functional ones — discriminable but not separable. Consciousness, in a sense, represents an interruption in the smooth operation of this circuit whereby the functions of stimulus and response become necessarily distinguishable. If, for example, the child, eager to handle another glittery plaything, should actually grasp the burning flame, the child immediately realizes that he or she has not grasped just another shiny object but rather something outside his or her experience, something novel or problematic. The child at this point is paralyzed, uncertain as to how to behave toward any shiny object, and the child will remain frozen until he or she reformulates an understanding of reality consistent with all, apparently inconsistent, sensory information. It is the need to reconcile the problematic within experience that necessitates mental functioning.

Of central importance to Dewey in this dynamic is that the reconciliation is not a passive, reflective matter but an active one — the result of a process of manipulation and experimentation. Of central importance to Mead is the point that the active reorganization of reality is the active reorganization of the self: the "me" that comes into view is an interpretation of the impulsive activities of the "I" as it attempts to reconcile a previous but suddenly problematic "me," understood as an objectified view of the self interacting within its social and environmental context, and a new "me," which must respond to its changed situation. This is not to say that mind or its consequence, self, are synonymous with immediate sensuous experience, only that as novel or problematic immediate sensuous experience calls the function of mind into operation, it also throws the meaning of individual identity into play. In this regard, sexual experience becomes all the more poignant, for when the mediation work of the socialized "me" is suspended long enough for the uncensored libido to dominate attention, it is very likely to be felt as acutely problematic.

The fact that the episode in sections 28 and 29 of "Song of Myself" is not just sexual but masturbatory only serves to dramatize what could also be said about other private, sensuous experience that is sufficiently intense to induce confusion. To begin with, the autoerotic nature of the passage conveniently collapses both stimulus and response — the internal and external aspects of experience — within the same subjectivity. For example, the "Flames and ether" that make a rush for his veins, helped by the "Treacherous tip" of him, are but responding to the poet's self, projected into the role of "prurient provokers stiffening" his limbs on all sides. The effect is that of a being seen as an organic, self-enclosed circuit in which "Parting [is] tracked by arriving." With the social — mediating — aspect of the self subordinated simply by the privatized nature of an autoerotic conceit, the result is a kind of word-model that foregrounds one function of consciousness, immediate impulse, "pure feeling." It is not a real subjectivity but a kind of heuristic by which subjectivity might be rendered more visible.

The choice of "quivering" as the verb to characterize the special quality of the process of identity reformation is uniquely appropriate. "Quivering" captures the electrified buzz of nerves straining in anticipation of the incomparable pleasure of a touch as well as the deeply fearful shivering and shaking of one brought to the "headland" to look down over the certain death of self entailed in any transformation. "Quivering" also invites the purely physical image of an organism in the throes of changing its form — or, in more human terms, the outwardly visible hyperkinetic motions of a mind violently reorganizing itself, shouting "I talk wildly . . . . I have lost my wits." The dangerous feeling of the "headland" and the disoriented feeling of "lost wits" combine to dramatize that problematic moment in experience when a prior organization of reality breaks down and the self is paralyzed until a new interpretation can be formulated to direct action. When the quivering comes to an end and the poet reaches an orgasm of "rich showering rain" fertile enough for sprouts to "take and accumulate" in a phallic image of "Landscapes projected masculine full-sized and golden," we discover that the direct consequence of the experience is intellectual: as the erotic and agitated lines of sections 28 and 29 give way to the equanimity of measured lines in section 30, the poet's aloof tone underscores the fact that the sensory cataclysm just concluded has left him with not only a new identity but new philosophical insights:

All truths wait in all things,
They neither hasten their own delivery nor resist it,
They do not need the obstetric forceps of the surgeon,
The insignificant is as big to me as any,
What is less or more than a touch?

Logic and sermons never convince,
The damp of the night drives deeper into my soul.

Only what proves itself to every man and woman is so,
Only what nobody denies is so. (*LV* 40)

The sequence of heightened sexual experience followed by reflection and insight is not an accidental juxtaposition found only at this point in the poem; it is a pattern whose repetition throughout "Song of Myself" marks it as an aspect of that work's deep structure. In section 2, for example, the mild auto-eroticism of the poet who has gone "to the bank by the wood and become undisguised and naked" and who a few lines later indulges himself in "A few light kisses . . . . a few embraces . . . . a reaching around of arms," leads immediately to the intellection of the poet who asks of his readers:

> Have you reckoned a thousand acres much? Have you reckoned the
>   earth much?
> Have you practiced so long to learn to read?
> Have you felt so proud to get at the meaning of poems? (*LV* 2)

An even more dramatic instance of this transaction whereby sensory stimulation leads to intellectual insight is the famous marriage of body and soul depicted in section 5:

> I believe in you my soul . . . . the other I am must not abase itself to you,
> And you must not be abased to the other.
> Loafe with me on the grass . . . . loose the stop from your throat,
> Not words, not music or rhyme I want . . . . not custom or lecture, not
>   even the best,
> Only the lull I like, the hum of your valved voice.
>
> I mind how we lay in June, such a transparent summer morning;
> You settled your head athwart my hips and gently turned over upon me,
> And parted the shirt from my bosom-bone, and plunged your tongue to
>   my barestript heart,
> And reached till you felt my beard, and reached till you held my feet.
>   (*LV* 5–6)

As in the episode concerning touch discussed above, the poet here, too, conceives of sensuous experience as the vehicle to an encounter with the soul. Although there is no apparent psychic turmoil, the absence of the kind of disorientation that marked the poet's confrontation of the problematic in that earlier discussed episode is in fact a function of the speaker's own calculation: the poet has consciously set aside previous organizations of reality as a condition of the sexual encounter. "Not words, not music or rhyme I want," he insists, "not custom or lecture, not even the best." With all culture-bound claims on his identity and perceptions willfully vacated, he is free to solicit something more fundamental and immediate, not the language of culture but its physiological precondition: "Only the lull I like, the hum of your valved voice." Even so — and like the previously discussed episode concerning touch — the immediate and dramatic consequence of the sexual reverie is new insight into himself and the universe:

> Swiftly arose and spread around me the peace and joy and knowledge
>   that pass all the art and argument of the earth;
> And I know that the hand of God is the elderhand of my own,
> And I know that the spirit of God is the eldest of my own,
> And I know that all the men ever born are also my brothers . . . . and the
>   women my sisters and lovers,
> And that a kelson of the creation of love;
> And limitless are leaves stiff or drooping in the fields,
> And brown ants in the little wells beneath them,
> And mossy scabs of the wormfence, and heaped stones, and elder and
>   mullen and pokeweed. (*LV* 6)

At the core of these experience-induced insights are some profound democratic affirmations. To begin with, an essentialism rooted in the primary sensual experience of individuals, particularly one that defines consciousness as partly a function of one's attempt to negotiate the social and material uncertainties of the environment, implies a larger philosophical argument for democracy. In essence, it is the view that democracy is preferable to all other forms of social organization because it alone is grounded in the existential necessity (and capacity) for human choice-making. To be sure, this argument is only latent in Whitman's pre-1860 conception of material selfhood; it is not until after 1860, as we shall see, that agency in that sense becomes central to his democratic vision. What is explicit in the poet's conception of natural democratic selfhood is that it offers no toehold for hierarchical distinctions; distinctions based on birth or class are secondary to the universal — and equal — capacity to feel. Indeed, hierarchies depend upon an ability to reduce the uniqueness of every human being, the infinite variety of potential human responses, to crude and simplistic classifications. By affirming the material, experiential self, Whitman recognizes our irreducible particularity as the essence of democracy and its central truth. Even more pointedly, purely intellectual distinctions, such as those captured by the currently fashionable phrase "cognitive elite" or the less fashionable notion of a caste of priests distinguished by a special ability to access the realm of mind, are abrogated by the inalienable ability of all to share equally in the sensuous "joy and knowledge that pass all the art and argument of the earth."[9] The reason "Logic and sermons never convince" is that they amount to a secondary layer of abstraction drawn from the primary layer of such immediate experience as the seemingly simple "damp of night [that] drives deeper into" the soul. Here Jefferson's deistic construct of "men created equal" takes a secular turn with no loss of moral force; however different are the feelings of each man and woman, no one feels any more or any less — or qualitatively any better — than another; thus "Only what proves itself to every man or woman is so."

3

"The Simple, Compact Well-Join'd Scheme"
Whitman's Democratic Cosmos

In the epigraph to part I, we heard John Dewey ask how we might "construe and interpret the natural environment . . . in order to get an intellectual warrant" for democracy, whether physical nature is hostile or indifferent to democratic aims or possibly willing to give us "an encouraging nod." For Whitman, nature seems to nod. Indeed, one might say that being attentive to those encouraging nods from nature — and translating them into poetry — is one of his chief literary missions. Perhaps more than any other American writer, he seems to construct his democratic vision around a view of nature as not only cooperative but authoritative as well.

This is not to say that Whitman originated the strategy of constructing nature in a way that permits it to serve as a vehicle for expressing other ideas. By deifying the poetic persona as part of his democratic mythology, Whitman seems to participate in what Lawrence Buell refers to as the "solipsistic tendency" in American literature. "Following Emerson's advice," Buell writes, "many of our authors seem to have built their own fictional universes," a move informed by "the romantic vision of the poet as a liberating god and the poem as a heterocosm, or second creation." [1] Thus, too, with ludic eagerness, Whitman puts himself forward as cosmological architect: "It is time to explain myself . . . . let us stand up. / What is known I strip away . . . . I launch all men and women forward with me into the unknown" (*LV* 70–71). Without arguing for the scientific value of such cosmological visions, Buell is quick to warn against "the modernist temptation to view their idea of the cosmology as *purely* metaphorical." Even though the transcendentalists regarded their own cosmologies as subjective impositions on nature, he says, they nonetheless believed that "the poet's approach was (or could be) metaphysically as well as metaphorically true." [2] Such a belief is not without merit. As M. H. Abrams has pointed out, poetic and metaphorical ideas have often challenged old conceptual boundaries and suggested new theoretical formulations and new and productive avenues of scientific research. And, the reverse is also true, as poets often move into new literary terrain with the aid of scientific borrowings.[3]

In the case of Whitman's vision of democracy, "scientific" or cosmological abstractions play several roles; in this chapter, I will explore two of the leading parts in the open drama he puts before us. First, in his conception of the "open road," Whitman constructs a poetic universe that seems nearly as diverse and relative as the physical universe itself. The question I will consider is: Does such a universe have a deeper human and social significance? More specifically, may we read his open road cosmology as a pragmatic argument that the relativity and diversity that are so necessary in physical nature are equally necessary in human society? Moreover, can nature serve in this way as an important model for political democracy and thus lend it, in Dewey's sense, an additional measure of authority? Second, in the poem he would eventually title "Crossing Brooklyn Ferry," Whitman creates a fictive environment that permits him to transcend temporal boundaries so that he might form an immediate and permanent bond with readers throughout time. But bonding throughout time is more than a poetic concern — it is a problematic at the heart of constitutional democracies. The question is why should a democratic people living today feel themselves bound by the wishes and words of those long dead. Why, in other words, should a two-centuries-old Constitution constrain the expressed will of a modern majority? In my discussion of "Crossing Brooklyn Ferry," I will consider the possibility that Whitman presents a metaphysics of time that reconciles this temporal paradox inherent in the idea of a constitutional democracy.

The Open Road

D. H. Lawrence once observed that "Whitman's transformation of the soul from a covert thing to be sought 'above' or 'within' into a 'wayfarer down the open road' was a great liberating act."[4] Lawrence's reference is to "Song of the Open Road," but Richard Chase, in his discussion of the Lawrence quote, makes the better point by arguing that that poem does not represent its material nearly as well as does "Song of Myself." Quoting the former poem, he further observes that "this impulse to provisional experiment and liberation, as well as the announcement that here, on the open road, 'is realization, / Here is a man tallied — he realizes here what he has in him,' makes Whitman's poem a classic statement of American Pragmatism." Though Chase believes that this limits Whitman (along with the entire American literary tradition) to an awareness of only "one philosophical question — namely, necessity vs. free will," the poetic idea of an open road, in fact, spotlights a web of philosophical, cosmological, and ultimately political concerns.[5] Dewey hints at this interrelationship in "The Development of American Pragmatism": "Pragmatism thus has a metaphysical implication. The doctrine of the value of consequences leads us to take the future into consideration [which in turn] leads us to the conception of a universe which is, in James' term 'in the making,' 'in the process of becoming,' of a universe up to a certain point still plastic."[6]

Dewey's writings suggest that he regarded "pragmatism" and "democracy" to be terms that described different aspects of the same reality: whereas pragmatism describes the philosophical (and metaphysical) assumptions that warrant democratic life, democracy describes the way humans should — and sometimes do — translate these assumptions into institutional form. For Whitman, democracy was sufficient to describe it all. Simply change Dewey's "pragmatism" in the preceding quote to "democracy" and we have a fairly good statement of Whitman's own philosophy. To be sure, Whitman's conception of the open road, his version of a universe "in the process of becoming," was not the premise from which he derived his ideas about democracy; rather, his conception of democracy informs his reading of the universe. Though he certainly avails himself of some of the best science that the nineteenth century had to offer, throughout his poetry, but especially in "Song of Myself," we more often find Whitman constructing a vision of the cosmos out of democratic assumptions and then deriving further insights about democratic life from the universe he has created. It is also true that Whitman's democratically grounded open road cosmology actually seems to anticipate some key elements of modern theoretical physics.

At the heart of Whitman's open road is a confluence of three essentially democratic ideas: equality, continuous process, and materiality (the antithesis of spiritualist ideas and the political hierarchies they support). Though the ideas are clearly related politically, their natural relation is far less obvious. Still, Whitman brings them together in section 31 of "Song of Myself" as "natural" facts, thereby inaugurating his conception of the universe as something "in the making":

I believe that a leaf of grass is no less than the journeywork of the stars,
And the pismire is equally perfect, and a grain of sand, and the egg of
   the wren,
And the tree-toad is a chef d'oeuvre for the highest,
And the running blackberry would adorn the parlors of heaven,

And the narrowest hinge in my hand puts to scorn all machinery,
. . . .
I find I incorporate gneiss and coal and long-threaded moss and fruits
    and grains and esculent roots,
And am stucco'd with quadrupeds and birds all over,
And have distanced what is behind me for good reasons,
And call anything close again when I desire it. (*LV* 41)

What becomes immediately clear is the implication of making materiality relevant to the problem of equality. Fundamental equality, he proposes, is the inescapable democratic conclusion we must come to when we recognize that we are all but different arrangements of the same material particles. But relating materiality to process also produces one of the most startlingly suggestive lines in Whitman's poetry: "I believe that a leaf of grass is no less than the journeywork of the stars." The journeywork process here is the process of creation. The poet's immediate intention is to undermine the myth of origins at the center of nondemocratic ideologies generally. Just as no originating breath of a masterful God during some magical moment of creation distinguishes humanity from the rest of existence, so does none distinguish one elite class or race of human from another. (His version of creation is not even the work of a master artisan but merely the steady, competent work of a "journeyman.") But the phrase "journeywork of the stars" also magnifies the sense of movement through both time and space that is already implicit in the idea of a creative process. That is, the process of material creation emerges as much more than a purely local event in an otherwise static universe, but instead the very condition that defines that universe. This becomes even more apparent as section 31 continues and the poet seems to exploit to radical effect the element of ubiquitous temporal and spatial movement he has just introduced. To dramatize the democratic ideal of material equality and the common bonds that equality should entail, the poet figures a universe in which it is impossible for any object to stand apart from him in either time or space.

In vain the speeding or shyness,
In vain the plutonic rocks send their old heat against my approach,
In vain the mastodon retreats beneath its own powdered bones,
In vain objects stand leagues off and assume manifold shapes,
In vain the ocean settling in hollows and the great monsters lying low,
In vain the buzzard houses herself with the sky,
In vain the snake slides through the creepers and logs,

In vain the elk takes to the inner passes of the woods,
In vain the razorbilled auk sails far north to Labrador,
I follow quickly . . . . I ascend to the nest in the fissure of the cliff.

(LV 41–42)

Just as it is useless for "objects to stand leagues off" and disguise themselves by "assuming manifold shapes," so is it useless for the mastodon to retreat back into history; it is temporally and spatially ubiquitous. Now, omnipresence in time and space is surely one of the oldest of theological conceptions, but its deployment here in an ideological system based partly in materialism is at least surprising. This is the poet who neither rejects scientific "facts" nor considers it necessary to confine his vision to scientific terms. True, it is a fiction — and a fiction constructed explicitly for ideological purposes — but the poet also teases out the cosmological implications of his fiction.

The poet's cosmology becomes even more recognizably modern a few lines later, when omnipresence in time and space gives way to a kind of directional flow following the arrow of time. We see this in the long catalog of section 33, one of the most majestic of the poem, which begins with a hyperexcited poet seizing the power in his own intuitions about the cosmos:

Swift wind! Space! My Soul! Now I know it is true what I guessed at;
What I guessed when I loafed on the grass,
What I guessed while I lay alone in my bed . . . . and again as I walked the
    beach under the paling stars of the morning.

My ties and ballasts leave me . . . . I travel . . . . I sail . . . . my elbows rest
    in the sea-gaps,
I skirt the sierras . . . . my palms cover continents,
I am afoot with my vision. (LV 43–44)

Once the poet is afoot, specific references to the main verbal idea of movement ("travel," "sail," "skirt") nearly disappear, along with the poetic "I," as both subject and verb seem to merge into a motional presence that grammatically subordinates most of the section. Diane Wood Middlebrook observes that this section signals the poet's turn from an exploration of the "Real Me," the "autocosmic boundaries of his own body," to "the theme of the macrospheric boundlessness of space and time."[7] It is a suggestive phrase, but the "Real Me," the poetic persona, does not entirely disappear: Of the catalog's 153 lines, over half are either prepositional phrases or subordinate clauses beginning with the conjunction "where," all of which simultaneously locate the poet at a seemingly infinite number of different spatial points. Ultimately, the disruption of spatial limits that allows the poet in motion to be everywhere at once makes linear time irrelevant — for when objects in space are no longer meaningfully separated, no measurement of the time required to bridge spatial separation can be of any use. Effectively, the poet has conflated time and space, so that when subject and verb reemerge at midcatalog, daydreaming at night in the poet's backyard, they do so as pure cosmic energy, obedient to no law other than their own.

Speeding through space . . . . speeding through heaven and the stars,
Speeding amid the seven satellites and the broad ring and the diameter of
    eighty thousand miles,
Speeding with tailed meteors . . . . throwing fire-balls like the rest,
Carrying the crescent child that carries its own full mother in its belly:
Storming enjoying planning loving cautioning,
Backing and filling, appearing and disappearing,
I tread day and night such roads.

I visit the orchards of God and look at the spheric product,
And look at quintillions ripened, and look at quintillions green.

I fly the flight of the fluid and swallowing soul,
My course runs below the soundings of plummets.

I help myself to material and immaterial,
No guard can shut me off, no law can prevent me. (*LV* 48–49)

The "space" the poet speeds through, alongside "tailed meteors," is a material universe in which both time and space are blurred, one marked by a continuous flow. It is also a universe that is derived from the democratic imperatives of equality, continuous process, and materiality. To that list we should add one more politically significant idea, eternal time. To begin with, Whitman uses the theological notion of eternity strategically, to undermine the creation narratives of competing mythologies. In section 44, he announces his own birth as the personification of a democratic god — the people consolidated into their poet. Since the logic of myth dictates that to be legally and ethically prior to other gods a democratic god must be temporally prior to them as well, the origins of the democratic god must be traced back to the mystery of eternity itself.

The clock indicates the moment . . . . but what does eternity indicate?

Eternity lies in bottomless reservoirs . . . . its buckets are rising forever
    and ever,

They pour and they pour all they exhale away.

We have thus far exhausted trillions of winters and summers;
There are trillions ahead, and trillions ahead of them. (*LV* 71)

Certainly, eternity is the very cosmic quintessence of democracy because it
levels all moments, giving each finite speck of time its equal share of infinity;
thus nothing within its boundless bounds may gain privilege based on loca-
tion in time. But as so often happens in Whitman's verse, the poet teases out
further implications of the idea so that its corollary, biological diversity, is now
seen in terms of its democratic value:

Births have brought us richness and variety,
And other births will bring us richness and variety.

I do not call one greater and one smaller,
That which fills its period and place is equal to any. (*LV* 71)

But Whitman's democratic myth of eternity is also a scientific one, as Joseph Beaver points out in *Walt Whitman: Poet of Science.* As Whitman proceeds to envision the actual birth of the democratic god, the conception of
eternity he draws upon is completely informed by the "nebular hypothesis"
gaining currency at that time in scientific circles. Just as Whitman made "genuine poetic use" of the best science of his age, he also made genuine political
use of that science, appropriating it to lend credibility to his conception of a
democratic world that began as a vaporous "huge first nothing" and developed only slowly through vast "bunches of ages": [8]

I am an acme of things accomplished, and I am the encloser of things
    to be.

My feet strike an apex of the apices of the stairs,
On every step bunches of ages, and larger bunches between the steps,
All below duly traveled — and still I mount and mount.

Rise after rise bow the phantoms behind me,
Afar down I see the huge first Nothing, the vapor from the nostrils of
    death,
I know I was even there . . . . I waited unseen and always,
And slept while God carried me through the lethargic mist,
And took my time . . . . and took no hurt from the foetid carbon.

Long I was hugged close . . . . long and long.

Immense have been the preparations for me,
Faithful and friendly the arms that have helped me.

Cycles ferried my cradle, rowing and rowing like cheerful boatmen;
For room for me stars kept aside in their own rings,
They sent influences to look after what was to hold me.

Before I was born out of my mother generations guided me,
My embryo has never been torpid . . . . nothing could overlay it;
For it the nebula cohered to an orb . . . . the long slow strata piled to rest
    it on . . . . vast vegetables gave it sustenance,
Monstrous sauroids transported it in their mouths and deposited it
    with care.

All forces have been steadily employed to complete and delight me,
Now I stand on this spot with my soul. (*LV* 71–72)

Whitman's use of nineteenth-century science serves as an additional argument for reading his democratic mythology in a materialist context. It also resolves the metaphysical paradox of a democratic creator, the "encloser of things to be," who is at the same time its own creation, "an acme of things accomplished." The "God" who carried him "through the lethargic mist" is no more a governing agent than are the stars who cleared room for him by keeping "aside in their own rings." The attribution of intention to God and stars functions merely as an assertion that the material forces of the universe are not (at least) hostile to the processes of democratic life. The true god in this section is the democratic self who stands "on this spot with my soul," the lone author of his own destiny.

Whitman's open road cosmos is, to be sure, an extrapolation of democratic ideas. But it is not wholly so, for it is also informed by the science of the day. As a hybrid of democratic and scientific thought, moreover, it becomes both a productive source of political insight and a prescient sketch of contemporary ideas in theoretical physics. The most compelling example of the latter is in the vision of the cosmos that eventually crystallizes in section 45 of "Song of Myself."

I open my scuttle at night and see the far-sprinkled systems,
And all I see, multiplied as high as I can cipher, edge but the rim of the
    farther systems.

Wider and wider they spread, expanding and always expanding,

Outward and outward and forever outward.

My sun has his sun, and round him obediently wheels,
He joins with his partners a group of superior circuit,
And greater sets follow, making specs of the greatest inside them.

(LV 73–74)

When these lines were published in 1855, the world was still sixty years away from Einstein's discovery that his theory of general relativity implied an unstable and expanding universe (a prospect so troubling to Einstein that he adulterated his theory with a "cosmological constant" in an embarrassing and futile attempt to stabilize the system); the world was yet sixty-seven years away from the time when Alexander Friedman would develop from general relativity an actual mathematical model of an expanding universe; and we were seventy-four years away from the moment when astronomer Edwin Hubble's observations would confirm that, indeed, the galaxies were flying apart and the universe was expanding.[9] Yet as Whitman gazed at the stars through the telescope of his own imagination, "Wider and wider they spread, expanding and always expanding, / Outward and outward and forever outward." The poet did not anticipate — in any meaningful scientific sense — the work of Einstein, Friedman, or Hubble. But neither is the visionary cosmos satisfactorily explained as an accident. When one complicates the progressive motion of an open road with a notion of a democratic eternity marked by the "nebular" origins of life, the premonition of an expanding universe rests just on the edge of the horizon. And when one conjoins that democratic eternity with a belief that the value of an endless succession of births is found in the "richness and variety" that results, the conclusion of an expanding universe seems, in retrospect, almost unavoidable. Of course, what is also unavoidable is an understanding that Whitman's expanding universe was, in part, the cosmic analogue of American imperialism, Manifest Destiny gone stellar. Yet even here we must concede that, for Whitman, American imperialism — which he likely read as the economic migration of mostly poor people into regions beyond the control of existing power structures — was itself an analogue for the energy and optimism that serve to renew life. Indeed, he makes this clear in the stanza that immediately follows:

There is no stoppage, and never can be stoppage;
If I and you and the worlds and all beneath or upon their surfaces, and all
    the palpable life, were this moment reduced back to a pallid float, it
    would not avail in the long run,

We should surely bring up again where we now stand,
And as surely go as much farther, and then farther and farther

A few quadrillions of eras, a few octillions of cubic leagues, do not hazard
    the span, or make it impatient,
They are but parts . . . . anything is but a part.

See ever so far . . . . there is limitless space outside of that,
Count ever so much . . . . there is limitless time around that.
Our rendezvous is fitly appointed . . . . God will be there and wait till we
    come. (*LV* 74)

However prescient Whitman's cosmology may seem, the most that it can be said to actually prove is that it is possible to draw the analogy between the way Whitman constructs democracy and the way science at the present time constructs the universe. After all, both are in some sense hypothetical. Moreover, neither is confirmed by its similarity to the other. Still, it is a highly significant analogy to draw. To see why, consider Dewey's question in the epigraph to part I. Dewey asked if "the world as an object of knowledge is at odds with our" democratic purposes or whether it is "willing to cooperate, that not only does it not say us nay, but gives us an encouraging nod?" [10] When we read Dewey carefully in the context of his often stated hostility to misguided belief in a stable and secure universe, we realize that he is not searching for an authoritative model of the universe from which he might derive principles to govern our social life. Nor is he constructing democracy as an inevitable law of nature. He advances no claim at all. Still, it is a useful question, for we can certainly imagine various conceptions of nature that might "say us nay." If, for example, we lived in a universe that the best empirical science demonstrated to be "closed," one in which first and final causes could be glimpsed through the telescope or diagrammed on a chalkboard, then it would not be unreasonable to believe that those physical laws could and should manifest themselves as the moral and political imperatives of social life. In such a world it would only make good sense to argue that the chaos and uncertainty of democracy undermine any attempt to harmonize with the natural order of things. But, of course, this is not the universe that we believe we live in. Our universe, at least as we currently perceive it, is a fluid, evolving, relative, self-creating place, a universe still in the making, an open road. And, of course, this belief also has consequences. At a very minimum, to believe that the cosmos is fluid and mutable is to doubt its capacity to ground stable and immutable moral principles. Or to put it somewhat differently, if we take seriously the idea that the universe we are a part of is still in the making, then we must consider it likely that we, too, are in the process of self-creation. Indeed, our continued life as a species may depend upon our willingness to see that process as fundamental to all aspects of human experience, our ability to drive that process by liberating the energies of all individuals, and then our capacity to intelligently organize ourselves socially to best engage in that process. The name we have for that process of continuous self-creation on a collective level is liberal democracy. The ultimate significance, then, of Whitman's open road cosmology, the analogy he draws between cosmic and democratic processes, is not in the accuracy of its representations. It is an argument that expresses in poetic terms the idea that reinventing ourselves socially is humanity's existential burden and the rationale behind individual liberty.

Aesthetic Time and the Constitutional Community in "Crossing Brooklyn Ferry"

Whitman's manipulations of time and space are also fictive devices made to operate locally within the universe of his poetry. In this sense, his treatment of time and space become interesting not as representations of the cosmos but as abstractions that have been made more plastic and thus more available for use as aesthetic instruments to resolve philosophical problems. One especially difficult philosophical problem confronting any democratic society concerns the often noted paradox in the idea of a constitutional democracy: at the core of constitutional government is the apparently undemocratic notion that it is proper and good for the people of one era to constrain the wishes of a majority in a subsequent era. Thomas Jefferson spoke to this problem when he observed late in his life that "some men look at constitutions with sanctimonious reverence, and deem them like the ark of the covenant, too sacred to be touched. They ascribe to the men of the preceding age a wisdom more than human, and suppose what they did to be beyond amendment. I knew that age well; I belonged to it, and labored with it. . . . It was very like the present, but without the experience of the present . . . and this they would say themselves, were they to rise from the dead. . . . Let us not weakly believe that one generation is not as capable as another of taking care of itself . . . the dead have no rights."[11]

But Jefferson was in the minority then, just as he is now. In American democratic theory, the dead *do* have rights. We have always conceived of both democracy and the nation as existing through time as well as in time. Previous generations may not govern us absolutely, but we do grant them a voice as historical texts, both legal and literary, which are routinely consulted for insight or direction. Everything from constitutional litigation to, say, the writing of this book attests that our practice of democracy places us in a continuous debate with the dead as well as the living — and those yet to live.

For the people of a democracy to think of themselves as bonded through time to past generations while also holding firm to the belief that it is their fundamental (if theoretical) right to immediately and continuously sever themselves from the past and chart a new course, they must at some level suspend their commonsense notions of time in favor of one that is more fluid or fictional. This describes the philosophical dilemma at the heart of Whitman's 1856 publication of "Crossing Brooklyn Ferry." Using the ferry ride from Brooklyn to Manhattan as a metaphor, Whitman offers a sustained meditation on the idea of transcending time in order to share sensuous experience, and hence identity, with past and future generations. And his conception of the "well-joined scheme" and its corollary image, the "float," effectively models a vision of a democratic nation in communion with its own heritage. To put this another way, Whitman's poem functions as a necessary fiction that reconciles the paradox of American democracy and American national continuity.

A necessary fiction, we should note at the outset, runs certain risks — in this case, criticism from those who are too often troubled by what seems to be a mystical logic that informs the poem. Betsy Erkkila, for example, one of the more sensitive of Whitman's critics, effectively glosses the critical consensus on the poem "as an attempt to invest the material world with the glow and glory of spiritual significance." Though she seems to endorse that view, she judiciously appends to it a kind of historicist reading. In the poem's "overarching concern with the problem of disintegration and union" conveyed by the pivotal "well-joined scheme," she contends that the poem's "overarching theme" permits it to read "also [as] a response to the fact of fracture in self and world at a time when traditional social structures were collapsing under the pressure of the new market economy." [12] This is no doubt true, just as it is true (as Erkkila herself has pointed out elsewhere) that fear of fracture also informed national political life. Nevertheless, Erkkila's critique fails to consider the temporal element of the problem — and the poem is, after all, concerned with the problem of time. More important, such commentary never goes beyond the issue of motivation. The presumption that the poem is essentially mystical seems to foreclose any need to evaluate Whitman's proposed resolution of these problems.

Be that as it may, Whitman opens the poem in a pensive state of wonder concerning the "hundreds and hundreds that cross" with him and even those "that shall cross from shore to shore years hence." The fact that he is replicating an act that will in turn be replicated by others many times in the future prompts him to reflect on what that act — crossing on the ferry — suggests of his connection to the multitude of strangers whose behavior he duplicates. His first insight, then, coming in section 2, concerns the paradox that though we are all disintegrated — both collectively and even individually reducible to discrete atomic particles — we are nevertheless linked by our mutual participation in some "well-joined scheme":

> The impalpable sustenance of me from all things, at all hours of the day,
> The simple, compact, well-joined scheme — myself disintegrated,
>   everyone disintegrated yet part of the scheme,
> The similitudes of the past and those of the future,
> The glories strung like beads on my smallest sights and hearings — on
>   the walk in the street, and the passage over the river,
> The current rushing so swiftly, and swimming with me far away,
> The others that are to follow me, the ties between me and them,
> The certainty of others — the life, love, sight, hearing of others.
>
> (*LV* 217–218)

A key feature of the poet's "well-joined scheme" is a certain conception of time. Here, Whitman seems to anticipate Henri Bergson's conception of *duree reelle*, or "real" or "pure" time, which that philosopher distinguished from the mathematical and spatial conceptions of scientific time (that is, time measured by the hands of a clock) by asserting, in T. A. Goudge's rephrasing, that real time is "a flowing, irreversible succession of states that melt into each other to form an indivisible process."[13] Bergson's "real time" is the experience of experience — the sense of movement one obtains from an immediate engagement with all the minutiae of life; an impression of linear progression is created by "glories strung like beads" when such beads are understood as the poet's sequence of responses to the "smallest sights and hearings — on the walk in the street, and the passage over the river." For Whitman, privileging concrete experience in this way — given "The similitudes of the past and those of the future" — seems to allow him to form a bond through time by establishing a commonality of experience with the "Others [who] will enter the gates of the ferry, and cross from shore to shore," and these others "will see the islands large and small." Indeed,

> Fifty years hence others will see them as they cross, the sun half an
>   hour high,
> A hundred years hence, or ever so many hundred years hence, others
>   will see them,

Will enjoy the sun-set, the pouring in of the floodtide, the falling-back to
the sea of the ebbtide. (*LV* 218)

Even as a Bergsonian conception of time privileges immediate experience
over abstraction, it still does not achieve quite the level of intimacy that Whitman would wish for his bond. Section 3 of the poem begins by taking a leap
from the assertion of a commonality of experience to the intimation of simul-
taneity of experience:

It avails not, neither time or place — distance avails not,
I am with you, you men and women of a generation, or ever so many
generations hence,
I project myself, also I return — I am with you, and know how it is.
Just as you feel when you look on the river and sky, so I felt,
Just as any of you is one of a living crowd, I was one of a crowd,
Just as you are refreshed by the gladness of the river, and the bright flow,
I was refreshed, (*LV* 218–219)

As is so often noted, Whitman's verb tense begins to shift here, with the future
rendered in the present tense while the present is relegated to the past.[14] A linear flow such as Bergson's, which permanently separates past, present, and future, no longer seems to operate in the poem. Clearly the poet is "defying
time," as Gay Wilson Allen has put it.[15] But he is also pointing out that, in one
respect, some experience persists through time — or that a strictly linear conception of flowing time is not sufficient to account for the way experience that
has been consolidated into texts seems to live on, continuously eliciting responses in the present.

It is important that the poem's redefinition of time is explicitly fictive. The
poet makes this clear when he opens section 5 with a direct address to the
reader: "What is it, then, between us? What is the count of the scores or hundreds of years between us?" (*LV* 220). It is a question he will answer some
forty-four lines later with the declaration that "What the push of reading
could not start is started by me personally, is it not?" (*LV* 223). In other words,
what is between him and his reader is "nothing substantial"; poet and reader
are only contiguous in the sense that they are both enclosed within the same
fictive time of the poem. The rules that govern the relationship between him
and his reader are wholly a function of the poem itself, they operate only
within the confines of the poem. The creation of aesthetic time is important,
however, not simply because it allows Whitman to establish what seems to be
a personal connection to his reader but because it provides him with an alternative temporal logic that has political significance. But that significance does

not begin to clarify until he reifies his conception of time in the more concrete image of the "float."

Whitman introduces the image of the float as the answer to a riddle. He seems to tease us: When he asks what is the nature of the thing that separates him from his readers in the opening to section 5, his immediate response to the rhetorical question is not an answer but the conditions that will serve to limit an answer: "Whatever it is, it avails not — distance avails not, and place avails not" (*LV* 220). The reader has already been asked to suspend common-sense expectations of time; now we are told that "distance" and "place" do not matter either. "Whatever it is," it does not obey commonsense notions of space. What it is comes six lines later:

> I too had been struck from the float forever held in solution,
> I too had received identity by my body,
> That I was, I knew was of my body, and what I should be, I knew I
>   should be of my body. (*LV* 221)

Whitman's float is a spatial as well as a temporal fiction. Though the "float forever held in solution" has long been recognized, as Allen phrases it, as "a metaphor for the salt water (or ocean) in the east river," critics have variously interpreted it as "Emerson's Over-Soul," "cosmic consciousness," the "womb and amniotic fluid," or other such tortured or quasi-mystical substances.[16] A more conventional interpretation produces a more coherent reading: dating back at least as far as Heraclitus, flowing streams and sea passages have been common metaphors for time. An obvious reading of "Crossing Brooklyn Ferry" would interpret the "float forever held in solution" as consistent with both. But following D. C. Williams, the philosopher J. J. C. Smart claims that both of these metaphors entail a deep misconception about the way time works. For Smart, they are representations of the "myth of passage" — falsehoods that suggest that we move in space relative to a time that somehow flows past us when, in the reality of contemporary theoretical physics, movement in space *is* movement in time.[17]

Significantly, Whitman's metaphor both borrows and undermines the "passage" convention: if time is a flowing stream or river of experience, Whitman's ferry does not flow with it or against it but crisscrosses over it — back and forth, sideways in Bergson's experiential time — from shore to shore. Indeed, as the poet looks to his own materials, he discovers a nonlinear form of enveloping experience that swirls around him: he notes the seagulls "high in the air floating with motionless wings" making "slow-wheeling circles" as they only gradually edge toward the south, "fine centrifugal spokes of light round the shape of my head in the sun-lit water," "the tremulous whirl of the wheels," and "The scallop-edged waves in the twilight, the ladled cups, the frolicsome crests and glistening" (*LV* 219-220). The result is a kind of temporal stasis where all movement seems locked within a closed system, while the cyclical repetition of similar movements that give pattern to change become now mere circularity — time flying in a holding pattern. Consequently, distance and place "avail not"; they no longer function as meaningful distinctions when space — in this case, the water the ferry travels on — has been reconceived as the metaphor for static time. As he did in the passages from "Song of Myself" previously discussed, the poet once again collapses time into space, or, to use a coinage of Stephen Hawking, time and space become a "singularity."

While the chief political value of Whitman's time/space fiction may be the way it reconciles the contradiction inherent in the idea of a constitutional democracy, it also suggests a number of additional democratic ideas, and it is worthwhile to digress a moment to consider them. Many reiterate or support points made in the previous two chapters, while others add dimension to Whitman's democratic float. First and most obvious is that when the matter of space is "well-joined" in a simple, compact scheme with time, it compels a recognition that the poet is ontologically identical to his readers who were, like him, "struck" from the same solution: he shares both their origins and compositional material. No argument for distinction or privilege can be grounded in nature. Second, the notion of aesthetic space-time, the infinity of a "float forever held in solution," provides no room for something prior to it. There is no first or final cause; the commonsense notion of causal sequences, if they exist at all in "Crossing Brooklyn Ferry," are but the discrete, localized transactions between such things as steamers and pilots, seagulls and sky, or rail and idly leaning passenger. No effect can be traced back to the work of some superagent, god, or force operating outside the bounds of Whitman's poetically conceived space-time.

This latter point has clear ethical implications. That is, no causal order — imagined as something extrinsic to the very natural environs of the poet's space-time conception — can be seen to authorize an ethical structure or motivate action within the system. "It is not upon you alone the dark patches fall," he says in section 6, "The dark threw patches down upon me also" (*LV* 221). As emblems of the evil the section proceeds to catalog, the cast shadows of clouds emerge spontaneously, position arbitrarily, and dissipate without reason. Good and evil (which is to say, cultural ideas) are wholly natural things in that they are sponsored by no supernatural being — except, perhaps, the poet, who, like his readers, "Played the part that still looks back on the actor or actress, / The same old role, the role that is what we make it, as great as we like, or as small as we like, or both great and small" (*LV* 222). Whitman's often misunderstood amorality comes down to this point: moral and ethical constructions are "natural" entities in that they are aspects of natural processes, not intrusions into nature by some supernatural other. They are not the regulatory standards of some creator but ways in which human beings within creation function as part of the self-regulating system that is nature. By professing everywhere in his poetry that good as well as evil are aspects of his cosmic identity, his natural inheritance, he is not arguing for moral neutrality; rather, he is acknowledging that good and evil are terms we use to assign value to our own strategies for living. It signals his refusal to see humanity as pawns in a dramatic contest between *super*natural forces of good and evil. Whatever role we play in that moral drama, he argues, it is one that we stage ourselves, playing "the part that still looks back on the actor or actress."

Third, Whitman's collapsing of space and time complicates the more naive notions of materialism that are sometimes attributed to him — especially as that materialism is connected with a "spiritual substance." In effect, the "matter" of space now becomes a manifestation of time — a point that is made explicitly by striking the poet's body (or any body) from the temporal solution as well as implied as a logical extension of the "well-joined scheme." Dewey, in *Experience and Nature*, expresses essentially the same idea when he asserts that "matter has turned out to be nothing like as lumpy and chunky as unimaginative prejudice conceived it to be" (*EN* 97). Properly conceived, it is a quality or character of interacting events. What lends matter its substantial, solid sense of permanency is only the fact that, from a human perspective, the rate of change is so slow. For Dewey, there is no categorical distinction between the solid but dull realm of hard "substances" and the precious, evanescent, and transient realm of phenomena (*EN* 96–97). Both are the observed qualities of temporal events.

This reconception of the role of time sheds further light on Whitman's conception of the soul discussed in chapter 2 and, by extension, the idea of political identity. When we place Whitman's "attempt," in Erkkila's phrase, "to invest the material world with the glow and glory of spiritual significance" in the context of his time/space fiction, we discover that the metaphor of "investiture" does not quite accurately describe the connection he imagines between body and spirit. In the opening lines of section 5, once the poet's body is struck from the temporal solution he can proclaim, "I too received identity by my body." The emergence of both body and "identity" — one of Whitman's many synonyms for soul — from the temporal solution suggests that both (if they can even be distinguished) are in some sense born of time. The poet's soul (or his "mind" or "identity") is not only to be understood in terms of its material origin but its temporal one as well. Moreover, the body appears to emerge prior to the soul, or perhaps simultaneously, if they were ever separate.

Again, Whitman seems to anticipate Dewey. Recall that Dewey first challenges the legitimacy of all dualisms, such as spirit versus matter or mind versus body (essentially, different expressions of the same dualism), by demonstrating that mental activity, however it be conceived as a spiritual entity, is nevertheless a natural function wholly necessitated by the human need to continuously recalibrate our responses to the environment in order to sustain life. Mind, as a natural activity, is distinguished from the strictly physical activity of the inanimate world, or the psycho-physical activities of the animate world, only by its increased level of "complexity and intimacy of interaction among natural events" (*EN* 214). Thus the question is begged: How was it that this natural function came to be dissociated from the material organ that performs it? Dewey's answer points to a temporal confusion:

> The idea that matter, life and mind represent separate kinds of Being is a doctrine that springs, as so many philosophic errors have sprung, from a substantiation of eventual functions. The fallacy converts consequences of interaction of events into causes of the occurrence. . . . "Matter," or the physical, is a character of events when they occur at a certain level of interaction. It is not itself an event or existence; the notion that while "mind" denotes essence, "matter" denotes existence is superstition. It is more than bare essence; for it is a property of a particular field of interacting parts. (*EN* 214)

One of the consequences, in other words, of struggling for life in a world that favors greater and greater ingenuity for survival is that the creatures who successfully adapt to that world by evolving that ingenuity will prosper. "Mind," therefore, is a consequence — an effect — of the natural preference for the function of thought. But everyday intuition reverses this temporal order: the fact of thought, commonsense dictates, presumes the antecedent existence of some agent causing the thought. The classic conception of mind, then, like its cousins spirit and soul, is the hypostatization of an eventual function — an erroneous substantiation that results when it is not understood as a temporal product, "a character of events in interaction" (*EN* 214).

The notion that identity, political identity, is, in Dewey's phrase, "a character of events in interaction" or a product of experiential transactions over time returns us to an examination of "Crossing Brooklyn Ferry" as a reconciliation in poetry of the paradox of a constitutional democracy. First, in a negative sense, it strips away nondemocratic conceptions of national identity. The "identity" the poet depicts as being received from the body, especially as that identity is understood politically as an American soul, can have no determinative antecedent existence grounded in class, race, ethnicity, or pristine cultural pedigree. It is not an ethereal and immutable substance preserved outside the bounds of time. In a positive sense, however, the poet has not eliminated the soul's grounding but shifted it into time: time, the time of each and every moment, becomes the site of the soul's origination.

In this context, Bergson's concept of "real time" as a sense of flow generated by the process of experience becomes more meaningful — not because it accurately defines time but because it highlights the way experience in time provides a fertile site for the generation of the soul of Whitman's "identity." This starts to become more clear when the poet establishes his identity with the reader in section 7:

> Closer yet I approach you,
> What thought you have of me, I had as much of you — I laid in my stores
>   in advance,
> I considered long and seriously of you before you were born.
> Who was to know what should come home to me?
> Who knows but I am enjoying this?
> Who knows but I am as good as looking at you now, for all you cannot
>   see me? (*LV* 222)

Here, the poet's fictive time has effected a liberation of experience; the separate experience of poet and reader, otherwise thought to be locked in time, now becomes portable through time. Consequently, there is a reciprocal movement: while the poet more closely approaches the reader, the reader's experience, in turn, moves toward him, for "Who was to know what should come home to me?" This reciprocal attraction between poet and reader upon the plane of his reconceived time has two immediate effects. First, it seems to intensify the poet's own sensory experience, as nothing seems to him "more stately" than "mast- / hemmed Manhatta," "river and sunset, and my scallop-edged waves of flood-tide" (*LV* 223). Second, it culminates in an apparently mystical bond, a perfect identity between reader and poet:

> Curious what gods can exceed these that clasp me by the hand, and with voices I love call me promptly and loudly by my nighest name as I approach,
> Curious what is more subtle than this which ties me to the woman or man that looks in my face,
> Which fuses me into you now, and pours my meaning into you. (*LV* 223)

The stuff of everyday experience, what Heidegger called *Faktizitat,* or facticity, becomes a necessary but not sufficient condition for identity. Complete identity, political identity, is a function of shared experience, a consequence of "fusing" meaning through time.

To share experience and thus fuse identity through time is to engage in a process of writing and reading texts, whether they be constitutional or literary. But it is decidedly not a form of critical reading. As Kerry C. Larson persuasively argues in his insightful analysis, "Crossing Brooklyn Ferry" cannot be read as a usable model of the reading process. Employing the metaphor of contractual negotiation to describe the necessary struggle between writer and reader over the meaning of a text, Larson makes the useful point that Whitman seems far more interested in establishing what Denis Donoghue called "contact" with his reader. Achieving contact, in Larson's reading, means achieving an intimate and uncritical bond with the reader, one that circumvents the need to negotiate contentious particulars and "thrives on the promise of indiscriminate receptivity." Although Whitman creates a feeling of closure by projecting a sense of an agreement reached with the reader, "the precise terms" of the understanding, Larson asserts, are "perhaps of less consequence than the process of assimilation itself." Thus: "The poem seems written under the constraint of a double imperative: it desires to affirm an unparalleled intimacy with its auditor that suggests him to be absolutely intrinsic to the poem's development at the same time it is moved to stipulate that those ties which bind listener to author are absolutely extrinsic to interpretative reflection. What Whitman would impress upon us is not a method of reading but its irrelevance." [18]

It seems to me that Larson's reading is fundamentally sound. The poem clearly does not offer a usable model of interpretation, nor does it attempt to determine the results of the assimilation process by asserting the "precise terms" that should organize it. When read as a purely local attempt at poetic communication, it would appear to fail in its aims. But there is nothing that demands that we so read it. When read instead as a celebratory and abstract representation of the process by which a culture, a people, a nation, consolidate their collective identity by assimilating a past, it succeeds quite well. Larson's own gloss describes that process even more economically. The "double imperative" of a constitutional, democratic nation is first to affirm an "unparalleled intimacy" with the authors of its past in a way that recognizes them as "absolutely intrinsic" to the nation's development. To overrule Jefferson, the dead do have rights, and they exercise them through our willingness to imagine our own experience as a continuation of the experience that they have distilled in their texts. But second, this continuity is a fiction motivated by the desire of many to find proof of our collective identity in our continuing conversation about the meaning of certain texts. However much — and in whatever ways — the precise terms of that collective identity may change through time and "interpretative reflection," these terms are extrinsic and quite irrelevant to the desire to bind ourselves to a shared past.

Still, democracy necessarily privileges the here and now, just as time, as we experience it, moves us progressively forward. Thus, as the poet opens his concluding section, he seems to restart time and space, returning the reader to conventional time through a series of commands that puts them back into regular motion. The river is told to "flow on," the waves are told to "frolic," the clouds are told to "drench," the crowds are told to continue to "cross," the "masts of Manahatta" are told to "stand up," and so on, until he returns once again to his theme:

> Appearances, now or henceforth, indicate what you are!
> You necessary film, continue to envelop the soul!
> About my body for me, and your body for you, be hung our divinest
>   aromas!
> Thrive, cities! Bring your freight, bring your shows, ample and sufficient
>   rivers!
> Expand, being than which none else is perhaps more spiritual!
> Keep your places, objects than which none else is more lasting!
>
> We descend upon you and all things, we arrest you all,
> We realize the soul only by you, you faithful solids and fluids,
> Through you color, form, location, sublimity, ideality,
> Through you every proof, comparison, and all the suggestions and
>   determinations of ourselves. (*LV* 224–225)

Poet and reader may both "realize the soul" through these objects because it is the experience of them — the infinite number of transactions between individual and environment — that defines identity; to the extent that these objects remain constant through time, they dangle the hope of an objective referent by which the poet may argue an identity, through time, with his reader. But no truly democratic conception of identity, however much it might want to ground itself in precedent, can allow the past a final say. The present always retains the right to create it all anew. Whatever of the past is latent in the objects of experience and whatever of the present is latent in the texts of the past, they remain silent until called forth for use by a present exercising the prerogative of interpretive liberty, "free sense":

> You have waited, you always wait, you dumb beautiful ministers! you
>   novices!
> We receive you with free sense at last, and are insatiate henceforward,
> Not you any more shall be able to foil us, or withhold yourselves from us,
> We use you, and do not cast you aside — we plant you permanently
>   within us,
> We fathom you not — we love you — there is perfection in you also,
> You furnish your parts toward eternity,
> Great or small, you furnish your parts toward the soul. (*LV* 225)

4

"Not Chaos or Death . . . . It Is Form and Union and Plan" *Laissez-faire and the Problem of Agency*

If we extrapolate the logic of Whitman's material conception of self, a self shaped through concrete experience, we come almost inevitably to an idea of human agency in which individuals attempt to manage their lives through purposeful action. The same is true when we reason back from his self-creating, process-oriented, open road cosmology. In both cases we reach ideas that would seem to urge us to believe that the capacity to formulate alternative courses of action and then choose among them is fundamental to human life. Such a belief is also essential to any conception of liberal democracy — particularly the version advanced by pragmatism. Yet the idea of human agency seems strikingly absent from Whitman's democratic vision in 1855 and 1856. The self he represents in the first two editions seems either to observe events from a distance or only passively participate in them. The self appears neither able nor inclined to exert influence on the course of its own career. In this chapter, I will explore two related aspects of Whitman's evisceration of human agency: first, I trace its origins to the peculiar demands of his poetic theory and to his romanticized conception of nature as safe; second, I consider how, in the absence of human agency, Whitman locates the animating force of his vision in the cosmos. The universe he spins into poetry appears to be governed by an "invisible hand" — linking it, in effect, to the laissez-faire ideas prevalent in Jacksonian America.

The Passive Self

The absence of agency manifests itself in many ways and on numerous occasions in Whitman's early work. Very often it shows up as an exaggerated form of passivity. In the famous sexual union between body and soul depicted in section 5 of "Song of Myself," for example, we see that "peace and joy and knowledge" simply "spread around" him so that he seems just as helpless to resist the new knowledge as he had been to resist the lover (*LV* 6). In section 30, he is even more explicit about his passive role in the acquisition of knowledge:

All truths wait in all things,
They neither hasten their own delivery nor resist it,
They do not need the obstetric forceps of the surgeon, (*LV* 40)

However consistent with strains of romantic, transcendental, or Quaker ideology this view of thought as a matter of passive reception may be, it runs decidedly against the pragmatist tradition embodied by Dewey and James — and, more to the point, against the dynamics of a conception of selfhood that is as dependent upon immediate experience as is Whitman's.[1] To recall the discussion of the poet's soul in chapter 2, in Whitman we have the condition of thought (immediate experience), we have an aspect of the cause of thought (problematic experience), and we have the effect of that cause and condition (thought itself), but we do not have the actual dynamics of the transaction. For Dewey, these dynamics were understood to be an active manipulation of and experimentation with the materials of existence. The only reason mind and identity exist is to make the resolution of problematic experience possible. In *Experience and Nature*, for example, he locates all human existence in a cross section between that which is stable and predictable in experience and that which is problematic, or as he preferred to say, "precarious": "The conjunction of problematic and determinate characters in nature renders every existence, as well as every idea and human act, an experiment in fact, even though not in design. To be intelligently experimental is but to be conscious of this intersection of natural conditions so as to profit by it instead of being at its mercy" (*EN* 61).

Nowhere in the first two editions of *Leaves of Grass* do we find a poet who must grapple between alternatives and decide among them. Decision-making cannot help but be there somewhere — for, as Dewey reminds us, it is an inescapable fact of existence — still it goes unrecognized by the poet and unincorporated into his phenomenology of democratic selfhood. We are left with an architecture of static being — that is, being without a motive for behavior. Even though he represents identity as the product of a dynamic process, it is a process that *happens to* the self.

Although many varied cultural, political, and biographical explanations might reasonably be advanced to account for Whitman's depiction of the self as passive in the first two editions of *Leaves of Grass*, it is in the first place a by-product of his own expectations of the medium of poetry. He had written in the 1855 preface that "the greatest poet has less a marked style and is more the channel of thoughts and things without increase or diminution, and is the free channel of himself" (*CRE* 719). This view of poetry does not stop at merely recognizing its power to record or organize immediate experience; it asserts that there is a level of poetry that actually *is* immediate experience. It is in this light that we should see the poet's highly eroticized flirtations with the soul in, for instance, sections 5 and 27–29 of "Song of Myself": as the "free channel of himself," the poet is not so much narrating an experience as he is attempting to have one. The passages are so highly charged with erotic impulse, so convincing, that there is no reason to doubt that he is riding the crest of an immediate sexual experience. But the mistake the poet appears to make is in believing that poetry or language is a "free channel" for that immediate experience or that the experience happens *in* language. In an often quoted passage from *Experience and Nature*, Dewey writes:

> Immediacy of existence is ineffable. But there is nothing mystical about such ineffability; it expresses the fact that of direct experience it is futile to say anything to one's self and impossible to say anything to another. Discourse can but intimate connections which if followed out may lead one to have an existence. Things in their immediacy are unknown and unknowable, not because they are remote or behind some impenetrable veil of sensation or ideas, but because knowledge has no concern with them. . . . Immediate things may be *pointed to* by words, but not described or defined. (*EN* 73)

As Dewey claimed in "The Reflex Arc Concept in Psychology" and elsewhere, the function of "knowledge" — which means all cognitive activities such as language-using or poetry-making — is to manage one's living situation. Mediation is always mediation for a purpose. One does not have an immediate experience through the medium of poetry but rather uses poetry, however unconsciously, to shape and manage an experience. Linguistic and narrative decisions organize the chaos and mystery of immediate experience into usable or safe or predictable "recognizable" objects. But because Whitman has conflated the mediation of experience through poetry with the very sensuous and immediate experience poetry would organize, his poetry fails to incorporate an understanding that the poet is an agent actively engaged in mediating. Hence though the effects of mediation are present in the poetry, he fails to account for such an agent in his metaphysical vision.

The omission of agency from a naturalistic metaphysics seriously undermines its usefulness as a warrant for democratic life; however "free" such an agentless metaphysics as Whitman's may be, it must nonetheless remain absolutely silent on the important democratic problems of individual motive and behavioral consequences. Put another way, an agentless metaphysics does not simply omit one aspect of a democratically conceived universe but also reveals itself to be blind to the very conditions of existence that make full democratic life both morally and materially superior to any other conceivable arrangement — for agents are only necessitated by a special kind of metaphysics, a certain kind of reality. Dewey makes this point by contrasting the various schools of rationalism, schools that depend upon the ability to reduce all existence to mathematical equations or predictable principles, with a more naturalistic conception:

> As against this common identification of reality with what is sure, regular and finished, experience in unsophisticated forms gives evidence of a different world and points to a different metaphysics. We live in a world which is an impressive and irresistible mixture of sufficiencies, tight completeness, order, recurrences which make possible prediction and control, and singularities, ambiguities, uncertain possibilities, processes going on to consequences as yet indeterminate. They are mixed not mechanically but vitally like the wheat and tares of the parable. . . . Qualities have defects as necessary conditions of their excellencies; the instrumentalities of truth are the causes of error; change gives meaning to permanence and recurrence makes novelty possible. A world that was wholly risky would be a world in which adventure is impossible, and only a living world can include death. (*EN* 43)

Dewey believed that all existence is a tension between the safe, predictable, and certain, on the one hand, and the dangerous, unpredictable, and unstable, on the other. Human intellect is a "naturally selected" ability to negotiate between these two categorical relations in order to stabilize human life. But so pervasive is this human need to stabilize and use the environment, ridding it of danger and uncertainty, that historically it has informed not only common work and thought but also many of our metaphysical conceptions of reality itself. The desire — the need — to live in a stable, predictable world often led thinkers to conjure up delusive metaphysical visions of the world as rationally ordered and ultimately safe. The various and tortured conceptions of rational, idealistic, and religious schools of thought ignore all that is random and precarious in life; in so doing, they foreclose a full appreciation of ourselves as beings naturally selected to respond to, act in, and thrive on a volatile world. We are, existentially, agents. Still, when we turn to Whitman's first two editions of *Leaves of Grass*, we find that it is not just agency that is missing; equally important, the precarious conditions that would make agency necessary are also either missing or muted.

At first blush, this might not seem to be the case. The autoerotic encounter of section 28, for example, seems to be the very quintessence of danger: the touch that quivers him to "a new identity" is, after all, an explicit acknowledgment that sexuality entails the certain danger of loss of self. It is just this danger that prompts the poet to fret about his senses having left him "helpless to a red marauder," even coming "to the headland to witness and assist against" him. But the episode pivots on one line that belies the danger it would pretend: "I went myself first to the headland . . . . my own hands carried me there" (*LV* 39). In the first clause, he appears to confess responsibility, the moral implication of agency; yet immediately in the second clause he relieves the "me" of such responsibility by displacing it onto his own "hands," which seem to have carried him there, willing or not. The effect is a paradox — an act that has been purposefully contrived by a passive agent. The "me" that carries the weight of identity would appear to be hostage to his own alienated hands as they grip the penis. But it is not so much a penis the hands grip but a pen, for even though the passage is in many respects a genuine sexual reverie, it is nonetheless a reverie conducted *in language* for the ideological purpose of parsing the self. And even though the poet may confuse such an exercise with immediate experience — a happy confusion in that it produces a nearly living allegory — the exercise is still governed by a visionary idea, not by internal pressures, however vividly felt or expressed. Here, all the danger and precariousness that might attend an actual erotic experience collapse safely within the confines of the controlled environment of the poem; conversely, here, too, all responsibility for choice-making an agent might otherwise be held to is lifted from the poem's speaker and disseminated throughout that same linguistic sphere. Like a ride on a roller coaster, where panic is induced for pleasure — and even the very real experience of fear is useless as a motive to guide a gondola whose course holds rigidly to the predictable gyrations of a track — Whitman is free to indulge, even exploit, sexual impulses without the need to manage their direction, for he has already subordinated their play within the poetry to a larger metaphysical apparatus. By troping the libido and its attendant dangers — transforming them into figures of speech to be used for ideological purposes — he does more than deprive his vision of the kind of animating mechanism necessary to sustain intelligent democracy; to the extent that the ideological machine is drawn inward so that it actually structures the free play of his own sexual responses, he not only insulates himself from the very private demands of his own sexuality but, as will become more clear in the next chapter, leaves the integrity of the vision itself vulnerable to newer, different, and more vital sexual experience.

Sexual danger is not the only form of the precarious that gets troped in Whitman's first two editions of *Leaves of Grass*. Perhaps the more obvious example of the way he elides the existential threat to life is his articulation of a philosophy of death. Whitman's ideas about death permeate his entire oeuvre; consequently, they are often favorite subjects of critical commentary. Even the most casual Whitman reader is likely to be familiar with the broad outlines of his death philosophy. In brief, death is not the antithesis of life but the mechanism by which life is continued throughout eternity; it is not to be feared as the instrument of divine retribution for sin but embraced as the proof of our own regeneration. Thus the poet of "Song of Myself" can confidently proclaim in section 48 that "No array of terms can say how much I am at peace about God and about death" (*LV* 79). The assertion, coming near the poem's conclusion — its figurative death prefiguring its rebirth — serves to introduce the poet's recapitulation of his philosophy in section 49:

And as to you death, and you bitter hug of mortality . . . . it is idle to try
    to alarm me.

To his work without flinching the accoucheur comes,
I see the elderhand pressing receiving supporting,
I recline by the sills of the exquisite flexible doors . . . . and mark the
    outlet, and mark the relief and escape.

And as to you corpse I think you are good manure, but that does not
    offend me,
I smell the white roses sweetscented and growing,
I reach to the leafy lips . . . . I reach to the polished breasts of melons.

And as to you life, I reckon you are the leavings of many deaths,
No doubt I have died myself ten thousand times before. (*LV* 80)

For those readers who are drawn to secular appropriations of typically religious notions, Whitman's philosophy of death may be intellectually quite satisfactory, if not quite emotionally satisfying. The idea that, materially, the life process can be properly understood as the continuous reorganization of a finite set of atomic particles is no less valid spiritually or important metaphysically simply because it is now a commonplace. For readers who are especially interested in the democratic implications of all such cosmological abstractions, Whitman's philosophy of death has much to offer. Larzer Ziff, to cite but one example, acknowledges that even though the "democracy of death is an old literary truism," Whitman deepens the idea by grounding his conception of spiritual democracy in the belief that latent in the idea of material death is a corporal, egalitarian soul that belies life's real and observable inequality; hence "[t]he great poet of democracy had to be the writer of the great poems of death."[2] Still, what Whitman's philosophy of death does not do, particularly as represented by the passage quoted above, is attempt to negotiate — or even express — the real, everyday, existential fear of dying. When the poet directly assures death that "it is idle to try to alarm me," he is not expressing an indifference to personal safety or a courageous willingness to risk known peril but an explicit refusal to grant metaphysical standing to the kind of precarious conditions that should elicit a reasonable fear. Even the bravado of the line — which from other, less boisterous poets might reveal terror by attempting to mask it — is by Whitmanian standards so restrained (even missing the ubiquitous exclamation mark) as to discourage a similar interpretation. Nor does the philosophy of death articulated in these lines seem to validate the act of mourning: however false such compensations may be, the common religious promise of eternal life amounts, at a minimum, to a recognition and affirmation of grief. But no such affirmation is clear when the consoling promise is not of everlasting consciousness but of reconstitution as "manure."

Though Whitman's philosophy of death did not substantially change throughout his poetic career, his poetic approach to death-grief did. Edward Butscher observes that "the essential paradox of Whitman resides in the fact that he achieved his greatest power in elegies and laments, in those very poems like 'In Midnight Sleep,' 'A Noiseless Patient Spider,' 'Out of the Cradle Endlessly Rocking,' and 'When Lilacs Last in the Dooryard Bloom'd' where subtle undercurrents of sadness and protest against man's mortal fate seem at their strongest." For Butscher, these poems do not represent a rejection of Whitman's own philosophy but rather instances when his perceptions about life and death are "at sharp variance with the underlying emotional and implicit awareness of them."[3] Butscher is certainly correct, but Whitman's elegies and laments were not written as homilies about his distanced philosophical conceptions of death but as literary instruments for organizing his own emotional responses to actual death. Whitman's immediate encounters with death would have a profound effect on his poetry, a point I will consider more fully in a subsequent chapter. But it is an impact that would come at a later stage in the poet's career. The poems Butscher cites (to which we should add nearly all of the *Drum-Taps* and "Sea Drift" clusters) were written after the 1855 and 1856 editions of *Leaves of Grass*. Moreover, by noting the tension between the poet's elegies and laments and his other (and earlier) treatments of death, Butscher draws attention to a larger transformation in Whitman's poetics. The incorporation of "undercurrents of sadness and protest" against mortal fate in these later poems, necessitated as they were by real circumstances, suggests that the self has been reconceived as the sort of being that must actively confront the precarious conditions of life and calibrate the most efficacious responses to it.

The Cosmic Agency of Laissez-faire

It would not be quite accurate, however, to say that Whitman failed in 1855 and 1856 to inform his poetry with any conception of agency. Rather, it is that individual agency has been displaced onto the cosmic whole. This becomes particularly clear when we examine the great catalogs. For instance, in section 12 of "Song of Myself," the poet begins a celebration of the nation's energy by relentlessly cataloging a seemingly infinite variety of individual acts.

> The butcher-boy puts off his killing clothes, or sharpens his knife at the
>   stall in the market,
> I loiter enjoying his repartee and his shuffle and breakdown.
>
> Blacksmiths with grimed and hairy chests environ the anvil,
> Each has his main-sledge . . . . they are all out . . . . there is great heat in
>   the fire.
>
> From the cinder-strewed threshold I follow their movements,
> The lithe sheer of their waists plays even with their massive arms,
> Overhand the hammers roll — overhand so slow — overhand so sure,
> They do not hasten, each man hits in his place. (*LV* 13)

The beauty of the passage resides in the poet's distance from his materials; he captures here not the struggle of labor to scratch out a living but a ballet of beautiful, muscular bodies in slow, synchronized motion. Timing and balance characterize all movement, from the implied rhythm of the butcher boy's repartee to the "even" play of the waists and arms of blacksmiths as they methodically alternate blows on the anvil. These are not human "acts" the poet has witnessed; as he phrases it himself: "I follow their *movements*" (emphasis added).

In *A Grammar of Motives*, Kenneth Burke offers a useful distinction between motion and action. Burke famously diagrams all philosophical thought, categorizing each school according to the way it privileges one or another of five dramatic elements: act, scene, agent, agency, and purpose. Though each philosophical approach in his "pentad" is uniquely useful in producing insight by focusing attention on only one aspect of human existence, each is also given to error precisely because its focus necessarily subordinates the other elements under its own terminological control. Materialism, for example, is the philosophy that "features" scene, or environmental conditions, so that it plays a determinative role in human conduct. To illustrate, Burke cites Hobbes's gloss of his own materialism in *Leviathan*: "Nature, the art whereby God hath made and governs the world, is by the *art* of man, as in many other things, so in this also imitated, that it can make an artificial animal. For seeing life is but a motion of limbs, the beginning whereof is in some principle part within; why may we not say, that all automata (engines that move themselves by springs and wheels as doth a watch) have an artificial life? For what is the heart, but a spring; and the nerves, but so many strings, and the joints, but so many wheels, giving motion to the whole body, such as was intended by the artificer?" [4]

For Burke, Hobbes is but a typical example of the "way in which materialism, or reduction to motion, is a treatment of personal motivations in terms of the *scenic*, explaining the *internal* in terms of *external* conditions." "Hobbes's intention," in other words, is "the reduction of will itself to terms of a scene mechanically determined." [5] Action, by contrast, consists of the willed activities of a critical consciousness. Of course, in "Song of Myself," the poet is the scene, is the cosmos. In an earlier section on the "open universe," I pointed out that Whitman had re-visioned the poetic ego as an omnipresent, omniscient personification of cosmic energy; in effect, he deified the poetic presence. The paradox of this deification is that though he is at this level omnipotent, he remains wholly subject to the "laws" that govern the natural environment — the scene with which his cosmic self is coextensive. In doing so, the poet deeds over to the cosmic scene any vestige of personal agency. In section 14, for example, he observes

> The sharphoofed moose of the north, the cat on the housesill,
>   the chickadee, the prairie-dog,
> The litter of the grunting sow as they tug at her teats,
> The brood of the turkeyhen, and she with her halfspread wings,
> I see in them and myself the same old law. (*LV* 15)

However Whitman imagined himself to be linked by the "same old law" to natural processes, it was a linkage he apparently felt was sufficiently secure to ground profound expressions of trust. Everywhere in Whitman, the poet willingly gives himself over to the security of natural process, but perhaps nowhere more explicitly than in his sea poetry and especially in those passages about the sea in "Song of Myself." In section 22, for instance, nature, as represented by the sea, is not the terror-filled place of many of Whitman's subsequent sea poetry, which exhilarates by conjoining the symbolic promise of inexhaustible life with the real certainty of personal annihilation; here, the specter of death raised by the "unshovelled and always-ready graves" is cradled within the crosscurrents of a nature envisioned as the grand choreography of benign and libidinal forces that ultimately continues all life:

> You sea! I resign myself to you also . . . . I guess what you mean,
> I behold from the beach your crooked inviting fingers,
> I believe you refuse to go back without feeling of me,
> We must have a turn together . . . . I undress . . . . hurry me out of sight
>   of the land,
> Cushion me soft . . . . rock me in billowy drowse,
> Dash me with amorous wet . . . . I can repay you.

> Sea of stretched ground-swells!
> Sea breathing broad and convulsive breaths!
> Sea of the brine of life! Sea of unshovelled and always-ready graves!
> Howler and scooper of storms! Capricious and dainty sea!
> I am integral with you . . . . I too am of one phase and of all phases.
>
> (LV 28)

Whitman could be safely "integral" with the "Howler and scooper of storms" because he is comfortably locked in a self embrace; the ultimate scene of nature the sea represents is coextensive with — governed by — the omnipresent cosmic self the poet continually projects throughout the poem: "I too am of one phase and of all phases." The episode is but one more of the poet's autoerotic fantasies, only here on a cosmic scale. And since the poet has projected his own regulatory presence onto nature, he may conceive of nature as an ordered and rational place, as he makes clear at the end of section 50: "Do you not see O my brothers and sisters? / It is not chaos or death . . . . it is form and union and plan . . . . it is eternal life . . . . it is happiness (*LV* 81).

The universe depicted here as a rationally conceived "form and union and plan" — "the same old law" that governed the poet — was a variant of the Enlightenment conception of "natural law" captured in Burke's citation of Hobbes's statement quoted earlier. But it is a conflicted, highly problematic variation of that conception. Competing views of nature mark the major fault lines in Whitman's vision; in Whitman, natural law was not just more gritty, more sensual, more sexual — perhaps more natural — than many Enlightenment thinkers would have conceived it to be, but his conception of nature included and even absolved the kind of "chaos" that others had ruled to be "unnatural." Yet Whitman's conception of nature was also normative in the sense that nature functioned as a vital, regulative presence whose scope of authority was total. What is really at conflict here is, on the one hand, a more modern and pragmatic understanding of nature as the partially random, indeterminate, ultimately unknowable, free, morally neutral, and infinitely open universe suggested by his democratic instincts and experience and, on the other hand, the residue of eighteenth-century assumptions of a closed, morally interested, and planned universe.

If Whitman had recognized the contradiction within his own cosmology, as a liberal, a patriot, and an antimonarchist he almost certainly would have attempted to "correct" his theory of nature by bending it toward a belief in natural law. As Sidney Fine and others have observed, some form of natural law was not only the prevailing moral and cosmological belief in colonial and antebellum America, it was buttressed by political necessity. "Belief in a higher law" than that represented by civil society, he observes, "was strengthened in the colonies by the necessity of establishing the validity of the American case in the struggle with England." Colonial leaders "insisted that the individual is in possession of certain inalienable natural rights that no government can abridge. . . . The theory of natural rights, as Charles Grove Haines has asserted, thus 'became the foundation for the concept of limited government.'"[6] Such a legal recourse to — and ultimate faith in — the rational mechanics of a higher natural order informed the philosophy of one of Whitman's intellectual idols (and his father's friend), Thomas Paine. "If we consider what the principles are that first condense men into society," Paine said in his famous reply to Edmund Burke's denunciation of the French Revolution, "and what the motives that regulate their mutual intercourse afterwards, we shall find, by the time we arrive at what is called government, that nearly the whole of the business is performed by the natural operation of the parts upon each other."[7]

The poet who is securely rocked in "billowy drowse" gives himself over to the same regulatory balancing act "performed by the natural operation of the parts upon each other." But there are consequences to the conception of natural law, as Dewey makes clear in *The Quest for Certainty*: "The doctrine that nature is inherently rational was a costly one. It entailed the idea that reason in man is an outside spectator of a rationality already complete in itself. It deprived reason in man of an active and creative office; its business was simply to copy, to re-present symbolically, to view a given structure. . . . It relegated practical making and doing to a secondary and relatively irrational realm" (*QC* 211–212). Such a conception of nature unavoidably impinges upon conceptions of human organization:

> Its paralyzing effect on human action is seen in the part it played in the eighteenth and nineteenth centuries in the theory of "natural laws" in human affairs, in social matters. These natural laws were supposed to be inherently fixed; a science of social phenomena and relations was equivalent to discovery of them. Once discovered, nothing remained for man but to conform to them; they were to rule his conduct as physical laws govern physical phenomena. They were the sole standard of conduct in economic affairs; the laws of economics are the "natural" laws of all political action; other so-called laws are artificial, man-made contrivances in contrast with the normative regulations of nature itself. *Laissez-Faire* was the logical conclusion. For organized society to regulate the course of economic affairs, to bring them into service of humanly conceived ends, was a harmful interference. (*QC* 211–212)

As Sidney Fine points out, this was precisely the case in Jacksonian America. Natural law was presumed to serve as final arbiter in more than just civil matters. "The classical economists," he asserts, "tended to describe the economic order as controlled by a set of natural laws analogous to those governing the physical order, and although they were by no means unqualified adherents of laissez-faire, they were inclined to argue that human interference with these laws would be productive of nothing but harm."[8] There is no dispute that in both Jeffersonian and Jacksonian democracy, laissez-faire was economic orthodoxy; indeed, as Fine notes, until the post–Civil War period there was no competing economic doctrine. It would have been quite extraordinary if Whitman had even been able to conceive of a vision of freedom that was not also, in some sense, a laissez-faire vision. M. Wynn Thomas is quite justified in observing of the great catalog of section 15 that "the whole panorama is implicitly presented as a celebration of the free spirit of economic liberalism, the laissez-faire capitalism of the mid-nineteenth century":[9]

> The pure contralto sings in the organloft,
> The carpenter dresses his plank . . . . the tongue of his foreplane whistles
>   its wild ascending lisp,
> The married and unmarried children ride home to their thanksgiving
>   dinner,
> The pilot seizes the king-pin, he heaves down with a strong arm,

The mate stands braced in the whaleboat, lance and harpoon are ready,
The duck-shooter walks by silent and cautious stretches,
The deacons are ordained with crossed hands at the altar,
The spinning-girl retreats and advances to the hum of the big wheel,

(*LV* 16)

The catalog, largely an itemization of discrete economic acts, ends some sixty-one lines later with the poet asserting, "And these one and all tend inward to me, and I tend outward to them, / And such as it is to be of these more or less I am" (*LV* 20).

Thus the speaker identifies with all the economic vitality he surveys. Moreover, by absorbing the sheer infinity of particular, disconnected acts into the singular, rhythmic movement of the catalog, the poet assumes the role of the "invisible hand," representing a multitude of private purposes as they become unified within a single, passively expressed, static being: "I am," the poet says, not "I do."

One of the commonplace criticisms of laissez-faire capitalism is that it celebrates the power and position of the individual by erroneously assuming that the "rationally selfish" choices made by private, atomistic selves contribute to the collective good, while the altruistic decisions of a collective must harm because they represent "irrational" intrusions into the natural, economic order. The appropriate response to laissez-faire doctrine, critics often assume, is to assert the ultimate moral authority of the collective over the individual's "rationally chosen" struggle for personal profit. This critique of laissez-faire individualism may be motivated by laudable moral impulses, but it is deeply misguided for, in truth, laissez-faire has nothing to do with any meaningful conception of individualism, individual choice, or even reason. Laissez-faire faith in the ultimately good and reasonable results of private, "selfish" choices is in fact a collectivist utopian fantasy purchased at the price of a real appreciation of the spontaneous and unique creative capacities of unpredictable human individuals. "Rational choice" in laissez-faire amounts to the assumption that individuals will unwittingly conform to a "logical" structure imposed on them by their own mechanical function within a closed and certain universe. Herbert Spencer, the great nineteenth-century laissez-faire theorist, put the issue plainly in *Social Statics* when he professed sympathy for the social scientist who must witness the foolishness of "political schemers," legislators, who "with their clumsy mechanisms," try to "supersede the great laws of existence. Such a one, no longer regarding the outside of things, has learned to look for the secret forces by which they are upheld. After patient study, this chaos of phenomena into the midst of which he was born has begun to generalize itself to him; and where there seemed nothing but confusion, he can now discern the dim outlines of a gigantic plan. No accidents, no chance; but everywhere order and completeness." [10]

Laissez-faire does, however, rely on one form of atomistic behavior. It is in the competitive acts of and between individuals that "the evolution of society" is presumed to proceed dialectically as if to fill out the outlines of some Hegelian-like order. But in this regard, Whitman has nothing to offer the laissez-faire theorist: though Whitman's vision on the global level may evince a laissez-faire determinism, as it functions on the local and particular level it does not. Whitman's characters do not seek competitive advantage over each other, nor does society "evolve" via the competitive process of natural selection. Most of Whitman's characters simply act without motive; when motive is present, it is invariably an emotional one—the scorn of street-people for a prostitute, the affection of a mother for her child, the lust of a red-faced boy or girl, the ubiquitous love of the poet for his reader. Whitman's characters do not negotiate with each other, exchange goods or services, or even join in complex interactions; most often, they reside in individual lines in a catalog, unaware of those who live in the lines above and below them.

So while it is fair to say that Whitman's vision represented by the 1855 and 1856 editions of *Leaves of Grass* retained some of the form of the laissez-faire ideology of his times, his democratic intuitions — and the democratic idiom he was inventing — were pushing him beyond that form to something much more complex. Though that vision, lacking as it was a meaningful conception of human agency, was not yet democratic in the fullest possible sense, the promise of completion was nevertheless there in the seeds of a newer conception of democratic existence. Democratic agency was latent in a conception of an open universe that mandated purposeful action; it was latent, too, in his understanding of the objectified, socially implicated aspect of self — the self that makes democratic community possible. And it was especially there in the poet's attempt to access his own soul, the ever-present but always concealed "I," the subjective aspect of the self — irreducible to any conception of external reason — that informs the unique and particular quality of his own impulses.

In one of Whitman's most famous editorial changes to "Song of Myself," he altered his self-announcement in section 24, which in the first three editions had read, "Walt Whitman, an American, one of the roughs, a kosmos," to "Walt Whitman, a kosmos, of Manhattan the son" (*LV* 31). The deletion of "one of the roughs" has been variously interpreted, but one of the more common assumptions is that it reflected Whitman's growing conservatism, a desire to distance himself from the "roughs" of New York City streets so as to assume all the more convincingly the role of "the good grey poet."[11] But the deletion also reflects a growing discomfort with Rousseauian primitivism, especially with the Jacksonian version wherein the primitive self was held to be a sufficient and complete model for democratic identity. Though Whitman's egalitarian ethic would always be rooted in a naturalistic essentialism, turmoil, both political and personal, would ultimately lead him to an understanding that the recognition of that essentialism only begins the struggle for full democratic life; full democracy, he would discover, in fact depends upon the antithesis of primitivism: the cooperation of free agents bound together by a shared allegiance to the tenants of a democratic culture.

This is a profound and disturbing realization, as Whitman's increasingly urgent plea for "fidelity" to the democratic faith demonstrates. It acknowledges that a free and democratic people are denied a guarantee of ultimate success; indeed, the implicit rejection of an Enlightenment faith in a rational order that guarantees success necessarily entails a serious challenge to the Jeffersonian assertion of "inalienable rights," particularly since they are grounded in a decidedly unnatural view of a rational nature. Cooperative democratic life, as Whitman would come to understand it, is more of a burden and an obligation than a natural license to pursue happiness — perhaps the same kind of existential mandate that compels all individuals to feed and clothe themselves under penalty of death.

In "Calamus" and again in *Sequel to Drum-Taps*, Whitman would explore the ways in which agency, the human capacity to act intelligently, is the natural response to this existential mandate. Interpreted in this sense, Jefferson's bill of inalienable rights might not actually be dissociated from nature after all — at least not from a nature recognized as precarious: surely a natural mandate to perpetually act in order to preserve life implies the innate means to do so and the natural right to have whatever freedom is needed to fulfill such a mandate codified by all the moral authority human beings can devise.

Crises and ReVisions
"Sea Drift," "Calamus," *Drum-Taps*, and
Sequel to Drum-Taps, 1859 – 1867

Thus we trace Fate, in matter, mind, and morals, —
in race, in retardations of strata, and in thought and
character as well. It is everywhere bound or limitation.
But fate has its lord; limitation its limits; . . . For,
though fate is immense, so is power, which is the other
fact in the dual world, immense. If Fate follows and
limits power, power attends and antagonizes Fate. . . .
For who and what is this criticism that pries into the
matter? Man is not order of nature, sack and sack, belly
and members, link in a chain, nor any ignominious
baggage, but a stupendous antagonism, a dragging
together of the poles of the Universe. He betrays his
relation to what is below him, — thick-skulled, small-
brained, fishy, quadrumanous, — quadruped ill-
disguised, hardly escaped into biped, and has paid
for the new powers by loss of some of the old ones.
— Ralph Waldo Emerson, "Fate"

5

"The Most Perfect Pilot"
The Problem of Desire and the Struggle for Poetic Agency

In 1857 Walt Whitman, the poet of boundless optimism, fell into a period of deep personal turmoil and depression that would last nearly three years. There are a number of plausible explanations for this melancholia. One, for example, is that he was struggling professionally, having lost his job as editor of the *Brooklyn Times* sometime in June of 1859. It was about this same time that he famously complained in his notebook of being in a "Slough" and needing "to stir — first for money enough, to *live and provide for* M——."[1] But most biographers agree that the primary cause of Whitman's "Slough" was sexual. Though drawn almost exclusively from interpretations of twelve early drafts of poems later included in "Calamus" (referred to by the critics as the "Calamus-Leaves" poems), the evidence is nonetheless compelling that during this time Whitman was deeply involved in a difficult romantic relationship with a man.[2] The particulars of Whitman's tortured romance have long been the subject of controversy. While most critics do agree that it was almost certainly a homosexual relationship, there is less agreement on whether the relationship was his first, consummated, or even requited. Whatever the details of the relationship may have been, it is clear that the episode had a powerful impact on Whitman. It was a crisis that threatened the poet with real loss — most concretely, of course, loss of a genuine flesh-and-blood love object, but perhaps more deeply, it threatened loss of the poet's sense of self. But possibly its most profound impact was in the transformative effect it had on Whitman's poetry and the vision it enabled, for not only did Whitman memorialize his conflict in verse, more important, he attempted to resolve it in verse as well.[3]

The problem, of course, is that the poetic style and vision Whitman had developed in 1855 and 1856 would hardly make an appropriate vehicle for resolving personal sexual conflict or conflict of any kind. The universe his verse was created to represent was fundamentally laissez-faire, which is to say that the self he imagined to live in that universe was also governed by laissez-faire principles, not *self*-governed. In fact, the peculiarly passive sexual persona that Whitman represents in his early erotic poetry seems especially ill-suited for such a task. In the famous section 5 of "Song of Myself," for example, the speaker documents his own passivity as he recalls for his more assertive lover how once in June "You settled your head athwart my hips and gently turned over upon me, / And parted the shirt from my bosom-bone, and plunged your tongue to my barestript heart" (*LV* 6). Or again, in section 28 of the same poem, he complains in mock protest of senses "Behaving licentious toward me, taking no denial, [/ . . . /] Unbuttoning my clothes and holding me by the bare waist" (*LV* 39). This erotic passivity is so characteristic of Whitman's early verse that it has led several modern critics to conclude that it is a function of Whitman's homoerotic desire to be taken by a man as if he were a woman.[4] But whatever the motivations informing Whitman's passive verse may have been, it is difficult not to conclude that that passivity (idealized or not) could not have served him when he needed to use his poetry to negotiate a real sexual crisis. The language of a passive self, whether it originated in an ideology, a psychological disposition, or a sexual ideal, was now a language he could not afford to sustain.

For Whitman to have resolved such a personal crisis in poetry, he would have needed to invent for himself a new, more functionally pragmatic form of poetic language, one deeply antithetical to the poetics of laissez-faire freedom he had pioneered. In this chapter, I argue that Whitman's crisis required him to develop what I would call "poetic agency," a verse form that was not exclusively concerned with representing the free play of cosmic and social forces but one that was designed to enable the self to negotiate the psychic dangers such forces entail — a language of self-governance. In its strictly personal application, this poetic process is one where the poem functions as a psychological tool to help the ego gain leverage over the internal and external conditions that would deprive the self of any power of autonomous action (however relative such autonomy may be). As it will be seen to operate in "Calamus," the primary focus of this chapter, this form of poetic creation entails the transference onto paper, as it were, of a kind of textualized version of the self, which the poet can then modify or restructure; once the fictionalized self has been altered in some idealized way, it becomes a suitable object of identification for the poet. The significance of this move transcends the personal and psychological value it held for Whitman himself. It precipitated a fundamental transformation in his vision of democracy. By equipping his verse with the power of agency, Whitman also, in effect, equipped the self in his democratic vision with the capacity to take the kind of action necessary to the intelligent management of human social affairs.

Whitman's Developing Vision and the Sea

In many ways, the significant stages of Whitman's vision, from its celebration of laissez-faire freedom to the documentation of struggle and subsequent invention of a poetic agency, all register as changes in his imagery of the sea. The poet who wrote the first two versions of *Leaves of Grass*, for instance, could hardly have found a more appropriate image for the laissez-faire universe — or a better metaphor for the way he saw himself in that universe — than his own romanticized version of the sea. Sometimes Whitman in 1855 and 1856 would represent the sea as a site of danger or tragedy, as in the frigate fight in sections 35 and 36 of "Song of Myself" or in the death of the "beautiful gigantic swimmer" in "Sleepers," but then it was not so much to explore its evil or malevolent depths as it was to skim from its surface a thin, sentimental form of heroism. More telling is the poet's depiction of a benign and amorous sea with "crooked inviting fingers" in section 22 of "Song of Myself." This sea the poet "resign[s]" himself to, has a "turn" with, allows to "Cushion me soft . . . . rock me in billowy drowse." And though it is a "Sea of unshovelled and always-ready graves! / Howler and scooper of storms!" he is nonetheless "integral" with it and, like it, "Of one phase and of all phases" (*LV* 28). In this sea, passive resignation makes sense, for here the poet found absolute security through complete envelopment within an implicitly balanced, implicitly logical, natural process.

But by 1859 and 1860 the sea, and the natural process it symbolized, offered anything but security. In two astonishingly powerful — and astonishingly personal — poems that Whitman published just prior to the third edition of *Leaves of Grass* (1860), the once benign sea suddenly became the "fierce old mother" and "the savage old mother," not the site of heroic deeds but the place where the poet first felt "the fire, the sweet hell within." In the first of these, "As I Ebb'd with the Ocean of Life," the poet walks the shores of his beloved "Paumanok" (Long Island) late one autumn day and becomes fascinated by lines of debris and sediment left on the sand by the ebbing tide. The refuse he sees provides the melancholy poet ample material with which to identify; "I too am but a trail of drift and debris," he writes (*LV* 321). The problem he identifies in this poem is at once deeply personal and literary. He suffers a deep depression induced by the awareness that he is somehow at war with himself, so alienated from some other version of himself that he must now contend with "the eternal self of me that threatens to get the better of me" (*LV* 319). But he casts this self-diagnosis in literary terms: at root, his problem has been the inadequacy of his poetry. The grand and sweeping verse of a poet who so enthusiastically identified with the "multitudes" of America's laissez-faire democracy has been utterly irrelevant to his own very private emotional condition:

> O baffled, balked,
> Bent to the very earth, here preceding what follows,
> Oppressed with myself that I have dared to open my mouth,
> Aware now, that, amid all the blab whose echoes recoil upon me, I have
> not once had the least idea who or what I am,
> But that before all my insolent poems the real Me still stands untouched,
> untold, altogether unreached, (*LV* 320)

By attributing personal turmoil to his choice of a poetic form that has proved unable to "touch" or "reach" his "real" self, he in effect charges poetry in general with the responsibility of resolving such conflict. Implicitly, he signals his intention to find such a poetic language. He does not find it in "As I Ebb'd with the Ocean of Life"; the most he can do is console himself with the weak parenthetic promise that "(the flow will return)" (*LV* 321). In another sea poem, however, he does begin to use verse to organize and direct the fragmented debris of the self. In "Out of the Cradle Endlessly Rocking," the loss of a love object is refigured as a childhood memory of the literal death of a mockingbird at sea — "the savage old mother" — so that, in Wordsworthian fashion, the recollecting poet can effect an identification with the bird's grieving mate that will liberate and inform his own poetic powers.

Death serves multiple functions in this poem. It is the metaphor for other forms of loss as well as the occasion for writing of those losses. But more deeply — and in marked contrast to Whitman's less intimate use of death imagery in the first two editions of *Leaves of Grass* — it is a "real," terrible phenomenon that is imagined as something beyond the poet's subjective experience, not a continuation of it. As such, it is an objective source of psychic pain so intolerable that it must be "re-mediated." It is the piercing grief that death brings, not the pleasing symmetry of the metaphysical conception of death, that the poet begs the sea to render up.

> A word then, (for I will conquer it,)
> The word final, superior to all,

Subtle, sent up — what is it? — I listen;
Are you whispering it, and have been all the time, you sea-waves?
Is that it from your liquid rims and wet sands?

Answering, the sea,
Delaying not, hurrying not,
Whispered me through the night, and very plainly before daybreak,
Lisped to me constantly the low and delicious word Death, (*LV* 350)

The importance of death-grief is the fact that it necessitates a re-mediation —
a conquering, as the poet puts it — through the active mediation of poetry.
Death is redemptive, in this sense, because it stirs to life the creative agency of
poetic language, which the "chanter of pains and joys" will put to transformative use: "Taking all hints to use them, but swiftly leaping beyond them"
(*LV* 344).

This is, to be sure, an example of poetic agency, but it is a narrower version
of the kind he will later develop. It points to a utilitarian conception of poetry,
one that recognizes that poetic language may be usefully employed for particular or localized purposes, such as the therapeutic negotiation of grief. And
there are other such examples in *Leaves of Grass*. For instance, when Whitman
redefines sexual desire in the "Calamus" poems as the bonding force that "creates" a democracy, he is exploiting poetic resources to write political doctrine.
But the broader conception of poetic agency I am interested in reads the narrow and particular representations of emotion mentioned previously as proto-
typical, generative of a new dynamic logic informing Whitman's metaphysics.
Poetic agency becomes the motive force that pervades and redefines Whitman's entire democratic vision, a redefinition that reaches down, on the one
hand, to the individual, reconceived as "agent," and up, on the other hand, to
the realm of nature, reconceived as volatile, mutable, and at least marginally
susceptible to the managerial efforts of human agents. It is not surprising that
in Whitman's later treatments of the sea he would imagine it neither as an
amorously enveloping symbol of a benign, laissez-faire nature nor as the "savage old mother" whose currents tear apart the helpless self and spew the wreck-
age upon the shore like so much debris at ebb tide. Rather, it is a place whose
volatility and danger calls forth a high degree of navigational skill — as in the
1867 poem "Aboard at a Ship's Helm" (ultimately included in the "Sea-Drift"
cluster along with "As I Ebb'd with the Ocean of Life" and "Out of the Cradle
Endlessly Rocking"). There, a "young steersman steering with care" through
a treacherous fog heeds the warning of an ocean bell and, tacking, "speeds

away gayly and safe." It is a fortunate maneuver, for the "precious wealth" the ship carries is itself another ship — the ever-voyaging "Ship of the body, ship of the soul" (*LV* 560).

Pragmatic Psychology

The most dramatic example of Whitman's use of poetic agency is in "Calamus." Here it is necessary to focus on how these poems functioned psychologically. There is, of course, no shortage of psychological interpretations of Whitman, especially the "Calamus" poems, that might be consulted. Unfortunately, much of the criticism of these poems is not helpful; whether psychological interpretations are grounded in French or Anglo-American theory, their very nature makes them highly vulnerable to an extreme sort of reductionism. This is, more often than not, equally true of psychological studies of Whitman. It is perhaps an occupational hazard of the psychoanalytic critic — one Dewey illuminates in *Human Nature and Conduct*: "The treatment of sex by psycho-analysts is most instructive, for it flagrantly exhibits both the consequences of artificial simplification and the transformation of social results into psychic causes. . . . They treat phenomena which are peculiarly symptoms of the civilization of the West at the present time as if they were the necessary effects of fixed native impulses of human nature."[5] What bothered Dewey was what he saw as the tendency of many psychoanalysts to reduce all variety of human behavior to some essentializing basic drive without regard to the ways these instinctual drives — or the more neutral sounding "impulses," as he preferred to call them — are shaped through their interactions within the environment. "Fear of the dark," for instance, "is different from fear of publicity, fear of the dentist from fear of ghosts, fear of conspicuous success from fear of humiliation," and so on. Though each may share similar physical manifestations, "each is qualitatively unique. Each is what it is in virtue of its total interactions or correlations with other acts and with the environing medium, with consequences."[6] Dewey was following the same lines he had established in his critique of the "reflex arc" theory in psychology, which I discussed in chapter 2. Now, however, rather than challenging the "stimulus-response" reduction of human conduct to the absolute determinism of environmental conditions, he is rejecting its opposite extreme: the notion that human conduct (and, by extension, individual identity) is the sum total of primitive drives. For Dewey, as for other pragmatists such as William James, neither the individual human being nor the individual's environment — both social and natural — could be understood in isolation of the other because they are both constantly evolving products of their own mutually modifying relationship.

This interest in seeing the individual in a mutually modifying relationship with his or her environment sets Dewey, James, and Mead squarely against both Lacanian and most examples of traditional psychoanalytic interpretation, as a brief digression into the canon of such critical approaches to Whitman illustrates. To begin with, one of the most artful uses of the Lacanian paradigm comes from Michael Moon in his discussion of the "Calamus" poetry. Basing his interpretation on Freud's assertion that male paranoia is an unconscious defense against homosexuality originating in the Oedipal situation, Moon's thesis is that in the third edition of *Leaves of Grass*, Whitman deliberately represents — or strategically cultivates for remedial purposes — this paranoia, which Moon reads as a cultural, not just an individual psychic, response. By dramatically representing the culturally inscripted paranoia of gender boundaries "becoming too painfully constrictive," "or a fear of the loss of boundaries altogether," the poet's purpose is understood to be an "invitation to readers to recognize the pain of the oppressive cultural constraints under which they are laboring and the exhilarating — but also perilous — pleasure of attempting to redraw these boundaries along other lines. The desire to lose *and* the fear of losing the boundary lines in force around self-definition and sexual definition are both strongly impelled by the third edition, in which Whitman aspires to extend the scope of his revisions of culture to include his readers' notions of their relation to such basal elements of mid-nineteenth-century American culture as nature and religion."[7]

The argument Moon produces to support this thesis is admirably elegant. For instance, with a sharp eye, he ferrets out the play involved in Whitman's use of the words "difference" and "indifference," building a connection between the psychic states the "Calamus" poems would seem to represent and the Saussureian structure that is assumed to organize the cultural unconscious that Whitman is supposedly attempting to reconfigure. But the artistry Moon praises is really his own. The reason he can so easily glide between intrapsychic phenomena and cultural dynamics is because, for Lacan, as is well known, the individual organism is at the outset little more than an empty subjectivity whose identity is but the "mirror" image of the culture — an inscription of cultural meanings produced in a linguistic economy that obeys the same principles that also govern the Oedipal determination of psychic meaning. Meanwhile, it is claimed, the real subjectivity behind the identifying "I" is forever cut off from objective apprehension (or completion in an authentic object of desire) by the endless succession of fictions the ego identifies with. Language, in this view, is not a tool the "real self" uses to organize the experience that constitutes it; rather, it is the medium in which the ego erects a false self, repressing authentic desire. Going far beyond the reasonable proposition that experience is mediated by language, this school of thought would seem to require us to believe that whatever presents itself as "genuine" human experience must necessarily be false.

Moon is correct, however, to join other critics in examining the intensity of emotional representations in the "Calamus" poems. These poems do pivot on a wide range of emotional states: exhilaration, anxiety, love, loneliness, euphoric anticipation, despondency, and, certainly, fear; but paranoia, understood as a delusional fear, unreasonable and unfounded, is not among the emotions "Calamus" dramatizes. Any fear may, of course, actually be delusional and therefore serve as an indication of paranoia, but without any evidence from the text to suggest that the fear is not based on reasonable judgment (and there is absolutely none), a convincing diagnosis that a given fear is unfounded requires an extratextual, biographical judgment that the poet was documenting very real anxiety, which is nonetheless unjustified by the circumstances of the poet's life — precisely the kind of biographical judgment Moon refuses to make. It is especially clear that, in this instance, the misrecognition of paranoia is wholly a function of the critic's reduction of the material to the demands of his theory and completely irrelevant to the text at hand.

The reductive tendency also plagues some of the best traditional examples of psychological criticism. For example, Edwin Haviland Miller, the first critic to apply psychoanalytic concepts in a systematic or rigorous manner, begins with the assumption that Whitman's material "has its origins in unconscious and infantile sources; hence the results are regressive imagery, fantasy, and reactivation of infantile longing."[8] The difficulty with this view is that the "look back" to the putatively definitive infantile state seems to demand a pathological finding. Thus "Calamus" cannot be read as the poet's successful and healthy attempt to assert control over his personal life but "an act of simplification, an evasive gesture, a retreat from nineteenth-century, and human, complexity."[9] Likewise, Stephen Black interprets the same cluster of poems as a fantasy in which "Whitman can take momentary comfort by imagining his return to an oral, pre-Oedipal phase prior to the conflicts with young and old men, prior to the separation from his mother."[10] The impulse to reduce can also be found in biographical critics such as David Cavitch; though he is less explicit or technical in his use of psychoanalysis, he does acknowledge his debt to both Miller and Black. His thesis that "Whitman gained his full power to write when he learned how to re-create his family relationships in the voice and structure of his poems" inevitably leads him to read the poetry as a screen upon which both past and ongoing family antagonisms are projected. In Cavitch's view, Whitman's poetry "entraps" him by perpetuating a pattern of family relations that "deprived him of an authentic emotional life."[11]

Attention to the psychological function of Whitman's poetry (or poetry generally) need not be reductive. Justin Kaplan, for example, uses the poetry to help explicate the many psychological tensions in the poet's life. Without explaining in detail, he makes what is nevertheless an intriguing claim that, "through poetry," Whitman "reconstituted himself and moved on to a new stage of composure and understanding."[12] Kaplan's worthwhile phrase urges us to look at the ways Whitman's poetry functions pragmatically as an instrument in the poet's psychological development. This is not to say that the text is a human psyche, let alone some primitivist cartoon of a human psyche. And though almost any text might offer an analyst suggestions as to the motives of the person who created it — indeed, texts such as the "Calamus" poems may even provide a great wealth of suggestions — all literary creations are nevertheless the conscious creations of writers who are quite capable of appropriating the psychic models the culture packages and harnessing them to literary conventions that predate the writer's own development.

While the "Calamus" poems do emerge out of psychological conflict, which, to some extent, they reflect, nevertheless they neither contain nor are reducible to that conflict. To the contrary, these poems are consciously constructed textual environments in which the poet has created fictionalized versions of the self. Liberated within the textual environment, the fictive self becomes subject to the manipulations and experimentation of the poet, who can employ all the literary devices the culture makes available to him. Once the conflict is "resolved" within the confines of the poem through the erection of "artificial" counterpressures ("countercathecting" structures, in psychoanalytic jargon) that represent verbally the imagined play of psychic motivations, the result is a newly created fictional self, available to the poet — or reader — to assimilate through the process of identification.[13]

A more appropriate heuristic tool with which to launch a productive and pragmatic psychological investigation of the "Calamus" poems is Freud's own "Mourning and Melancholia." Melancholia (not paranoia, as Moon would have it) is the striking emotional quality we find in such poems as "Calamus. 9."

Hours continuing long, sore and heavy-hearted,
Hours of the dusk, when I withdraw to a lonesome and unfrequented
   spot, seating myself, leaning my face in my hands;

Hours sleepless, deep in the night, when I go forth, speeding swiftly the
country roads, or through the city streets, or pacing miles and miles,
stifling plaintive cries;

Hours discouraged, distracted — for the one I cannot content myself
without, soon I saw him content himself without me;

Hours when I am forgotten, (O weeks and months are passing, but I
believe I am never to forget!)

Sullen and suffering hours! (I am ashamed — but it is useless — I am
what I am;)

Hours of my torment — I wonder if other men ever have the like, out of
the like feelings?

Is there even one other like me — distracted — his friend, his lover, lost
to him?

Is he too as I am now? Does he still rise in the morning, dejected,
thinking who is lost to him? and at night, awaking, think who is lost?

Does he too harbor his friendship silent and endless? harbor his anguish
and passion?

Does some stray reminder, or the casual mention of a name, bring the fit
back upon him, taciturn and deprest?

Does he see himself reflected in me? In these hours, does he see the face
of his hours reflected? (*LV* 379–380)

Freud defines melancholia by distinguishing it from the more routine pat-
terns of mourning following the loss of a love-object. Though both mental
states will to some extent involve "painful dejection, cessation of interest in
the outside world, loss of the capacity to love, [and an] inhibition of all activity," melancholia is marked additionally by "a lowering of the self-regarding
feelings to a degree that finds utterance in self-reproaches and self-revilings,
and culminates in a delusional expectation of punishment."[14] In fact, a low-
ered self-regard is an unmistakable feature of "Calamus. 9.," for though the
poet here mourns the estrangement of his lover's affections — "the one I cannot content myself without, soon I saw him content himself without me" —
his self-described dejection is accompanied by a kind of resigned acknowledgment of his own worthlessness. For instance, he does not qualify his
lament of the "Hours when I am forgotten" with a protest against the injustice
of being consigned to oblivion (which we might otherwise expect from the
brash poet so accustomed to asserting his own ego), only the meek, parenthetical claim that "I believe I am never to forget." Even more explicitly, a low-
ered self-regard registers in the curious confession, wrought from the poet's

"Sullen and suffering hours!" that "(I am ashamed — but it is useless — I am what I am;)." Clearly, we see here the degree to which the corrosive force of his own malignant torment has become directed entirely inward; while many critics have assumed that the poet's "shame" derives from his sense of guilt over the commission of homosexual acts, such a moralistic reading of the line renders it completely irrelevant to the poem's central concern with the problems of loss and loneliness. This, rather, is the poet of "As I Ebb'd with the Ocean of Life" coming face to face with the scattered debris of a shattered self: "I too am but a trail of drift and debris." The humiliating confession, "I am ashamed — but it is useless — I am what I am," merely underscores his certainty that what he *is* is nothing, or at least nothing of any worth. Loss of a love-object, for this poet at this time, is complete loss of self.

Freud postulates that a melancholic reaction to the loss of a love-object — which results in a corresponding loss of self — actually suggests a previous rupture in the particular relationship in question. He hypothesizes that when some "real slight or disappointment" shatters the "attachment of the libido to a particular person," or object-relationship, without actually bringing an end to the relationship, allowing the libido to displace itself onto another object, the free libido instead withdraws into the ego itself. Once there, however, the withdrawn libido serves "to establish an *identification* with the abandoned object. Thus the shadow of the object fell upon the ego, and the latter could henceforth be judged by a special agency, as though it were an object, the forsaken object. In this way an object-loss was transformed into an ego loss and the conflict between the ego and the loved person into a cleavage between the critical activity of the ego and the ego as altered by identification." [15] Consequently, when the love-object is actually lost, the loss is felt to be a loss of self — is, in fact, a loss of the self that had identified with the abandoned object.

The problem of melancholia that "Calamus. 9." articulates is also, then, a problem of identification, as the query the poet initiates on line 7 — and continues to the poem's end — makes clear. When he "wonder[s] if other men ever have the like, out of the like feelings? / Is there even one other like me — distracted — his friend, his lover, lost to him?" he is attempting to resolve the melancholia that occasioned the poem in the first place by searching for the perfect, in other words, identical, reader/lover whose experiences so match those the poem articulates that the poet is permitted to wonder in the final line if the reader might "see himself reflected in me? In these hours, does he see the face of his hours reflected?" This is a complex and clever — yet perfectly readable — psychological maneuver. The poet has not attempted to find a substitute love-object with which to identify (a move that Freud and common sense reminds us would be extremely painful) but has merely transferred to the speaking persona of the poem an emotional state identical to his own and then designated that persona an object of identification for some fictional reader. The poem establishes a kind of three-point circuit of identifications in which the real-life poet and a hypothetical reader jointly identify with the melancholy persona of the poem. The poem's speaker (a fictional construct not to be confused with the "real" Whitman) functions to enable an imaginary reader to supplant the (presumably "real") former lover as an object of identification.

"Calamus. 9." represents a highly significant turn in the poet's fictionalized developmental process. This is so not because we find any evidence that the poet is recovering from his melancholic state; its value lies in the fact that by creating a poetic persona that is available to both fictive reader and real poet as an object of identification, the poem models the structure that the poetic ego will utilize in its reformation of identity. But before examining this process in greater detail, it is useful to take a step back and try to reconstruct how, hypothetically, the poet's crisis of identification might have developed. Such a reconstruction is possible when we recognize that, when arranged by their thematic or emotional content, the twelve original "Calamus-Leaves" poems establish a kind of developmental pattern.[16]

To begin with, there are just a few poems in "Calamus-Leaves" that, compared to the others in the group, are so free of obvious emotional conflict that they may serve as the collection's touchstone of unambivalent tenderness and passion. "Not Heat Flames up and Consumes," for example, is an innocently romantic assertion that the forces of nature cannot compare with the intensity of the narrator's own affection. "Does the tide hurry, seeking something, and never give up?" he asks on line 7, "O I the same;"

> O nor down-balls, nor perfumes, nor the high rain-emitting clouds, are
>   borne through the open air,
> Any more than my Soul is borne through the open air,
> Wafted in all directions, O love, for friendship, for you. (*LV* 384)

The tenderness, which the poet here represents as a quality of his own experience, is the same emotional abstraction he projects onto strangers in "What Think You I Take My Pen in Hand?":

> What think you I take my pen in hand to record?
> The battle-ship, perfect-model'd, majestic, that I saw pass the offing
>   to-day under full sail?

The splendors of the past day? Or the splendor of the night that envelops
    me?
Or the vaunted glory and growth of the great city spread around me? —
    No;
But I record of two simple men I saw to-day, on the pier, in the midst of
    the crowd, parting the parting of dear friends;
The one to remain hung on the other's neck, and passionately kissed him,
While the one to depart, tightly prest the one to remain in his arms.

                                      (*LV* 399–400)

Though they offer similar celebrations of male love, the two poems differ
in several respects. For example, the parting motif of "What Think You I Take
My Pen in Hand?" prefigures the separation narratives of many of the other
"Calamus" poems (and perhaps recasts the permanence of alienation as
merely a benign and temporary parting). But the most compelling aspect distinguishing the latter from the former poem — from nearly every other poem
Whitman wrote — is the preoccupation with the discovery of new material.
The inflated drama behind the question "What think you I take my pen in
hand to record?" only reveals that Whitman has projected onto an imagined
reader his own sense of surprise that essentially private sexual emotion could
justifiably supplant the "vaunted glory" and cosmic "splendors" that characterized, say, "Song of Myself," as the legitimate focus of poetic attention.

That Whitman would be surprised to discover a shift of his own poetic attention should serve to remind the reader of the extent to which Whitman had always identified himself with the personified, but public and political, content
of his poetry. A shift in poetic content signals a much deeper shift in the poet's
self-identification — a shift toward a new identification necessitating the
abandonment of a prior identification (not simply, at this point, an integration
of identifications). Two other poems underscore the depth of this transformation. "When I Heard at the Close of the Day" features the poet torn between the affections of his imagined audience and those of his lover, with the
lover clearly winning out. Whitman opens the poem lamenting that "When I
heard at the close of the day how my name had been received with plaudits in
the capital, still it was not a happy night for me that followed"; indeed, nothing satisfies him until, several lines later, he can rest secure:

For the one I love most lay sleeping by me under the same cover in the
    cool night,

In the stillness, in the autumn moonbeams, his face was inclined toward
    me,
And his arm lay lightly around my breast — And that night I was happy.
    (*LV* 381–382)

The implicit question the poet seems compelled to raise is which love object is sufficiently satisfying to relieve the tension he experiences as unhappi-
ness. His answer — the poem — is testimony (not totally incredible) that the
psychic investment that had held him to his old persona has weakened, allowing the free libido to be displaced onto the new object, his lover. In
"Recorders Ages Hence," we see him driven to rewrite his public image in
conformity with his new identification by explicitly admonishing

You bards of ages hence! when you refer to me, mind not so much my
    poems
Nor speak of me that I prophesied of The States, and led them the way of
    their glories;
But come, I will take you down underneath this impassive exterior — I
    will tell you what to say of me;
Publish my name and hang up my picture as that of the tenderest lover,
    (*LV* 380)

This, again, is not simply a career change. It is a dramatic rupture in the poet's
sense of a cohesive identity — all too blithely captured in "That Shadow My
Likeness":

That shadow, my likeness, that goes to and fro, seeking a livelihood,
    chattering, chaffering,
How often I find myself standing and looking at it where it flits;
How often I question and doubt whether that is really me;
But in these, and among my lovers, and caroling my songs,
O I never doubt whether that is really me. (*LV* 404)

Whatever critical suspicions are aroused by Whitman's dubious protest
that he "never doubts" the identity of the "real me," they are best channeled
into an appreciation of just how wrenching this kind of psychic disintegration
can actually be. This is the poet, the reader will recall, who wailed on Pau-
manuk's shore "that, amid all the blab whose echoes recoil upon me, I have
not once had the least idea who or what I am" (*LV* 320). In this light, it is possible to understand the anxiety that must have compelled him in "Calamus.
8." to renounce all the public and political sources of meaning that had previously organized his life:

Long I thought that knowledge alone would suffice me — O if I could but
  obtain knowledge!
Then my lands engrossed me — Lands of the prairies, Ohio's land, the
  southern savannas, engrossed me — For them I would live — I would
  be their orator;
Then I met the examples of old and new heroes — I heard of warriors,
  sailors, and all dauntless persons — And it seemed to me that I too had
  it in me to be as dauntless as any — and would be so;
And then, to enclose all, it came to me to strike up the songs of the New
  World — And then I believed my life must be spent in singing;
But now take notice, land of the prairies, land of the south savannas,
  Ohio's land,
Take notice, you Kanuck woods — and you Lake Huron — and all that
  with you roll toward Niagara — and you Niagara also,
And you, Californian mountains — That you each and all find somebody
  else to be your singer of songs,
For I can be your singer of songs no longer — One who loves me is
  jealous of me, and withdraws me from all but love,
With the rest I dispense — I sever from what I thought would suffice me,
  for it does not — it is now empty and tasteless to me,
I heed knowledge, and the grandeur of The States, and the example of
  heroes, no more,
I am indifferent to my own songs — I will go with him I love,
It is to be enough for us that we are together — We never separate again.

(LV 378–379)

It is not necessary to assume — as an overly strict reading of Freud might
tempt us to do — that the melancholia we find in "Calamus" originates in
some previous disenchantment in Whitman's love relationship that predates
the poet's actual separation from his lover. Based solely on the evidence of the
poetry itself, we can easily hypothesize that Whitman's melancholic loss of self
was in fact a kind of freak accident of the poet's occupation. In short, given the
fact that he had always identified himself with the specifically public, political,
and cosmic content and theoretical purpose of his poetry, a psychological crisis was inevitable when an intense emotional relationship made it urgent that
he utilize poetic language for the very contradictory purpose of shaping private emotion. Indeed, the emotional demand that he "surrender" poetic language to such a contradictory purpose, enclosing private desire within an exclusively public medium, seemed to require the abandonment of his previous

understanding of poetic meaning — and his identification with it. The loss of the real-life lover who had served to anchor the complex of emotions informing the new poetic object he had come to identify with left an empty self searching anxiously for a new identification around which a new self might be built. It is this traumatic process that he memorializes — while denying the inescapable trauma of it   in "O Living Always, Always Dying."

O love!
O dying — always dying!
O the burials of me, past and present!
O me, while I stride ahead, material, visible, imperious as ever!
O me, what I was for years, now dead, (I lament not — I am content;)
O to disengage myself from those corpses of me, which I turn and look at, where I cast them!
To pass on, (O living! always living!) and leave the corpses behind!

                                                                                                (*LV* 396)

Whitman's Poetry and the Reformation of the Self

The new love object Whitman found to replace his lost lover was in fact a fictional construct of the general reader. In the analysis of "Calamus. 9." that began my larger discussion of the poet's struggle for an autonomous ego, I asserted that by creating a poetic persona that is available to both fictional reader and real poet as an object of identification, the poem structures the process that the poetic ego will utilize in its reformation of identity. We see this process begin in "Calamus. 16." where the poet, apparently quite disconcerted, directly addresses the reader:

Who is now reading this?

May-be one is now reading this who knows some wrong-doing of my past life,
Or may-be a stranger is reading this who has secretly loved me,
Or may-be one who meets all my grand assumptions and egotisms with derision,
Or may-be one who is puzzled at me.

As if I were not puzzled at myself!
Or as if I never deride myself! (O conscience struck! O self-convicted!)
Or as if I do not secretly love strangers! (O tenderly, a long time, and never avow it;)

Or as if I did not see, perfectly well, interior in myself, the stuff of
    wrong-doing,
Or as if it could cease transpiring from me until it must cease. (*LV* 386)

The poetic persona we see here, with his confession of guilt, doubt, and self-revulsion, contrasts sharply with the grandiose "kosmic" Whitman of earlier verse. Likewise, the imagined reader seems far less the idealized citizen of the poet's idealized America than an uncomfortable representation of the often hostile real public Whitman was more likely to encounter. Moreover, the poem does not conclude in triumph but in a double defeat; as the poet admits that he is helpless to control the drives that determine his behavior, we observe that he is also helpless to reformulate the culturally determined moral content of these drives.

In "Are You the New Person Drawn toward Me?" however, the poet begins to imagine a new relationship with the reader. Or to be more accurate, he reconstructs the reader as a projection of his own desire and thereby facilitates the process of identification:

Are you the new person drawn toward me, and asking something
    significant from me?
To begin with, take warning — I am probably far different from what you
    suppose;
Do you suppose you will find in me your ideal?
Do you think the friendship of me would be unalloyed satisfaction?
Do you suppose I am trusty and faithful?
Do you see no further than this facade — this smooth and tolerant
    manner of me?
Do you suppose yourself advancing on real ground toward a real heroic
    man?
Have you no thought, O dreamer, that it may all be maya, illusion?
O let some past deceived one hiss in your ears, how many have prest on
    the same as you are pressing now,
How many have fondly supposed what you are supposing now — only to
    be disappointed. (*LV* 382)

The imagined hostility of a real reader has now given way to the innocent but presumably eager solicitations of an imaginative one, just as the skittish, self-deriding poet has been supplanted by a slightly inflated but judicious and authoritative idealized one. The "new person" the poet confronts is really the reflected wish of the poet to see the "newness" of his own new persona validated by the desire of an imagined reader or lover. To accomplish this, the poet has constructed a fictional lover out of the material of his own desire. In so doing, not only has he created a new poetic persona, he has also created for himself a substitute object, a reader or lover uniquely suitable for him to identify with.

We are now in a position to understand the role the poet's fictional identification plays in the larger process of ego formation. The psychoanalyst David Rapaport has asserted that the ego owes its "relative autonomy" to the "derivative motivations" that it structures to guarantee against "drive slavery," on the one hand, and "stimulus slavery," on the other, continuously playing one force off the other. What Rapaport calls "Activity" refers to the relative capacity of the ego to exhibit that autonomy through the control of drive demand.[17] The initial "passivity" of the "Calamus-Leaves" poems — the sort of condition Rapaport describes as, in part, "*the helpless-passive experience of tension*" — we find in the consuming dejection of "Hours continuing long, sore and heavy-hearted" in "Calamus. 9." Passivity is also unmistakable in the poet's complete subjugation to drive tension, marked by his lament in the same poem, "it is useless — I am what I am," or in the poet's "wrong-doing" in "Calamus. 16," which despite his "self-convict[ion]" will still not "cease transpiring from me until it must cease." These two poems, like others discussed, represent a poet excessively vulnerable to external stimuli, helpless to manage the drives that determine his life.

The creation of a substitute object in the form of an imaginative reader or lover who exists within the confines of the poem is important to understand psychologically because it models the ego structure, which enabled the poetic persona to reassert control over drives the poetry represents as debilitating.[18] The poet reveals his development of an active posture in the poetry in two ways: his ability to reroute drive tension when the object is absent and his ability to forestall involuntary response even when his fictional object is present. That is, activity is manifested first in his ability to escape the paralysis of anxiety that marked many of the poems quoted earlier once drive energy could be discharged through its representation as poetic objects that might be freely accepted by imagined readers; in this sense, he effectively achieves a kind of imaginary consummation. This is the fundamental organizing strategy of "Calamus" as represented in "In Paths Untrodden" and "Scented Herbage of My Breast" but perhaps most lovingly captured in the poet's tender assertion in "Roots and Leaves Themselves Alone" that, until accepted by the reader, his love poems are but "Roots and leaves themselves alone":

Buds to be unfolded on the old terms;
If you bring the warmth of the sun to them, they will open, and bring
    form, color, perfume, to you,
If you become the aliment and the wet, they will become flowers, fruits,
    tall branches and trees, (*LV* 383)

The second manifestation of activity, the poet's representation of an ability to forestall passive discharge in the presence of the fictionalized drive object, is the very counterpressure that permits the poet to adopt the coy, aloof stance toward his reader or lover in "Are You the New Person Drawn toward Me?" This representation of the poet's ability to resist submission to the lover (which is to say, regulate the conditions of the relationship) also informs "Whoever You are Holding Me Now in Hand," a poem that elaborates the nature of the poet/reader transaction. In that poem's second and third stanzas, for example, he cautiously asks:

Who is he that would become my follower?
Who would sign himself a candidate for my affections? Are you he?

The way is suspicious — the result slow, uncertain, may-be destructive;
You would have to give up all else — I alone would expect to be your
    God, sole and exclusive,
Your novitiate would even be long and exhausting,
The whole past theory of your life, and all conformity to the lives around
    you, would have to be abandoned;
Therefore release me now, before troubling yourself any further — Let go
    your hand from my shoulders,
Put me down, and depart on your way. (*LV* 368)

What we see here is not a poet who has privatized a cultural pathology, a move Michael Moon was concerned to have Whitman avoid, but one doing something infinitely more complex — and something of the opposite; he was enclosing private desire within a particularly public entity, the space he and his reader/lover could cohabit. In the process, however, he imported into that space the ego structure necessary to manage that relationship and the economy of desire that organizes it. This explains the inclusion of at least one poem in the "Calamus" cluster, "Calamus. 31." (later divided by stanza into two poems, "What Ship Puzzled at Sea" and "What Place Is Besieged?"), which appears to have nothing whatsoever to do with love or desire:

What ship, puzzled at sea, cons for the true reckoning?
Or, coming in, to avoid the bars, and follow the channel, a perfect pilot
    needs?
Here, sailor! Here, ship! take aboard the most perfect pilot,
Whom, in a little boat, putting off, and rowing, I, hailing you, offer.

What place is besieged, and vainly tries to raise the siege?
Lo! I send to that place a commander, swift, brave, immortal,
And with him horse and foot — and parks of artillery,
And artillerymen, the deadliest that ever fired gun. (*LV* 398–399)

Despite its seemingly anomalous subject matter, this poem is quite appropriate to the "Calamus" problem: the "most perfect pilot" and brave "commander" are personifications of the poetic ego's assertion of authority over
the forces of desire — an attempt to manage at least the intrapsychic half of a
nature that Dewey reminds us is eternally precarious. But for the most part in
"Calamus," agency or management is less an abstraction the poet exclusively
focuses on than a practice the poet employs in the fictional territory he creates
for himself and his "public." To the extent that this public entity — the poetic
construct of a poet/reader relationship — is imagined to be democratic and
political, it cannot escape coming under the jurisdiction of that same ego
structure — which is to say that however the poet links his vision of democracy to that economy of desire, he cannot avoid structuring that vision around
the principle of human agency that is the very meaning of "ego."

    This is precisely the case, as the poet, having worked free of the supposed
categorical boundaries that he imagined kept public vision separate from private desire, reassumes the public role he had "sever[ed]" himself from in
"Calamus. 8." Now he is not so content to define that public role as merely being the visionary "incarnation" of the people, the passive medium through
which the people's own natural, and inevitably progressive, revitalizing instincts were consolidated, expressed, and thereby harnessed for public use —
the role he imagined for himself in the 1855 preface. There he had claimed
that, in his role as visionary poet (as distinguished, by the way, from what we
know of Whitman's actual partisan political conduct), "He is no arguer . . . he
is judgment," which is to say he merely codifies, uncritically, the judgment already latent in the social body he incorporates, while not taking up political
positions within that body (*CRE* 713–715). He moves, albeit tentatively, to actually govern the nation he incarnates by asserting a normative role for the
ideal of America he has abstracted — an implicit but unmistakable recogni-

tion that not all "versions" of America are worthy of the name and, more troubling still, that the preferred ideal is not guaranteed success either by natural process or by virtue of its consolidation into poetry.

He had signaled the move to visionary governance in "Whoever You are Holding Me Now in Hand" by articulating the very formidable political obligations that are to bind the poet and his reader: "You would have to give up all else — I alone would expect to be your sole God, sole and exclusive, standard, [/. . . /] The whole past theory of your life, and all conformity to the lives around you, would have to be abandoned" (*LV* 368). This is not to say that the poet does not still, in some sense, "incarnate" the people. The new theory he would establish as a governing standard is not anything he believes to be an alien imposition but one, though perhaps unacknowledged, he regards as existing "latent in all men," as he puts it in "To the East and to the West":

To you of New England,
To the man of the Seaside State, and of Pennsylvania,
To the Kanadian of the north — to the Southerner I love,
These, with perfect trust, to depict you as myself — the germs are in all
     men;
I believe the main purport of These States is to found a superb
     friendship, exalté, previously unknown,
Because I perceive it waits, and has been always waiting, latent in all men.
                                                                              (*LV* 401)

Here, he is content merely to "depict" himself as the exemplar of the "superb friendship" he defines as the foundational principle of "These States." In "The Prairie-Grass Dividing," he begins *demanding* "the most copious and close companionship of men" commensurate with the natural power of the land itself:

The prairie-grass dividing — its own odor breathing,
I demand of it the spiritual corresponding,
Demand the most copious and close companionship of men,
Demand the blades to rise of words, acts, beings,
Those of the open atmosphere, coarse, sunlit, fresh, nutritious,
Those that go their own gait, erect, stepping with freedom and
     command — leading, not following,
Those with never-quell'd audacity — those with sweet and lusty flesh,
     clear of taint, choice and chary of its love-power,

> Those that look carelessly in the faces of Presidents and Governors, as to
> say, *Who are You?*
> Those of earth-born passion, simple, never constrained, never obedient,
> Those of inland America. (*LV* 394–395)

Throughout "Calamus" the poet had been attempting to form an identifying bond with his reader by searching for that special community where desire informs civic life. In "This Moment Yearning and Thoughtful," he speculates wistfully on the prospect of somehow joining "men in other lands" with
whom he might become "brethren and lovers" (*LV* 393); in "I Dream'd in a
Dream," he fantasizes about a "new City of friends," "invincible to the attacks
of the whole rest of the earth" and dominated by "the quality of robust love"
(*LV* 400–401); and in "A Promise to California," he reinterprets the myth of
national expansion to warrant his own migration to the West "to teach robust
American love; / For I know very well that I and robust love belong among
you, inland, and along the Western Sea" (*LV* 398). But the public approbation
of the libido he yearns for in these poems is obviated in "The Prairie-Grass
Dividing" because it has been legitimated through refiguration as the preem-
inent power in nature — a nature whose correspondence with the human social environment it is the poet's job not to recognize but to achieve. Poet and
public may no longer depend upon the happy accident of their mutual resi-
dence within a natural matrix of desire to guarantee their bonds. Rather, social bonds are a product forged with the energy of untamed desire that has
been harnessed for that use by a "demanding" executive poet. The idea of a
unity of poet and public, achieved through the regulation of desire, finally begins to crystalize as a vision of the state.

Such a refiguring of desire offers a rich source for democratic meanings.
But as politically fruitful and as morally significant Whitman's particular
transformation of private desire into public principle is, the greater value is
that it inscribed within the democratic ideal he was attempting to articulate
the mechanism it most needed — human agency. Still, in 1860, it was the love,
desire, and the "City of Friendship" that they made possible that most concerned Whitman, not any capacity for governance. Clearly, as "I Hear It Was
Charged against Me" makes plain, even though the poet seemed to intuit how
far the political implications of poetic agency might reach, he was not interested in developing them:

> I hear it is charged against me that I seek to destroy institutions;
> But really I am neither for nor against institutions;

(What indeed have I in common with them? — Or what with the
    destruction of them?)
Only I will establish in the Mannahatta, and in every city of These States,
    inland and seaboard,
And in the fields and woods, and above every keel little or large, that
    dents the water,
Without edifices, or rules, or trustees, or any argument,
The institution of the dear love of comrades. (*LV* 394)

Nevertheless, the fortuitous advent of agency within the poet's vision opens
up his democratic ideal to an engagement with problematic historical experience. As we shall see, it will be the poet's negotiations of the very dramatic,
historical, and tragic experience of the Civil War that will both reshape his understanding of the vision's content and open up avenues of cultural and institutional criticism that could not exist within the shackles of a laissez-faire
democratic theory.

6

"To Learn from the Crises of Anguish"
Tragedy, History, and the Meaning of Democratic Mourning

The introduction of agency into Whitman's poetics was, as we have seen, the result of his need to manage his own psychic chaos. With the Civil War, however, came social and political chaos. By using his newly transformed poetry to grapple with such a public crisis, it was inevitable that the effort would register as a fundamental alteration in the social and political vision his poetry had originally been designed to express. This is indeed the case, as Whitman's Civil War poetry marks a significant advancement toward his vision of democracy as people acting collectively and pragmatically to secure a meaningful freedom.

In many respects, Whitman's use of poetic agency serves as a signal that the gap that had seemed to separate his political practice from his political vision was beginning to close. In practice, Whitman had been anything but passive. In his highly partisan editorial career with various Democratic newspapers — and especially in his support of William Leggett and the radical "Loco Foco," or equal rights, faction of the Democratic Party — he was the very essence of rhetorical agency. In fact, his strident advocacy of a host of controversial positions in the 1840s and early 1850s seems to have gotten him fired regularly from various newspaper and writing jobs.[1] Now the vision, once hamstrung by its laissez-faire underpinnings, could be reimagined to make such advocacy essential to the success of democracy.

In this chapter, I will attempt to distinguish three ways in which agency seems to register as a social (rather than a psychological) dynamic in Whitman's most compelling wartime works, *Drum-Taps* and "When Lilacs Last in the Dooryard Bloom'd" (initially published in *Sequel to Drum-Taps*). First, and perhaps most basically, poetic agency permits him to represent diverse and atomistic people consolidating themselves into a collective in order to engage in purposeful action. Second, the tragedy of the Civil War seems to have led Whitman to the realization that social life is shaped by human events and decisions, not natural processes — that human history is not natural history.

It is the capacity for agency in his poetry that permits him to incorporate that realization in his democratic vision. He was able to imagine the possibility — the imperative — of struggling within an uncertain and dangerous world to fashion a more humane life. And third, the assassination of President Abraham Lincoln brought Whitman to an understanding that the very contentious nature of democratic life inevitably left it vulnerable to deep and potentially indelible division; beyond the particular historical causes of the Civil War, the life of any democratic nation is in perpetual jeopardy of dissolution. Democracy itself, then, might be understood as a kind of necessary tragedy. The continuation of a democracy depends upon perpetual acts of social reconciliation. In "When Lilacs Last in the Dooryard Bloom'd," Whitman models this act of reconciliation; in so doing, he exemplifies poetic agency in its most refined and noble form.

Agency, Social Identity, and Purposeful Action

As the poet mobilized himself in preparation for the uncertainties of civil war, he carried into his visionary mechanics a conception of circumstances that were just precarious enough to warrant the employment of his newfound agency. The result is a dramatic shift in the poet's conception of the nexus of action and political identity. This is immediately evident in the critically "neglected" poems that first call the North to arms at the beginning of *Drum-Taps* — poems that, as M. Wynn Thomas has cogently argued, are reflective of Whitman's use of verse for political advocacy. Critics have tended to ignore these poems, Thomas observes, because they are "[u]neven in quality and apparently belligerent and chauvinistic in tone . . . indeed the best that is customarily said of them is that they represent the work of a man who as yet knew nothing of the vile and shocking realities of war." [2] Looking deeper into these early war poems, Thomas reads them as a celebration of the North's repudiation of its own undemocratic cultural traits, which the war against an undemocratic South may have signaled. Consequently, they "are far from simple" but are "full of Whitman's hopes and uncertainties about the outcome of the nation's internal struggle to determine the extent and nature of its commitment to democracy." [3] Pushing Thomas's insight in a slightly different direction, we may also read the poems as an implicit repudiation of the undemocratic strains in Whitman's own laissez-faire democratic vision. Having inculcated through "Calamus" the means of poetic agency, he now regarded it as the poet's responsibility to work for the success of that historically specific democratic struggle, in effect, modeling the collaborative action essential in a democratic society. In other words, the poet needed to negotiate the contingencies of the national crisis that, after all, threatened the fundamental coherence of the nation, his visionary model.

Even a poem whose form seems typical of many found in the first two editions of *Leaves of Grass* registers the influence of agency through subtle structural inclusion of purpose. In "First O Songs for a Prelude," for example, the introductory poem of *Drum-Taps*, the poet recurs to his most characteristic literary technique, the urban catalog, as he celebrates how his beloved "Manhattan, my own, my peerless! [/ . . . /] threw off the costumes of peace" and "led to war" (*LV* 453). In the fifth stanza he approvingly observes:

To the drum-taps prompt,
The young men falling in and arming;
The mechanics arming, (the trowel, the jack-plane, the blacksmith's
     hammer, tost aside with precipitation;)
The lawyer leaving his office, and arming — the judge leaving the court;
The driver deserting his wagon in the street, jumping down, throwing
     the reins abruptly down on the horses' backs;
The salesman leaving the store — the boss, book-keeper, porter, all
     leaving;
Squads gathering everywhere by common consent, and arming;
The new recruits, even boys — the old men show them how to wear their
     accoutrements — they buckle the straps carefully;
Outdoors arming — indoors arming — the flash of the musket-barrels;
The white tents cluster in camps — the arm'd sentries around — the
     sunrise cannon, and again at sunset;
Arm'd regiments arrive every day, pass through the city, and embark from
     the wharves;
(How good they look, as they tramp down to the river, sweaty, with their
     guns on their shoulders!
How I love them! how I could hug them, with their brown faces, and
     their clothes and knapsacks cover'd with dust!)
The blood of the city up — arm'd! arm'd! the cry everywhere;
The flags flung out from the steeples of churches, and from all the public
     buildings and stores;
The tearful parting — the mother kisses her son — the son kisses his
     mother;
(Loth is the mother to part — yet not a word does she speak to
     detain him;)

The tumultuous escort — the ranks of policemen preceding, clearing
   the way;
The unpent enthusiasm — the wild cheers of the crowd for their
   favorites;
The artillery — the silent cannons, bright as gold, drawn along, rumble
   lightly over the stones;
(Silent cannons — soon to cease your silence!
Soon, unlimber'd, to begin the red business;)
All the mutter of preparation — all the determin'd arming;
The hospital service — the lint, bandages, and medicines;
The women volunteering for nurses — the work begun for, in earnest —
   no mere parade now;
War! an arm'd race is advancing! — the welcome for battle — no turning
   away;
War! be it weeks, months, or years — an arm'd race is advancing to
   welcome it. (*LV* 454–455)

Like the catalogs of Whitman's early poetry, this, too, seeks to represent a diverse and inclusive society. But both the strategy and its effect are different. The catalogs of "Song of Myself," for example, strove for radical diversity by the seemingly endless enumeration of an inexhaustible variety of human beings and motives, which suggested, by sheer overpowering accumulation, the boundlessness of social life itself; in those catalogs, discrete social facts represented nothing particular so much as the infinite particularity of human types in an explosion of purpose that spread in all directions. But in this catalog, inclusion entails exclusion. Manhattan is set apart from all the nameless other places it must lead. And as the real municipality of Manhattan is bound spatially by its own city limits, the human boundary of the poet's Manhattan is the circumference shaped by the polar points of an infinity of social opposites, all drawing in along traversing axes to a hub formed in a single moment of purposeful action: the working-class "mechanics" who join the middle-class "lawyer" and "judge"; the "salesman" who joins "the boss, book-keeper, porter"; the "new recruits, even boys" who submit to the tutelage of "old men"; the double antitheses of gender and age as "mother" and "son" both join and part in a reciprocal kiss; all the men who have volunteered are joined by "women volunteering for nurses"; indeed, all that is "outdoors arming" is also "indoors arming." What is represented is not the infinite accumulation of atomistic particularity but "squads" of binary oppositions, tethering themselves together "everywhere by common consent." For the first time in *Leaves of Grass*, an exclusively defined community is joined together by fidelity to a common purpose for action.

But if this poem conveys the idea that that joining is spontaneous, unprecipitated by any cause other than shared, pent-up enthusiasm, other poems supply an agent. In "City of Ships," Manhattan is again the setting for a feverish display of war passion; now the poet must rouse his beloved city to action. After reminding the city of its preeminence in the world, he concludes by commanding:

> Spring up, O city! not for peace alone, but be indeed yourself, warlike!
> Fear not! submit to no models but your own, O city!
> Behold me! — incarnate me, as I have incarnated you!
> I have rejected nothing you offer'd me — whom you adopted, I have adopted;
> Good or bad, I never question you — I love all — I do not condemn anything;
> I chant and celebrate all that is yours — yet peace no more;
> In peace I chanted peace, but now the drum of war is mine;
> War, red war, is my song through your streets, O city! (*LV* 490)

In "Beat! Beat! Drums!" — perhaps the most belligerent of all the calls to arms — the war drum he beats and the bugle he blows "stop for no expostulation," doing their job rather crudely by subordinating all hesitant or reflective voices to the "ruthless force" of rhythmic sound: "So strong you thump, O terrible drums — so loud you bugles blow" (*LV* 487). But in "City of Ships," the poet chants a much more sophisticated protocol for leadership, which the drum rhythms merely punctuate. Still, it is also a paradoxical protocol. The problem at the heart of "City of Ships" is essentially the one Kenneth Burke refers to in *A Rhetoric of Motives* as the "ambiguities of substance." To identify A with B, for example, by persuading them that they share identical interests, is, Burke argues, to make A and B "substantially one," or "consubstantial." But substance, he reminds us, has always been a highly problematic philosophical concept, inextricable from a myriad of internal contradictions. Yet even so, a "doctrine of *consubstantiality*, either explicit or implicit, may be necessary to any way of life. For substance, in the old philosophies, was an *act*; and a way of life is an *acting-together*; and in acting together, men have common sensations, concepts, images, ideas, attitudes that make them *consubstantial*."[4] By commanding the city to "Spring up," Whitman is but naming the "deed," the action, implicit in the city's identity: "be indeed yourself, warlike." In other words, he attempts to persuade them that the quality of action he has named derives from the constitutive ideal that unites them as a city — and what should, therefore, unite the city with the poet. As Burke further explains, "[i]dentification is compensatory to division. If men were not apart from one another, there would be no need for the rhetorician to proclaim their unity."[5] In fact, the poet's need to insist that the city "incarnate me as I have incarnated you" — a recognition that the polity has failed to identify with him in return — points to two paradoxes of democratic agency. First, the very need for rhetorical agency acknowledges that dissent is endemic within the entity he would unite under a particular ideal (the ideal he himself symbolizes); to "incarnate" the poet is then to choose to identify with the ideal he represents and exercise its attendant praxis. Second, even though there may be functional distinctions among the various roles played by agents at any given time in a democracy and even though poets or other executives may serve as the loci of motivational energy, nevertheless democratic agency is necessarily conceived of as a pervasive capacity; action is imagined as a "reciprocal" dynamic, a necessarily mutual decision to incarnate the other — or not.

History as Denatured Tragedy

To incarnate, in good faith, a decision within a political body — to accept ownership of and responsibility for that decision — is to incarnate the consequences of that decision as well. The particular consequences of the "red war" the poet sings is the "reality" of death and brutality, which critics such as James E. Miller Jr. assert, reasonably enough, stunned Whitman into a more sober, unsentimental understanding of the tragedy of war.[6] Certainly the poet's loss of innocence provides *Drum-Taps* with many of its most dramatic images. In "A March in the Ranks Hard-Prest, and the Road Unknown," for example, the poet marches in the "sullen" ranks of a defeated and retreating army along a "road unknown" in darkness until they come upon an old church that has been converted into an "impromptu hospital." What he sees inside transcends "all the pictures and poems ever made," including, presumably, his own: "Shadows of deepest, deepest black, just lit by moving candles and lamps" and one large torch whose "wild red flame" illuminates a young soldier who is bleeding to death from a gunshot wound to his abdomen. After the poet "stanch[es] the blood temporarily," he surveys the rest of the scene:

> Faces, varieties, postures beyond description, most in obscurity, some of
>   them dead;

Surgeons operating, attendants holding lights, the smell of ether, the
   odor of blood;
The crowd, O the crowd of the bloody forms of soldiers — the yard
   outside also fill'd;
Some on the bare ground, some on planks or stretchers, some in the
   death-spasm sweating;
An occasional scream or cry, the doctor's shouted orders or calls;
The glisten of the little steel instruments catching the glint of the torches;

$$(LV\ 494)$$

Before he leaves, he bends down to the young soldier whose bleeding he has
just stanched, whereupon the boy gives him a final "half-smile" and dies.

However mawkish these images may strike the modern reader, it seems
closer to the mark to say that the poet's language stretched to melodrama not
to exaggerate the tragic reality of war he actually saw but in a futile effort to
keep up with it. It is often remarked that in much of his Civil War poetry, Whitman anticipates the modern movement by his frequent willingness to rely on
nothing more than stark images, as though narrative language itself was completely impotent to render the meaning of such an unspeakable horror. "The
Artilleryman's Vision" actually uses narrative language to anticipate modernity in another way. Long after the war is over and while his wife lies sleeping
next to him, a veteran artilleryman wakes in the middle of the night to a "fantasy unreal," the haunting memory of "All the scenes at the batteries [that] rise
in detail before me again." As the "vision presses upon" him, he reports:

I see the gaps cut by the enemy's volleys, (quickly fill'd up — no delay)
I breathe the suffocating smoke — then the flat clouds hover low,
   concealing all;
Now a strange lull comes for a few seconds, not a shot fired on
   either side;
Then resumed, the chaos louder then ever, with eager calls, and orders of
   officers;
While from some distant part of the field the wind wafts to my ears a
   shout of applause, (some special success;)
And ever the sound of the cannon, far or near, (rousing, even in dreams a
   devilish exultation, and all the old mad joy, in the depths of my soul;)
And ever the hastening of infantry shifting positions — batteries, cavalry,
   moving hither and thither;
(The falling, dying, I heed not — the wounded, dripping and red, I heed
   not — some to the rear are hobbling;)

Grime, heat, rush — aid-de-camps galloping by, or on a full run;
With the patter of small arms, the warning *s-s-t* of the rifles, (these in my
    vision I hear or see,)
And bombs bursting in air, and at night the vari-color'd rockets.

(LV 506–507)

Critics often comment on this poem's realistic representation of battlefield
detail as well as its psychologically realistic documentation of posttraumatic
stress disorder (a condition not recognized medically until the early twentieth
century). There is also a haunting realism to the abruptness of the poem's final
line that does not attempt closure but seems, rather, to suspend meaning as
though it hovered beyond reach amid the dangers of rockets and bombs bursting in midair. But the significant problem at the center of this poem is the seeming paradox that real horrors of war have generated a "fantasy unreal." The
very realism of the vision seems to belie its status as fantasy, as the veteran's
continuous present-tense assertions that "I breathe" or "I hear" or, especially,
"I see" the raging battle he describes, have the effect of erroneously locating
his past experiences in the present moment. Conversely, his acknowledgment
that what he sees is but a "fantasy unreal" opens the question of how faithfully
his vision corresponds to the history it seems to represent. In short, the overpowering brutality of actual history has usurped the imagination, collapsing
any possible distinction in the poem between reality and vision.

However Whitman's epiphany concerning the real brutality of war may
have affected him personally, it also presented him with a philosophical dilemma that "The Artilleryman's Vision" puts sharply into focus. The problem
is central to *Drum-Taps*. Simply stated, the poet must answer the companion
questions of what is the relation between history and nature and how does
that relation correspond to his visionary ideals? In the metaphysical vision of
the 1855 and 1856 editions of *Leaves of Grass*, the poet had conflated history
and nature. He had invested historically contingent, laissez-faire Jacksonian
America with the authority of unalterable but benign nature. Doing so, as
I argued in the second chapter, was, in many respects, altogether appropriate — indeed, it was often altogether unavoidable. After all, there is great
value in exploring the potential warrant nature may offer democratic conceptions of cooperative life; moreover, our conceptions of nature are already implicated in the historical contingencies of cultural ideals. Still, the terms "human history" and "natural history" do not name quite the same things;
as Whitman's poetry demonstrates, however impossible it may ultimately be
to disentangle them, the great sin in failing to try is that it leaves solipsism

insulated from critical scrutiny. It was by being so completely unaware of any distinction between history and nature that the poet was able to transfer so completely individual human agency to the mechanical operations of an impersonal and unassailable laissez-faire nature. But conversely, as will be seen later, it was the poet's introduction of agency into his vision — and especially the concomitant inclusion of the precarious conditions of existence that necessitate agency in the first place — that made it necessary for the poet to recognize one of nature's hybrids, human history: the peculiar realm created by the endless interactions and consequences of human choice-making that combine to render each successive moment of human life just a little unprecedented and unpredictable. Further, not only did the introduction of agency necessitate an awareness of history, but it also compelled him to reimagine a self capable of making history.[7]

How useful any conception of nature is as a model for progressive ideals (however its historical contingency is recognized) depends on how amenable to successful living "real" nature seems to be at the moment. For the poet of *Drum-Taps*, brutal, bloody, and violent nature — or the history he conflated with nature — was certainly not a place where life could enjoy much success. So given the poet's previous reliance on the perfect correspondence between nature and the ideal, the problem of a violent and unacceptable reality first presents itself to the poet as an anomaly, a failure of correspondence. In "Year That Trembled and Reel'd Beneath Me," for example, reversals in the Union's war fortunes in 1863–1864 prompt the poet to note the lack of correspondence between his most immediate experience of nature, the weather, and his moral expectations of reality.[8]

> Year that trembled and reel'd beneath me!
> Your summer wind was warm enough — yet the air I breathed froze me;
> A thick gloom fell through the sunshine and darken'd me;
> Must I change my triumphant songs? said I to myself;
> Must I indeed learn to chant the cold dirges of the baffled?
> And sullen hymns of defeat? (*LV* 505)

Here, the real problem of potential "defeat" is figured in the poem as confusion, as the poet considers the prospect that he might need to "learn to chant the cold dirges of the baffled." What is baffling is that the very fact of defeat, confounding nature's grant to the Union of a moral right to victory, would seem to raise the possibility that there exists a second or parallel nature — a morally false, alternative nature — which appears to belie the empirical reality of that nature he encounters through the senses as weather. Rather than challenging the basic logic of correspondence theory, the poet adopts a metaphoric strategy that reconciles the moral failure implicit in defeat by linking it with a fictive hostile nature. At the same time, he cannot avoid raising the possibility that real nature may also be fictive. The warm summer wind is belied by the air that "froze me," and "the sunshine" is pierced by a "thick gloom" that "darken'd me."

Whitman's consternation over such confusing and recalcitrant climactic conditions as the summer wind, freezing air, sunshine, and thick gloom is neither accidental nor idiosyncratic. In his insightful discussion of the role weather plays in *Drum-Taps*, Thomas reminds us that actual weather conditions were already a very large factor in the progress of the war and a predictably significant concern of Whitman's war poetry. Moreover, in putting the idea of weather to use in his poetry, Whitman had to negotiate between two very conflicting cultural assumptions about its meaning — one, an earlier and more superstitious "primitive climatology" that attempted to "classify cultures according to climate," and the other, the promising yet volatile and imprecise new nineteenth-century science of meteorology.[9] The weather was as unstable symbolically and ideologically as it was in fact. "As such," Thomas writes, "[i]t suggestively corresponded to Whitman's own relation to wartime events. Both psychologically and ideologically, he was in constant danger of being overwhelmed and undermined by the arbitrariness of events. His emotional survival depended on maintaining a teleology of conflict, on being credibly able to make the bewildering story of the war, as it actually unfolded, conform to his majestic vision of History, wherein the triumphant ineluctable progress of American democratic society was assured."[10]

Whitman's problem, as Thomas implies, goes beyond the uncertainties of weather. Elsewhere in *Drum-Taps*, we see that the poet is also troubled by the prospect of a morally unstable cosmos. For example, in "Quicksand Years" the apparent occasion is, once again, the prospect of Union defeat. Now failure is not explained by a grounding in an alternative nature but is refigured as the possession of time and history itself:

Quicksand years that whirl me I know not whither,
Your schemes, politics, fail — lines give way — substances mock and
    elude me;
Only the theme I sing, the great and strong-possess'd Soul, eludes not;

One's-self, must never give way — that is the final substance — that out of
all is sure;
Out of politics, triumphs, battles, death — What at last finally remains?
When shows break up, what but One's-Self is sure? (*LV* 479)

As in "Year that Trembled and Reel'd Beneath Me," the problem here too is
how to authenticate — or even explain — a reality that does not exhibit the
moral properties the poet had come to expect of it. But whereas time in that
previous poem (the particular "year" that trembled beneath him) was figured
merely as the temporal address ("your wind") of a morally active and interested nature, here the use of the second-person possessive "Your" conveys
the deeper sense that history (the quicksand years) actually owns responsibility for its "schemes" and "politics" that fail. Failure — which is to say moral
falsehood — has been transferred from nature to history. But the epistemological consequences of failure are similar in both poems, only now it is the reality of history (not nature) that has become suspect. The reality of temporal
"substances mock and elude" him because they are but "shows" that eventually "break up," leaving the poet with no other recourse but to reify the ideal,
the "theme" he sings, as the "final substance."

In "Crossing Brooklyn Ferry," Whitman conceived identity as a transaction between the particularity of real experience and an ideal construction, a
transaction made possible by the creation in poetry of fictive time. Actual history — that is, the particularity of living experience — was not thereby denied, as it has been in the two poems just discussed; rather, its claim to the status of real was validated as a necessary component in the creation of meaning.
Set against the earlier poem's treatment of real living experience, the failure of
these two *Drum-Taps* poems to recognize the authenticity of experience in
time is disappointing: they amount to an attempted escape from all that is un-
pleasant in any given moment. Still, what is striking about the poet's concept
of historical experience in "Crossing Brooklyn Ferry" (and, indeed, in all of
Whitman's early poetry) is that it is not fully historical. In Whitman's early
poetry, the march of human time was imagined as a developmental or progressive process, an extension of the process that was supposed to inform natural change. Since all change was conceived to be developmental, even such
tragedies as a shipwreck or the drowning of a swimmer could be understood
as benign expressions of an inevitable dialectical progression toward some
better existence. But the very notion of human agency that was now operating
in Whitman's poetry entails a view of history — history as, in Sidney Hook's
phrasing, dependent "in some respects upon what human beings do or leave

undone."[11] Beneath the escapist impulse that appears to ride the surface of these two poems from *Drum-Taps* is the deeper, more profound recognition that tragedy — especially the tragedy that humans manage to inflict on themselves — cannot be charged to a morally disinterested nature.

For Sidney Hook, perhaps Dewey's most able and prolific student, the recognition that life is innately tragic is a prerequisite for historical understanding (as well as a central insight of pragmatic philosophy). By the recognition of tragedy, however, he does not mean "merely sensitivity to the presence of evil or suffering in the world, although all tragic situations to some degree involve one or the other."[12] In *Pragmatism and the Tragic Sense of Life*, Hook defines tragedy in specifically human terms as a phenomenon of moral decision. All genuine moral decisions, he observes, are not choices between good and evil but rather between competing goods (understood as values), competing rights (understood as obligations), or between the good and the right that may come into conflict in any concrete situation. Even the most "intelligent" resolution of genuine moral problems always involves a frustration or outright rejection of some authentic good or right, the consequences of which are almost certain to be, in varying degrees, painful and tragic. History is, at least in part, the record of a seemingly infinite number of sometimes intelligent, and sometimes unintelligent, human choices and the even greater number of their often tragic consequences ricocheting through time. But, Hook asserts, "to put a gloss of reason over the terrible events which constitute so much of the historical record," as, for instance, Hegelian history does (along with any conception of a laissez-faire nature), only "vulgarizes tragedy. For it attempts to console man with a dialectical proof that his agony and defeat are not really evils but necessary elements in the goodness of the whole." Hook goes on to add that "no metaphysics which asserts that the world is rational, necessary and good has any room for genuine, inescapable tragedy."[13] This, expressed inversely, is the logical imperative behind Whitman's accidental insight. It was the poet's confrontation with the tragedy of war that was to lead him to the recognition of human history's conceptual distinction from nature but also to the subsequent recognition of the moral disinterestedness of nature itself, a discovery whose ultimate consequence was to liberate the poet's democratic vision from its subservience to the dictates of a laissez-faire conception of nature.

One of the complaints that is often heard about Whitman's poetry concerns what some regard as its cloying optimism. The same complaint, elevated to the status of criticism, is often leveled at pragmatic philosophy. The assumption is that they are both so exceedingly temperamentally optimistic that they naively reduce the complex, tragic, and ultimately insoluble mystery of existence either to a "problem" perfectly amenable to earnestly applied intelligence or to a happy scenario of evolutionary progress. Recently, for example, John Patrick Diggins resurrects this charge in *The Promise of Pragmatism* in order to challenge "one of the most questionable assumptions of American pragmatism, Dewey's organic vision of progress." According to Diggins, Dewey's reliance on the principles of evolution as an analogue for human history led him to erroneously see humankind as arising "[f]rom the womb of raw nature" to become "an 'organism' of intelligent adaptation, a progressive elevation away from bondage to instinct to rational control and eventually to community and human solidarity."[14] Diggins is certainly correct in his response to the Dewey he glosses that there is nothing in science, history, or human intelligence to warrant such a mindless confidence; he is also certainly correct that, as one of the historical consequences of human intelligence, modernity evinces more alienation than community. But as Hook suggests in his essay on the tragic, such views do not get Dewey, pragmatism — or Whitman, as I shall argue later — exactly right. Having asserted that a recognition of the tragic was implied in Dewey's understanding of the function of intelligence, Hook goes on to observe that "intelligence may be optimistic when it deals with the control of things, but the moral life by its very nature forbids the levity and superficiality which has often been attributed to the pragmatic approach by its unimaginative critics."[15] For Hook, optimism is simply an enabling disposition that permits inquiry to proceed. The pragmatic conception of intelligence "is more serious, even more heroic, than any other approach because it doesn't resign itself to the bare fact of tragedy or take easy ways out at the price of truth. Where death does not result from the tragic situation, there are always consequences for continued living which it takes responsibly without yielding to despair. It does not conceive of tragedy as a preordained doom, but as one in which the plot to some extent depends upon us, so that we become the creators of our own tragic history. We cannot then palm off altogether the tragic outcome upon the universe in the same way as we can with a natural disaster."[16]

In the light of Hook's observation, note that nature turns in *Drum-Taps* from being the continuation of human ideals to being the problematic setting in which these ideals must prove themselves; the sense of the tragic does not produce a sense of despair. In fact, the poet seems to return to his earlier optimistic outlook in "Solid, Ironical Rolling Orb," a poem that appeared only in 1860:

Solid, ironical, rolling orb!
Master of all, and matter of fact! — at last I accept your terms;
Bringing to practical, vulgar tests, of all my ideal dreams,
And of me, as lover and hero. (*LV* 522)

The exuberant tone of the poem suggested by the first line's clipped cadence, the exclamation marks, and the oddly epiphanous quality to his declaration that "at last I accept your terms" recalls the form, but not the content, of Whitman's characteristic optimism. It is not the optimism of a poet secure in his place in a rationally ordered universe but of an author confident in the "practical" viability of his ideals, even when put to use in conditions warped by irony. In "Long, too Long America," he demonstrates a more sober appreciation of the vulgarity of such practical testing, revealing in the process a view of the ideal as an educational product, a "conception" that results from struggle.

Long, too long, O land,
Traveling roads all even and peaceful, you learn'd from joys and
     prosperity only;
But now, ah now, to learn from crises of anguish — advancing, grappling
     with direst fate, and recoiling not;
And now to conceive, and show to the world, what your children
     en-masse really are;
(For who except myself has yet conceived what your children en-masse
     really are?) (*LV* 495)

Here, too, the poet exhibits his confidence. But the confidence he expresses is not the prophet's confidence in the clarity of his vision. What he expresses is a kind of parental confidence in his "children en-masse" to learn successfully the lessons that the "crises of anguish" will teach. What is taught through the tragic struggle of experience, as the play on the word "conceive" implies, is a new conception of collective identity. The poem seems to suggest that that identity, the outcome of the "crises of anguish," is assured as the poet exhorts the collective to "show" or become what they already "really" are — an identity that he already recognizes. This is the familiar pose of the parent as coach; the poem is not so much about assurance but reassurance — a rhetorical form that not only admits of but is necessitated by the real possibility of failure. Thus the ironic play of the parenthetical final line revolves around the tension between the poet's version of "conception" as an imagining in faith and hope and the collective's version of "conception" as the creation, through struggle, of an unprecedented self. Put another way, the two come together as a conception of agency as both a vision and the will to realize it.

Mourning the Politically Tragic

The great value of Hook's essay on the tragic is in its reminder of just how central the recognition of inescapable tragedy is to pragmatic philosophy. Yet if it has a shortcoming, it is Hook's failure to propose an adequate response to tragedy beyond the admonition to strive to thoughtfully reduce tragic reality and then stoically face what remains. Pragmatism's "categorical imperative," he writes, "is to inquire, to reason together, to seek in every crisis the creative devices and inventions that will not only make life fuller and richer but tragedy bearable." [17] Hook's own interpretation of that imperative points him to a search for solutions to problems that satisfy because they are more inclusive, more responsive to the greatest number of interests possible. While not gainsaying that response in the least, the poet of *Drum-Taps* nevertheless reaches beyond it to minister to the tragic residual that cannot be remediated by inclusion in any intelligent solution. Whitman demonstrates the special form of agency that tragedy calls forth. At the core of human life, the poet would seem to have us know, there is a dimension of terror, pain, and suffering that, for the very reason that it is beyond any "resolution," demands some means by which its corrosive influence can be managed. Such is the achievement of *Drum-Taps*, for as the poet attempts to reconcile the violence and death of the Civil War — the quintessence of tragedy, as Hook would define it — he also implicitly models a generic social response to the tragic element inherent in any morally conscious pursuit of democracy. The poet will deepen the significance of Hook's call for the "creative devices and inventions" that will make "tragedy bearable" by assuming the full ministerial responsibilities of an agent-poet who would offer himself as a national bard.

One of the most poignant illustrations of the poet's recognition of ministerial responsibility in *Drum-Taps* is "Come Up from the Fields Father." The setting of the poem is a "prosperous" Ohio farm on an autumn day, "all calm, all vital and beautiful." Against the backdrop of the day's irrelevant beauty, a father and mother are called by their daughter to the front door to receive a letter from Pete, their "dear son."

> Fast as she can she hurries — something ominous — her steps trembling;
> She does not tarry to smooth her white hair, nor adjust her cap.
>
> Open the envelop quickly;
> O this is not our son's writing, yet his name is sign'd;

O a strange hand writes for our dear son — O stricken mother's soul!
All swims before her eyes — flashes with black — she catches the main
　　words only;

Sentences broken — *gunshot wound in the breast, cavalry skirmish, taken*
　　to hospital,
At present low, but will soon be better. (*LV* 488–489)

What is curious thus far is that, even though the poem is ostensibly a summons addressed to the "father" to come up from the fields to receive the news
of his son's wounding, his presence can only be assumed. He has not, nor will
he be, represented as a family character. The mother's physical and emotional
responses are objectively described by an omniscient and sensitive narrator
(as are, in subsequent lines, the anxiety and grief of the remaining children).
But while the father is absent, the omniscient poet is there — or at least sufficiently present to interrupt the narrative line, first to comment and then later
to correct the narrative record and inform the reader (though not the family)
that the letter is factually wrong and that Pete is dead.

Ah, now the single figure to me,
Amid all teeming and wealthy Ohio, with all its cities and farms,
Sickly white in the face, and dull in the head, very faint,
By the jamb of the door leans.

Grieve not so, dear mother, (the just-grown daughter speaks through
　　her sobs;
The little sisters huddle around, speechless and dismay'd;)
See, dearest mother, the letter says Pete will soon be better.

Alas, poor boy, he will never be better, (nor may-be needs to be better,
　　that brave and ample soul;)
While they stand at home at the door, he is dead already;
The only son is dead. (*LV* 489)

The absence of the father combined with the presence of a strong and intrusive poetic voice suggests that the poet has actually assumed the paternal
function in the narrative — and subsumed that function into his own visionary responsibility. That reading is bolstered by the poet's apparently spouse-
like responsiveness to the mother's vulnerability, the sad and intimate portrait
of her sickly white face, dull head, and faint demeanor, which he permits to
exclude all competing images: "Ah, now the single figure to me." In this
sense, *where* the father is being summoned from is as important as the fact that

he is being summoned, for in calling the father from work in the fields, the family is in effect calling him — or the poet who would assume his place — to a new kind of work, caregiving.

> But the mother needs to be better;
> She, with thin form, presently drest in black;
> By day her meals untouch'd—then at night fitfully sleeping, often waking,
> In the midnight waking, weeping, longing with one deep longing,
> O that she might withdraw unnoticed — silent from life, escape and withdraw,
> To follow, to seek, to be with her dear dead son. (*LV* 489)

Of course, caregiving is not a gendered activity — a point implicitly underscored by those critics who occasionally and appropriately refer to the Whitman of such Civil War poems as "The Wound-Dresser" or as the "great Mother-man." Here, however, the poet has borrowed all the ministerial content latent in the nineteenth-century cultural stereotype of the father and inscribed it within the poetic function. He does not model that function, but his failure to do so only throws into relief the pragmatic imperative to ameliorate the paralysis of such grief — a function the poet would appear to be preparing himself for by refusing to valorize the representation of a mother's withdrawal into death when the humane truth is that she "needs to be better."

The mother's wound that must be made "better" in "Come Up from the Fields Father" is a wound to the memory; in particular, silence has functioned to privatize her grief, locking it in memory, by foreclosing any possibility of either expunging that grief through expression or redefining it through language. Significantly, the poet will demonstrate in "Pensive on Her Dead Gazing" that the appropriate response to such privatized grief is to transfer it to the social sphere, where (public) language may function to reshape grief into a public memory of the private-becoming-public tragic burden of preserving the very precondition and character of sociality in union. The impotent grief of a single, silent mother is subsumed by the mythological abstraction of motherhood, whose authoritative voice can command all of nature to "absorb" the heroic dead, memorializing them in soil.

> Pensive, on her dead gazing, I heard the Mother of All,
> Desperate, on the torn bodies, on the forms covering the battle-fields gazing;
> As she call'd to her earth with mournful voice while she stalk'd:

Absorb them well, O my earth, she cried — I charge you, lose not my
  sons! lose not an atom;
And you streams, absorb them well, taking their dear blood;
And you local spots, and you airs that swim above lightly,
And you essences of soil and growth — and you, O my rivers' depths;
And you mountain sides — and the woods where my dear children's
  blood, trickling, redden'd;
And you trees, down in your roots, to bequeath to all future trees,
My dead absorb — my young men's beautiful bodies absorb — and their
  precious, precious, precious blood;
Which holding in trust for me, faithfully back again give me, many a year
  hence,
In unseen essence and odor of surface and grass, centuries hence;
In blowing airs from the fields, back again give me my darlings — give my
  immortal heroes;
Exhale me them centuries hence — breathe me their breath — let not an
  atom be lost;
O years and graves! O air and soil! O my dead, an aroma sweet!
Exhale them perennial, sweet death, years, centuries hence.

$$(LV\,526-527)$$

Without intending to, by his conceit of a universal mother who consecrates
the soil with her "mournful voice," commanding it to hold "in trust" the "precious, precious, precious blood" of her "young men's beautiful bodies" so
that they might permeate the land "centuries hence," the poet supplies metaphoric logic to one of Lincoln's more powerful rhetorical claims. At Gettys-
burg, the president had asserted that the words of the living are impotent to
consecrate land that has already been hallowed by the deeds of the heroic
dead. Lincoln's logic would appear to assume that social memory is the construct of some biochemical process rather than the product of human linguistic agency — logic reminiscent, perhaps, of Whitman's own familiar philosophy of death, articulated here once again as the composting of material
necessary for the continuation of life. But Whitman has more than restated his
own death philosophy, he has appropriated it for political purposes: death is
now to be mourned, and the "mother of all" functions not so much as a natural principle, innately harmonious to the unalterable processes of the natural
order, but as the personified social will, dressed up in the kind of grand
mythological garb likely to underscore the ritual significance of its memorial-

izing task. It is the poet's words — cast as those of the social and commemorative construct of a transcendental mother — that consecrate the ground, designating particularly (as do the very memorable words of Lincoln) the deaths of soldiers as having sufficient social meaning to demand their preservation in public memory.

The need to heal by reconstructing social memory recurs as a problem throughout *Drum-Taps*. Whitman's most famous *Drum-Taps* poem, "The Wound-Dresser," begins as a treatise on the proper uses of memory. Though written no later than 1865, the poet imagines himself a former nurse sometime in the future who, now an "old man bending" years after the war has ended, comes upon the "new faces" of children who ask him to recall his experiences. From the vantage point of this imagined future, the poet (speaking in the future's present tense) "resumes" the past in order to respond to their questions. What they specifically want the poet to remember for them is the heroic adventure of war. Time, however, does not preserve such things in memory:

> But in silence, in dream's projections,
> While the world of gain and appearance and mirth goes on,
> So soon what is over forgotten, and waves wash the imprints off the sand,
> In nature's reverie sad, with hinged knees returning, I enter the doors —
>   (while for you up there,
> Whoever you are, follow me without noise, and be of strong heart.)
>
> (*LV* 480)

As the poet leads his imagined auditors solemnly through a gallery of images that feature the poet as nurse lovingly washing and dressing the wounded, the reader becomes aware of the poet as poet performing the ministerial role of his own metaphoric "waves," which "wash the imprints" of the trivial and false memory of a war without tragedy "off the sand" of public consciousness.

"America has always taken tragedy too lightly," wrote Henry Adams in *The Education of Henry Adams*. "Too busy to stop the activity of their twenty-million-horse-power society, Americans ignore tragic motives that would have overshadowed the Middle Ages; and the world learns to regard assassination as a form of hysteria, and death as a neurosis, to be treated by a rest-cure." [18] Though Adams was referring to the more common understanding of tragedy as the disastrous consequences of foolish or evil decisions, the observation, if true, might as easily apply to the kind of tragedy that Hook describes as the sacrifices that must necessarily be made when values collide in experience. What makes this a fair critique of American culture in particular, is that the classic American preoccupation with the present and the new, which has typically disposed American historians to mine the past for its continuities with the present, tends to undermine the moral standing of history's unchosen alternatives, foreclosing an appreciation in the present of the full tragic cost of historical choices. Ironically, perhaps, the obliteration of the tragic in memory is actually exacerbated to the extent that the consequences of any decision are morally unassailable — the preservation of the Union, for example, or especially the abolition of slavery that followed the end of the Civil War: for the very unarguable value of such consequences reconciles too easily the problematic in history, so that the tragic moral necessity of deciding to wage a war that slaughtered over 600,000 human beings seems no longer to be a decision at all but rather one more sad inevitability of an American historical process that — as fatuously sanguine views of the present would appear always to confirm — is seen to be powered by some transcendental moral energy.

The need to rescue the tragic past from the majoritarian exigencies of the moment may inform "Ashes of Soldiers," a poem in which the speaker would at first appear to be trying to isolate the meaning of tragic death from its social context to make it, as it were, the private possession of the poet himself:

> But aside from these, and the crowd's hurrahs, and the land's
>   congratulations,
> Admitting around me comrades close, unseen by the rest, and voiceless,
> I chant this chant of my silent soul, in the name of all dead soldiers.
>
> Faces so pale, with wondrous eyes, very dear, gather closer yet;
> Draw close, but speak not.
>
> Phantoms, welcome, divine and tender!
> Invisible to the rest, henceforth become my companions;
> Follow me ever! desert me not, while I live. (*LV* 511)

The poet who so rarely (if ever) sanctions a reading of himself as a completely private self, wholly distinct from "the crowd's hurrahs," seems to be eschewing his beloved social realm in favor of the presumably lonely company of "Phantoms, . . . divine and tender" who are "invisible to the rest." But a more fruitful reading is that he is really eschewing the perceptual present, conceived socially as all that is invisible to majoritarian democracy with its perpetual fixation on the immediate. This is not a privatizing poet. He is a national bard who, as the visionary of a civilization's past as well as its present and future, counts it his responsibility to recognize and mourn the tragic phantoms of its history.

Sweet are the blooming cheeks of the living! sweet are the musical voices
    sounding!
But sweet, ah sweet are the dead, with their silent eyes.

Dearest comrades! all now is over;
But love is not over — and what love, O comrades!
Perfume from the battle-fields rising — up from fœtor arising.

Perfume therefore my chant, O love! immortal Love!
Give me to bathe the memories of all dead soldiers.

Perfume all! make all wholesome!
O love! O chant! solve all with the last chemistry.

Give me exhaustless — make me a fountain,
That I exhale love from me wherever I go,
For the sake of all dead soldiers. (*LV* 511–512)

The oddly mixed metaphor, "silent eyes," which the poet uses to describe
the "sweet dead" he juxtaposes to the "sweet musical voices" of the living,
makes no literal sense (eyes do not literally speak). Politically, it makes perfect
sense, for to have silent eyes is to have a voiceless vision. It is significant that
the poet, whose own conception of his poetic mission is to speak the vision of
a people, would here decline to speak for the voiceless dead. Instead, he
speaks to them, honorifically baptizing them in loving recognition while simultaneously recognizing their silence. In this context, silence deserves a special reading: in a liberal democracy, all politics is not persuasion, and no decision is the result of a perfect consensus. To silence a vision — as opposed to
silencing a voice — is not to suppress dissent but to choose against empower-
ing a particular policy; that is, to render someone's visionary hopes politically
dead. But the paradox of democratic life is that the very fragmentation that it
promotes — and that defines much of its health — also ravages the tenuous
unity upon which it depends for its very survival.

    Love, of course, had always been Whitman's answer to such disunity, but
here he has taken the additional step of incorporating it into a more elaborate,
ritualized process. While so much of *Drum-Taps* may be more literally read
as modeling the psychological logic of the mourning process, which attempts
to reconcile the living to the fact of their own survival through a compensatory ritual that honors the dead by making them symbolically "wholesome,"
the significance does not rest there. The public function he understood his
words to perform — and the very public and cataclysmic circumstances that
united his own grief with the nation's — opened up his poetic constructions

to deeper insights into social logic. The mourning process, Whitman's war poetry demonstrates, must also have its moral and political analogues in democratic life: a ritual recognition of the multitude of tragic phantoms (the material interests sacrificed, the moral obligations "reasonably" disregarded) that may issue as much from intelligent reflection as from majoritarian prerogative. In either case, the poet demonstrates, the unity of a democratic society — the continued willingness of all of its citizens to submit to the will of the whole — is the achievement of a perpetual gesture of reconciliation, the fulfillment of a duty to acknowledge genuine tragedy in necessary change.

Mourning as a Democratic Process

"When Lilacs Last in the Dooryard Bloom'd," Whitman's great elegy mourning the death of President Lincoln, has perhaps generated as much or more comment and praise than any other single poem he wrote. Its uncharacteristic (for Whitman) formalism, its borrowings from classical elegy, and its orchestration of a trinity of symbols (western star, lilac bush, singing hermit thrush) to achieve personal or social renewal through a reconciliation with death have all received extensive comment. And so have the poem's "silences." Many critics have pointed out, for example, that the circumstances of Lincoln's death, even his name, are not mentioned at all — an observation that prompts many to concur with James E. Miller Jr. that the "poem is only incidentally about its subject. The real subject is death." [19] In a very thoughtful reading of the poem, Kerry C. Larson points up a far more significant silence. While commending the poem's attempt to devise "a medium proper to the task of reintegrating death back into life," an effort that results in "a conjunction of nuanced judgment and unabashed compassion," Larson is nevertheless compelled to conclude that "in certain key respects the silence of 'Lilacs' is devastating": "As in the case of *Drum-Taps*, it bears repeating that Whitman's elegy discerns absolutely no purpose served in the killing of those young men who continue to haunt the mind's eye 'as in noiseless dreams'; it uncovers no truth vindicated by their 'white skeletons,' no cause defended. Still more striking than the mere content of this implied verdict is, however, the silence which accompanies it, a silence which appears to indicate that even if the elegist can or will not speak on behalf of the Union purportedly upheld by the death of Lincoln and his soldiers, neither can he bring himself to speak against it." [20] In one sense, Larson is certainly correct. In both *Drum-Taps* and "When Lilacs Last in the Dooryard Bloom'd," Whitman scrupulously avoids any device that achieves social reconciliation through the construction of a settled meaning or the expression of a higher purpose. But rather than regarding this to be a weakness of Whitman's poetry, I judge it to be a significant visionary accomplishment.

At the heart of an elegy's attempt to console and reconcile through the articulation of a meaning is the fundamentally commercial metaphor of exchange: the meaning of a death is conceived as the value of the thing purchased by the death. Reconciliation, in this sense, is essentially the repossession of psychic (or social) equilibrium made possible when mourners are offered the consolation of "purpose." In the postwar political context in which the poem was written, Whitman clearly understood that such a formula for meaning could only produce a particularly divisive kind of reconciliation. Since it is the positive moral value of the victory that reconciles the victors to the losses they suffered to achieve it, sustaining the positive value of those losses (and its corresponding power to recompense the victor) depends wholly upon an ability to sustain the negative moral stigma that attaches not only to the vanquished cause but to the vanquished people as well. In a civil war, the tragedy is ironically compounded when the losers, effectively precluded from gracefully redefining their own identity in ways compatible with reintegration into the whole, are left to consolidate themselves as a people by "perversely" celebrating the very aspects of their political culture that the winners have deemed to be demonic. Even so, certainly such calculations of meaning are often quite necessary, even unavoidable; in the particular case of the American Civil War, where slaveholding and its many attendant evils needed to be firmly demonized, such calculations were appropriately articulated by others. But as a general matter, superior force does not guarantee superior morality, and history is replete with "assertions of meaning" that are only transparent justifications of brute power. More important, as a visionary matter — and especially for a poet eager to reconcile a fragmented nation — the use of such a divisive metaphor to construct meaning could only institutionalize the very social and political fault lines the poet was attempting to repair. By shaping social grief into an elegy that mourns without meaning, "When Lilacs Last in the Dooryard Bloom'd" negotiates this very difficult problem of reconstruction. By modeling a ritual of response to the death of the victorious Lincoln in the aftermath of the Civil War, the poet also structures an ethical response to the perpetual, low-burning civil war — the inevitable fractiousness — that defines a vigorous political democracy.

Whitman's use of a formalized symbolic structure certainly distinguishes his Lincoln elegy from the poetry of mourning in *Drum-Taps*; nevertheless, it shares with those other poems a logic whereby grief is negotiated through a restructuring of memory. For instance, the symbols introduced in the poem's first section — the falling (but eventually rising) western star and the perennial blooming lilac of "Ever-returning spring" — serve in classical fashion as reminders of life's cyclical nature and therefore as tokens of renewal intended to compensate for loss. (Interestingly, what is renewed is not life but death or, rather, the memory of death: "I mourn'd . . . and yet shall mourn with ever-returning spring" [*LV* 529].) In this sense, it is not unlike "Come Up from the Fields Father" or other *Drum-Taps* poems in which a destructive form of grief is depicted as a failure of memory. Likewise, the formula for grief-work in "Lilacs" is also much the same as the one that operates in *Drum-Taps*, a poetic process by which private grief may be managed through its transformation into an ordered public experience. Yet "Lilacs" differs from these other poems in that it is primarily concerned with public (rather than private) grief; Whitman attempts to structure the public and symbolic response to continuing social loss into an ongoing memorial process. The origins of grief itself are significantly more social in "Lilacs," just as its resolution is explicitly more political.

The public nature of grief becomes clear in section 2, where it is figured as a private emotional response to the poet's disconnection from the symbol of public power and group identity. But though grief begins as a private matter, it does not remain so, for it is the poet's inconsolable private grief that moves him to invest symbolic value in the western star and begin the process of making his elegy accessible to the public as a model for social and political grief.

> O powerful, western, fallen star!
> O shades of night! O moody, tearful night!
> O great star disappear'd! O the black murk that hides the star!
> O cruel hands that hold me powerless! O helpless soul of me!
> O harsh surrounding cloud, that will not free my soul! (*LV* 529)

In this, the most despairing of all sections of the elegy, the poet depicts his experience of grief as a melancholic "powerless[ness]." Significantly, he represents the loss that precipitates his impotence as both a visual and an auditory separation from the emblem of public power (a conjunction of senses that reflects Whitman's concern with the linkage between vision and voice). The disconnection is visual in that the "powerful" and "great" western star, symbol of the nation's chief executive, has fallen from view, "disappear'd" behind "the black murk" to leave the poet perceptually blinded in "shades of night" and enveloped by a "harsh surrounding cloud." The disconnection is auditory because the poet speaks only to himself (and the eavesdropping reader);

he seems unable to address the star directly, as he will later, but instead speaks about it. Moreover, he is not stricken by an internal paralysis but restrained externally by the "surrounding cloud that will not free" his soul. This suggests that, from the outset, the poet conceives that the "powerless," "helpless" state that attends his despair, his visual blindness and vocal impotence, is also a social condition. That is, the real Lincoln had symbolized and thus facilitated a sense of national identity (at least for the Union), a social soul; Lincoln's death, then, threatens a disintegration of that national identity and is experienced by the poet as a real (and perhaps permanent) separation from the social aspects of his own personal identity.

But the poet's social or national alienation will not last. Tellingly, when the star is eventually reintroduced in the poem much later in section 8, the poet's relationship with the Lincoln symbol has significantly changed. Most strikingly, the darkness of night that had earlier collaborated with the "black murk" to prohibit vision ceases in section 8 to be a hindrance:

> O western orb, sailing the heaven!
> Now I know what you must have meant, as a month since we walk'd,
> As we walk'd up and down in the dark blue so mystic,
> As we walk'd in silence the transparent shadowy night,
> As I saw you had something to tell, as you bent to me night after night,
> As you droop'd from the sky low down, as if to my side, (while the other stars all look'd on;)
> As we wonder'd together the solemn night, (for something I know not what, kept me from sleep;)
> As the night advanced, and I saw on the rim of the west, ere you went, how full you were of woe;
> As I stood on the rising ground in the breeze, in the cool transparent night,
> As I watch'd where you pass'd and was lost in the netherworld black of the night,
> As my soul, in its trouble, dissatisfied, sank, as where you, sad orb,
> Concluded, dropt in the night, and was gone. (LV 532)

The once seemingly impenetrable darkness of section 2 has now become "the transparent shadowy night" and the "cool transparent night," a change that enables vision. The poet recalls that "I saw" the star had something to say, "I saw" how "full of woe" it was, "I watch'd" where it passed in the sky; as the resulting vision brings intimate connection between the poet and his symbol, the power of sight even extends to the other stars, which "all look'd on."

Moreover, with vision and intimacy come cognition and power — and a liberated voice able to address his symbol directly: "Now I know what you must have meant, as a month since we walk'd."

The poet's reconnection with the western star comes at the very midpoint of the poem; it is the pivotal transformation within the mourning process that the elegy models. This centrality makes it especially important to understand what this reconnection does — and does not — mean. It is also important to understand the process that led to this transformation. First, the poet's reconnection with his Lincoln symbol should not be read as a complete national reconciliation or a final reconnection with (and within) the society that the Lincoln star would seem to represent. Whitman does not by poetic fiat simply reverse the political rupture and resulting loss of identity that initially triggered the grief. He does, however, suggest that he has reconnected with the larger meaning of the star, what the symbol would have said if only the poet had been prepared to hear it. Although he refuses here to divulge the star's meaning, he seems to hint that he has come to realize, at least, that social reconciliation does not depend upon reclaiming the actual symbol (retrieving, as it were, the dead Lincoln) but rather on retrieving the memory of all that the star had come to signify. We see that he anticipates this epiphany when we turn back to examine the passages between the star's introduction in the second section and the liberation of the poet's vision and voice when the star is reintroduced in section 8. Essentially, in the intervening sections the poet embarks on a narrative journey of ritual significance; at its conclusion, he comes to the seemingly paradoxical awareness that while the president's death is the solemn occasion for consolidating a sense of national identity, the president himself is not the substance of that social unity.

Whitman begins his ritualized narrative journey in section 5 by following Lincoln's coffin on its multistate journey to the grave — after first introducing the symbolic lilac bush in section 3 and the solitary hermit thrush in section 4. As the traversing coffin threads its way in section 5 through the "old woods," amid "the grass in the fields," and past such other natural or bucolic signposts as apple orchards and "yellow-spear'd wheat," the poet attempts to bind the nation's natural geography in much the same way he will attempt to bind its social geography (*LV* 530). In section 6, the coffin "passes through lanes and streets" of "cities draped in black" to link communities together in seemingly contiguous "processions long and winding," until the vision of unity is buttressed by harmonious sound (*LV* 531). At the same time, the poet participates in his poetic reconstruction of the nation by merging with his own narrative in order to stand

With the waiting depot, the arriving coffin, and the sombre faces,
With dirges through the night, with the thousand voices rising strong and
    solemn;
With all the mournful voices of the dirges, pour'd around the coffin,
The dim-lit churches and the shuddering organs — Where amid these
    you journey,
With the tolling, tolling bells' perpetual clang;
Here! coffin that slowly passes,
I give you my sprig of lilac. (*LV* 531)

Here, as the nation's people become symbolically (albeit superficially) unified
by their subsumption into a single class of mourners, the poet is liberated
from the solitary confinement of private grief through his participation in
public ceremony and the restorative rituals of nature and natural recurrence
(as marked by his gift of the lilac sprig). Soon, however, he acknowledges that
the significance of the funeral lies more in the momentary social harmony it
produces than in the body inside the coffin. He must turn his attention in section 7 to the job of untangling the deep ambiguities that inhere in the Lincoln
symbol. He must remind us that the significance of the dead president resides
in his public identity, his representation of the whole. He must also lay the
groundwork for a deeper and more complete resolution by distinguishing between the dead Lincoln and the living nation — in a sense, freeing Lincoln the
man from his symbolic burden by shifting our attention to the life-and-death
cycle of social life:

(Nor for you, for one, alone;
Blossoms and branches green to coffins all I bring:
For fresh as the morning — thus would I chant a song for you, O sane
    and sacred death.

All over bouquets of roses,
O death! I cover you over with roses and early lilies;
But mostly and now the lilac that blooms the first,
Copious, I break, I break the sprigs from the bushes;
With loaded arms I come, pouring for you,
For you and the coffins all of you, O death.) (*LV* 531–532)

One begins to sense here that the operative criterion behind the poet's choice
of the lilac as symbol is not so much its chance appearance at Lincoln's spring-
time death but its copiousness, making it uniquely suitable for memorializing
"coffins all" in the same fashion as Lincoln's. As the proper object of mourn-

ing is now reconceived to be all those vulnerable to the eventuality of death (that is, everyone) — in effect expanding into a group to coincide with the universalized class of mourners — the "categorical" distinction separating the mourners and the mourned evaporates. Here is both the ambiguity and the value of the Lincoln symbol — and the meaning the star would convey. The narrative facts that permit this conflation of mourners and mourned, living and dead, are explicitly political. As the death of a president already suggests (as no other individual's death can) the metaphoric death of the people he or she "represents," so it is also true that such occasions bring the people as close as they probably ever come to something like a unified consciousness — even if that unity means little more than an "acute recollection" of their shared symbols of identity. In one sense, the poet has achieved, at the midpoint of his Lincoln elegy, the unlikely image of a people unified by their mutual participation in a political rite of perpetually mourning their own perpetual death.

The notion of a people being unified through the act of mourning their own death is indeed an odd one. It highlights many of the same issues and questions that were raised earlier in the chapter in my discussion of *Drum-Taps*. In what sense, for example, are we always politically dying (beyond the historically specific instance of civil war)? Or in what way is the formula for grief-work that Whitman sketches in "Lilacs" relevant to the problem of political and social renewal that is clearly his larger concern? We can answer the question of what it means politically to be perpetually dying by extending Hook's notion of the tragic. Hook reasoned that the tragic element of democratic (and moral) life is in the fact that it necessitates choices among various and competing conceptions of the good or the right. This is true enough; but when considered in the light of the more recent habit of equating ideological positions with political, religious, cultural, racial, or ethnic identities, Hook's view of the tragic aspect of democratic life becomes even more unsettling. Democracy inevitably requires that some ideas — even ideas that many people regard as central to the way they define themselves and a vital means of connection to others — are rejected by the majority. For ideological or cultural minorities, life in a pluralistic democracy can easily be experienced as a continuous repudiation of themselves as a people. Moreover, this sense of deep alienation must surely be exacerbated when we consider that, in actual fact, most political conflict is ultimately resolved by some form of power — the democratic ideal of consensus reached through reasoned debate notwithstanding. (And some degree of raw power is as much a feature of democratic electoral competition as it is of undemocratic martial conflict as in the

Civil War.) Often, the losers in a democratic struggle come away feeling not that their ideas are being rejected after fair consideration but that the ideological heart of their human identity (their "soul," some would say) has come under lethal attack from a tyrannous majoritarian other. For them, the democratic process threatens cultural death. Here, the dramatic images of decaying post–Civil War southern culture found in writers such as Tennessee Williams or William Faulkner seem also like a rendering of the deep fears of countless other marginalized cultural minorities engaged in a "death-struggle," from fundamentalist Christians to Puerto Rican nationalists to nineteenth-century orthodox Mormons. The paradox is that, even though deep alienation (or political death) is often an inevitability (even a necessity) of democratic life, it is also clearly dangerous. Left unreconstructed, the deep and violent political emotion that accompanies this kind of political defeat threatens the constitutional integrity of the social body — ironically, at those very moments when it seems to the majority that the democratic processes are functioning most effectively. Such a deep and legitimate sense of loss, however necessary or inevitable, cannot help but appear to a political minority as evidence of the essential fraudulence of the constitutional structure that governed their defeat. Such fraudulence, however erroneously perceived, is certainly reason enough to avoid participation in the social and political life of the nation. And therein the tragedy is compounded, for it is one of the axioms of liberal democracy that it depends upon an authentic diversity of values and opinions — differing perspectives whose very sincerity demands a certain recalcitrance in the face of persuasion.

In "When Lilacs Last in the Dooryard Bloom'd," Whitman offers a resolution to this paradox of democratic life by drawing a parallel between two notions of reconciliation. On the one hand, he would reconcile (in the sense of bringing together) the hostile factions of the war-ravaged nation. On the other, he would reconcile (in the sense of fostering acceptance) grieving victims to their plight. The formula for healing grief becomes simultaneously a prescription for healing division. The process began, as we have seen, in the first eight sections of the elegy, where the poet cleverly manipulates the symbolic western star in order to transform grief for the fallen Lincoln into a larger sense of grief for the entire nation. Then, in sections 9 through 13, the poet forestalls reconciliation by seeming to luxuriate in his grief. Eventually, the poet confronts the necessity of reconciliation in section 14, as he treats two new figures in the poem, the "thought of death" and the "sacred knowledge of death," to the ministrations of the singing hermit thrush.

Section 14 begins as the poet sits at "the close of day" and observes the "large unconscious scenery of my land."[21] After solemnly marking "the summer approaching with its richness" to transform the American vista he surveys, he announces, " — lo! then and there,"

> Falling among them all, and upon them all, enveloping me with the rest,
> Appear'd the cloud, appear'd the long black trail;
> And I knew Death, its thought, and the sacred knowledge of death.
>
> Then with the knowledge of death as walking one side of me,
> And the thought of death close-walking the other side of me,
> And I in the middle, as with companions, and as holding the hands of
>   companions,
> I fled forth to the hiding receiving night, that talks not,
> Down to the shores of the water, the path by the swamp in the dimness,
> To the solemn shadowy cedars, and ghostly pines so still.
>
> And the singer so shy to the rest receiv'd me;
> The gray-brown bird I know, receiv'd us comrades three;
> And he sang what seem'd the song of death, and a verse for him I love.
>
> From deep secluded recesses,
> From the fragrant cedars, and the ghostly pines so still,
> Came the singing of the bird.
> And the charm of the singing rapt me,
> As I held, as if by their hands, my comrades in the night,
> And the voice of my spirit tallied the song of the bird. (*LV* 535–536)

The cathedral-like mustiness of "the fragrant" and "solemn shadowy cedars, and ghostly pines so still" that vault high above the "deep secluded recesses" of the "swamp in the dimness" to offer sanctuary in "the hiding receiving night, that talks not" provides an appropriately religious setting for the poet's ritual of reconciliation. The symbolic meaning of the companions he leads to this church is not generally contested by critics: "the thought of death" seems to represent the raw, existential fear of death, while "the sacred knowledge of death" appears to be the poet's terminology for a more emotionally remote, intellectualized conception of death (or, as some critics argue, the intellectual content of the hermit thrush's emotion-charged song).[22]

The agency in this ceremony, the action that will complete the mourning process and make reconciliation possible, is the duet sung by the hermit thrush and the poet's spirit: as the poet puts it, "And the voice of my spirit tallied the song of the bird." The song the bird sings is a tribute to "lovely and soothing death," which implores the "strong deliveress" to "come unfalteringly" "when thou must indeed come." Because the song comes at an important stage in the reconciliation process, it is worth noting here that it has occasionally been a target of disapproving critics. David Cavitch, for example, thinks that the "long carol is flat and static," while Kerry Larson regards the "largely unremarkable" song as full of "stale archaisms [that] further imply the poet's remoteness."[23] More approvingly, however, Gregory Eiselein focuses less on either the aesthetic quality or intellectual complexity of the song; instead, he draws attention to how it functions in the mourning process that Whitman advances, pointing out that the song "is an affirmation of the inevitability and peacefulness of death [that] . . . prepare[s] the poet to recall the painful memories of the war and its carnage."[24] For Eiselein, the song's value is in the role it plays in the essentially cyclical mourning process that Whitman sets forth in "Lilacs" and other poems.

Eiselein's insightful reading of Whitman's vision of dignified and moral grief-work is particularly instructive because it suggests how that process also functions as a model for social and political healing. Eiselein argues that, in sharp contrast to predominant nineteenth-century modes of mourning, Whitman refuses to envision a form of consolation that was either purchased through the good behavior of the bereaved or based upon the assurance of an afterlife. "Whitman refuses to make rational or spiritual sense out of the war deaths or to attach to them a positive meaning." Instead, he sets up "a flexible, open-ended mourning process. . . . Its progressive cycles move from an initiating sorrow (grief, sadness, despair) which induces mourning to a moment of acceptance and reconciliation which yields a peaceful solace, and back to painful memories which begin the process over again."[25] Eiselein maintains that, although the poet "projects no end to the mourning process," his cyclical pattern does, nevertheless, allow for a gradual amelioration:

> the key moment is the reconciliation or acceptance, the point at which the poet or the mourner embraces death, evil, or the sources of death, evil, separations, and loss, whether that source is located in the self, in another, an enemy, or in the structures of the universe. . . . Rather than declaring the lost love object dead or promising a future reunion with family in heaven, Whitman urges a merging, not with the lost love object, but with the cause of loss — spiritual evil, rebelliousness, the South, the dark side of the self, and death itself. In Whitman's view, reconciliation to the source of death and loss accomplishes two things in the mourning process. First, it brings an intellectual awareness and spiritual understanding of what

Donald Pease would call the "law of regeneration": all die; in death all is merged, averaged, composted, re-formed; and life begins again and again out of death. Second, and consequent to the understanding of the law of regeneration, reconciliation with the source of death and loss brings a peaceful consolation that allows the cyclical mourning process to continue to "incessantly softly wash again, and ever again," and provides mourners with a space in which to create a new beginning and a fresh meaning out of the debris of war and death.[26]

By these lights, it becomes clear that the importance of the thrush's song is more in how it achieves its ends than in its aesthetic value or its philosophical content. The quality of the song that some critics find mundane may, ironically, be the means by which it "merges" mourners with the source of their loss. The song's doctrinal simplicity, combined with its repetitive, monotonous cadences, does not challenge the individual intellect to maneuver through a maze of recondite insights. Quite the opposite: the deliberately mantric, hypnotic musicality of the verses works to synchronize an otherwise disparate congregation in a single moment of shared emotion. The first stanza of the bird's song is sufficient to illustrate the point:

Come lovely and soothing Death,
Undulate round the world, serenely arriving, arriving.
In the day, in the night, to all, to each,
Sooner or later, delicate Death. (*LV* 536)

The rhythmic "undulations" that envelop the small congregation comprised of the poet and his companions who have gathered in the swamp's secular cathedral carry just enough of a charismatic charge to effectuate the social bonding — while remaining structured like no Pentecostal service ever is by the priestly bird who leads the responsive recitation (the generally garrulous poet having taken his place in the chorus). One immediate effect of this essentially public ritual is to democratize grief by formalizing the reminder that the socially disruptive appearance of unequal loss is always an illusion of the moment — that though death may seem to strike capriciously, in the fullness of time its reach is unanimous.

Whitman's formula for grief-work becomes even more profound when we consider its political and social consequences. First, seeing Whitman's treatment of mourning in democratic terms serves as a useful reminder that a great deal of political and cultural struggle has a genuinely tragic dimension — a recognition that should, at a minimum, school in victors a habit of respect, even reverence, toward their foe. Second, the call to merge mourner with the source of loss makes a ritual and an imperative of one of democracy's saving truths, sometimes hidden by the savageries of the moment. In democracy, the sources of loss, political death, and potential alienation are the majority itself and the political process that regulates social life. In Whitman's vision of the mourning process, the losers of a political struggle are given a ceremonial vehicle for gradually and gracefully reimagining their connection to the larger political community. To be consoled by coming to an awareness of the "law of regeneration" is, in political and cultural terms, to find solace in the ideological neutrality of the democratic process itself — the process by which, over time, all political and ideological identities die and are reborn as something else. Eiselein observes that Whitman's goal "is to bring the bereaved to a place of new beginnings, to give to the bereaved the *process* and the *language* that will enable them to construct for themselves a meaning that makes sense of death and that lends value to their daily living." [27] The observation is no less accurate or no less poignant when read in the light of the continuous struggle to redefine the meaning of personal and political identity in a democratic society.

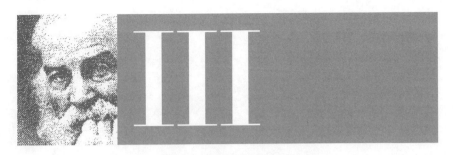

III

Prophet of Democracy
Democratic Vistas, 1871

*Feudal systems, which at their best are models for the
apportioning of responsibility among leaders and led,
have maintained themselves by predicting anarchy and
threatening loss of face to dissidents. Political systems
have thrived on the provocation of manifold and morbid
doubt; economic systems on the guilty hesitation to
initiate change. Yet political, economic, and technical
elites, whenever they have accepted the obligation to
perfect a new style of living at a logical point in history,
have provided men with a high sense of identity and
have inspired them to reach new levels of civilization.*
— *Eric Erikson,* Childhood and Society

"The Divine Literatus Comes"
Religion and Poetry in the Cultivation of Democratic Selfhood

Irrespective of Whitman's attitude toward the real American nation in the spring of 1865, it is nevertheless clear that the experience of writing "Calamus," *Drum-Taps*, and *Sequel to Drum-Taps* had the effect of permanently altering his poetic grammar — and thus the vision of an ideal America he was capable of rendering in poetry. Critics often regard this change in the poet's career as a diminution in his ability, perhaps the consequence of a growing conservatism, a desire for a more "respectable" reputation, or just plain exhaustion. But while it is true that by 1865 he had already composed his greatest poetic works (with the exception of "Passage to India"), perhaps the real change marked by these three works was not so much a diminution as a complication, not a subtle repudiation of the vision his earlier poetics affirm but a need to confront the many tensions it embodies. While the sweeping idealistic conceptions of Whitman's early work seem either irrelevant or antithetical to his more clipped and realistic late work, it may be more appropriate to treat this shift as marking a necessary doubleness in a coherent and comprehensive vision. Moreover, because the truths his vision speaks are at once opposed to each other yet also mutually dependent, it would have been practically impossible for the poet to discover them in such depth at the same moment in his career. On the one hand, the language of agency Whitman develops while coming to terms with the experience he manages in *Calamus* would seem to be an indispensable element in any mature vision of democratic life; the same appears true of his recognition in *Drum-Taps* that human history cannot be treated as simply another expression of a balanced and ultimately safe natural history. On the other hand, it seems equally true that, had the poet been in full possession of these realizations in 1855, it is not likely that he could have produced such a rich and deeply insightful vision of democracy's cosmic dimensions as "Song of Myself."

Whitman's "doubleness" is also in many ways America's doubleness, as the nation has always struggled to reconcile its ambitious ideals with the ugly realities that seem to belie them. By 1867, more troubled than he had ever been by America's doubleness, Whitman turned to prose in an attempt to resolve the contradiction between the obligations that democracy entails and the freedom it necessitates — to reconstruct his very vision of democracy in a way that accounts for both its promise and its failure. The result is his very complex and difficult essay "Democratic Vistas."

That Whitman should have turned to prose at such a time suggests a special anxiety over the complexities and contradictions of American democracy. His democracy was initially — and ultimately remained — a poetics, an aesthetics realized through a vision "inconceivable" outside of poetic language. Certainly one of the virtues of Whitman's poetic language is its suitability for representing the pluralism of a democratic universe. In Whitman's poetry, meaning is heaped upon meaning, and every scrap of sight and sound is collected in a radically "indiscriminate" attempt to include everything that happens to fall within the panoramic scope of the poet's vision. The effect is a vision of the democratic universe that seems nearly as infinite, open, and self-determining as its larger cosmic analogue, a universe also constantly in motion. These same virtues also open up the poetry to a range of interpretations far wider than anything the poet might have planned. By contrast, in much of Whitman's prose — especially, perhaps, his later prose — he trades this pluralistic universe for a monistic one. It seems that, for Whitman, prose writing often entailed a special burden of precision. To arrive at a single meaning in a sentence required the relentless elimination of alternative or competing meanings. The need to "get it right" bred a near infinity of modifiers and subordinating clauses. Consider, for instance, just one sentence from the 1872 preface to *Leaves of Grass*, one in which he speculates on the role science will play in a new, more democratic religion: "But (to my mind) Science — and may be such will prove its principle service — as evidently prepares the way for One indescribably grander — Time's young but perfect offspring — the New Theology — heir of the West — lusty and loving, and wondrous beautiful" (*CRE* 744). Stripped of its qualifiers, the sentence might have read "But science just as obviously prepares the way for an indescribably grander religion, the 'New Theology.'" It is almost as though he dreads the finality of a period, lest the reader exit the sentence with some misconception: about the status of this view as an opinion, about the potential significance of this particular "service" of science, about the temporal parentage of "the New Theology," about its cultural parentage, about its lusty and loving personality, or, finally, about the marvelous quality of its beauty. To be sure, much of Whitman's prose is stylistically similar to his poetry; still, when choosing to write what he thought of as prose, the evidence of his texts frequently suggests that he was in pursuit of a refined, singular meaning as he attempts to consolidate his vision of democracy.

In *Democratic Vistas*, Whitman makes just such an attempt. He strives to orchestrate a multiplicity of dualities and tensions, both in America and in his vision of it, into a single conception of democratic culture, one that imagines the individual self as unique and free only in the context of participation in a democratic society. What emerges is his most profound and sustained meditation on democratic life; it is a comprehensive theory of democratic culture and also an ambitious program, informed by his own native pragmatism, for the re-mediation of American culture and the full democratization of American society.

In this chapter, I will attempt to piece together the elements of that pragmatic program, beginning with its democratic poetics — Whitman's understanding of how imaginative literature functions (and should function) to promulgate the cultural assumptions that govern social life. Next, I will consider the centerpiece of *Democratic Vistas*, Whitman's interrelated models for democratic self and society that shape the substance of the cultural assumptions he would have literature promote. Finally, I will explore how Whitman's conception of democratic culture culminates in the notion of a secular, democratic religion. To experience democracy religiously, Whitman seemed to believe, was to come to a deep emotional and spiritual understanding of the complex material ties that bind people together in a web of mutual obligation.

Aristocratic Literature and the Fossilization of Power

Much of Whitman's insight in *Democratic Vistas* comes as a response to Thomas Carlyle's 1867 polemic against democracy, "Shooting Niagara: And After?" Whitman had always understood that democracy could only be justified by a faith that every human being possessed a natural capacity for self-governance; thus he was content in "the simple idea that the last, best dependence is to be upon humanity itself, and its own inherent, normal, full-grown qualities" (*PW* 374). But Carlyle, of course, had no such faith; inflamed by the enactment of Disraeli's Reform Bill, he argued that the slide toward greater and greater democracy in Britain and America was like shooting Niagara in a barrel. Human beings, he was sure, had no native gift for self-governance, and democracy only exacerbated their worst instincts:

This is called the Constitutional system, Conservative system, and other fine names; and this at last has its fruits, — such as we see. Mendacity hanging in the very air we breathe; all men become, unconsciously or half or wholly consciously, liars to their own souls and to other men's; grimacing, finessing, paraphrasing, in continual hypocrisy of *word*, . . . clearly sincere about nothing whatever, except in silence, about the appetites of their own huge belly, and the readiest method of assuaging these. From a population of that sunk kind, ardent only in pursuits that are low and in industries that are sensuous and *beaverish*, there is little peril of *human* enthusiasms, or revolutionary transports, such as occurred in 1789.[1]

"I was at first roused to much anger and abuse by this essay from Mr. Carlyle," Whitman wrote in a footnote to his *Vistas*, "so insulting to the theory of America." Even so, he had to acknowledge that he "had more than once been in the like mood" (*PW* 375). Several passages later, for example, he casts his own thoughts as the words of a "foreigner, an acute and good man" he had met before the war, and quotes him as saying

> "I have travel'd much in the United States, and watch'd their politicians, and listen'd to the speeches of the candidates, and read the journals, and gone into the public houses, and heard the unguarded talk of men. And I have found your vaunted America honeycomb'd from top to toe with infidelism, even to itself and its own programme. . . . I have everywhere found, primarily, thieves and scalliwags arranging the nominations to offices, and sometimes filling the offices themselves. . . . Of the holders of public office in the Nation or the States or their municipalities, I have found that not one in a hundred has been chosen by any spontaneous selection of the outsiders, the people, but all have been nominated and put through by little or large caucuses of the politicians, and have got in by corrupt rings and electioneering, not capacity or desert. I have noticed how the millions of sturdy farmers and mechanics are thus the helpless supple-jacks of comparatively few politicians. And I have noticed more and more, the alarming spectacle of parties usurping the government, and openly and shamelessly wielding it for party purposes." (*PW* 386)

Whitman's "mood" may indeed have been similar to Carlyle's, but here his diagnosis was not. Where Carlyle saw a democratic herd whose "low-minded" instincts made it highly vulnerable to rhetorical seduction, Whitman saw a corrupt political establishment that retained its power by excluding the "common man," those "sturdy farmers and mechanics." For Carlyle, too much democracy; for Whitman, too little. Still, Whitman's critique was not exclusively systemic. In an earlier passage, he had to "[c]onfess that everywhere, in shop, street, church, theatre, barroom, official chair, are pervading flippancy and vulgarity, low cunning, infidelity — everywhere the youth puny, impudent, foppish, prematurely ripe — everywhere an abnormal libidinousness" (*PW* 372). Like Carlyle, Whitman saw about him a nation of individuals ill-suited for democracy; unlike Carlyle, as we shall see, he did not regard the behavior that troubled him as something essential to human nature or democratic practice.

Carlyle's famous remedy for the excesses of democracy was to call for leadership from the "Aristocracy of Nature," those few who are equipped to live a "heroically human life" because they have been endowed by God with "wisdom, human talent, nobleness and courage." [2] Literature, particularly biography, becomes especially important in this regard, for, as Carlyle argues in *On Heroes, Hero-worship, and the Heroic in History*, it is in the great literature of the past that we find the heroic principle exemplified. [3] At first blush, Whitman would seem to offer a prescription that closely tracks Carlyle's reliance upon the heroic: in order to remedy "these lamentable conditions, to breathe into them the breath recuperative of sane and heroic life," he proposed "a new founded literature" (*PW* 372). But it is on just this point that Whitman turns most dramatically from Carlyle's solution — and in the process articulates a strikingly modern understanding of literature's political dimension. The imperative of Whitman's "new literature" was not to return to the past but rather to break from it, for it was "not merely to copy and reflect existing surfaces, or pander to what is called taste — not to amuse, pass away time, celebrate the beautiful, the refined, the past, or exhibit technical, rhythmic, or grammatical dexterity — but a literature underlying life, religious, consistent with science, handling the elements and forces with competent power, teaching and training men" (*PW* 372). Like Carlyle, Whitman was interested in the moral function of literature, the "teaching and training of men." That literature has such a moral function to perform has been a staple of Western criticism since Aristotle. What distinguishes Whitman's treatment of literature's moral dimension is his recognition that aesthetic "taste" encodes the values of a historical "past," while moral education, properly conceived, should prepare people to live in the present. What literature teaches, he suggests, is not an ahistorical conception of virtue but one that is, to some extent at least, historically contingent. More significant still is Whitman's understanding of both the inevitability and pervasiveness of literature's moral function. The moral process in literature is not limited to entertainingly packaged exhortations to do good, which the reader may choose to ignore; rather, literature transmits the entire shared epistemology of a civilization — an epistemology, moreover, that is always in service of political and historical needs. In the opening paragraphs of the essay, for example, he writes that "few are aware how the great literature penetrates all, gives hue to all, shapes aggregates and individuals, and, after subtle ways, with irresistible power, constructs, sustains, demolishes at will" (*PW* 366). For support, he turns to ancient Greece and medieval Europe:

> Nearer than this. It is not generally realized, but it is true, as the genius of Greece, and all the sociology, personality, politics and religion of those wonderful states, resided in their literature or esthetics, that what was afterwards the main support of European chivalry, the feudal, ecclesiastical, dynastic world over there — forming its osseous structure, holding it together for hundreds, thousands of years, preserving its flesh and bloom, giving it form, decision, rounding it out, and so saturating it in the conscious and unconscious blood, breed, belief, and intuitions of men, that it still prevails powerful to this day, in defiance of the mighty changes of time — was its literature, permeating to the very marrow, especially that major part, its enchanting songs, ballads, and poems. (*PW* 366)

By describing the totalizing, "saturating," "permeating" influence of literature on the "conscious and unconscious" beliefs and even "intuitions" of an entire people, Whitman has described something like the modern conception of culture. Or more precisely, he has conflated culture with the rhetorical forms by which culture is manifested and perpetuated. In this, too, Whitman was not entirely original. In Hippolyte-Adolphe Taine's *The History of English Literature* (the English translation of which appeared in 1871, just a few months after Whitman's publication of the full *Democratic Vistas*), Taine argued that a work of literature reflects not only the race and historical moment but also the "milieu" of its origins.[4] But whereas for Taine, culture was something inert in literature — something it passively reflected — for Whitman, literature was culture's shaping force. Even though Whitman agreed that literature bore the marks of its historical origins, he was far more interested in (or aware of) the ways in which literature (and language) institutionalizes and perpetuates the values and power relations it encodes, long after their historical moment has passed. "[I]t is strictly true," he wrote, "that a few first-class poets, philosophs, and authors, have substantially settled and given status to the entire religion, education, law, sociology, &c., of the hitherto civilized world, by tinging and often creating the atmospheres out of which they have arisen" (*PW* 366–367). And therein lies the problem, for what these "first-class poets" and others have institutionalized is an imaginative conception of the individual as a subservient being who must find his or her place within a feudal, hierarchical political system: "Dominion strong is the body's; dominion stronger is the mind's. What has fill'd, and fills to-day our intellect, our fancy, furnishing the standards therein, is yet foreign. The great poems, Shakspere included, are poisonous to the idea of the pride and dignity of the common people, the life-blood of democracy. The models of our literature, as we get it from other lands, ultramarine, have had their birth in courts, and bask'd and grown in castle sunshine; all smells of princes' favors" (*PW* 388).

Whitman saw that the disease that afflicted democracy was indeed, as Carlyle might have put it, democracy's reliance upon individuals who were in the main ill-equipped to govern themselves. But for Whitman, this was a point of social, not individual, criticism. Or more to the point, Whitman did not believe there to be a meaningful distinction between the two. The problem with the common man was the feudal ideas that informed his character — much the way the common woman of America suffered from "this fossil and unhealthy air which hangs about the word *lady*" (*PW* 389). Clearly, Whitman understood that individual human identity must reconcile itself to the political and economic norms of its social environment; thus no "[p]eople [who] have been listening to poems in which common humanity, deferential, bends low, humiliated, acknowledging superiors" can reasonably be regarded as prepared for egalitarian self-government (*PW* 412). Political criticism, in other words, is in the first instance literary criticism, which is to say, cultural criticism; it is the culture that supplies the fictive models of identity appropriate to the political system in which the individual resides. America's political dysfunction is a result of it seeming

> singularly unaware that the models of persons, books, manners, &c., appropriate for former conditions and for European lands, are but exiles and exotics here. No current of her life, as shown on the surfaces of what is authoritatively called her society, accepts or runs into social or esthetic democracy; but all the currents set squarely against it. Never, in the Old World, was thoroughly upholster'd exterior appearance and show, mental and other, built entirely on the idea of caste, and on the sufficiency of mere outside acquisition — never were glibness, verbal intellect, more the test, the emulation — more loftily elevated as head and sample — than they are on the surface of our republican states this day. The writers of a time hint the mottoes of its gods. The Word of the modern, say these voices, is the word Culture. (*PW* 395)

By using the word "culture" as a pejorative, Whitman has in mind, of course, the more narrow conception commonly associated (then as now) with elitist Victorian theories of education. The very word itself prompts him to immediately quip that "we find ourselves abruptly in close quarters with the enemy" (*PW* 395). Ironically, Whitman's rationale for disdaining the Victorian conception of culture links him to the more modern school of cultural criticism at the same time that it functions as a critique of many of its excesses. For instance, in asking the elitists of his time whether "the processes of culture" — that is, morally educative fictions — were "rapidly creating a class of supercilious infidels," he certainly anticipates the twentieth-century insight into the fictive and ideological quality of selfhood (*PW* 395). By pointing out that these processes of culture were actually subjugating the as yet unrealized democratic America to the hierarchical forms of feudal society — a society kept alive through the artistic conventions it gave rise to — he also demonstrates an intuitive appreciation for the intricate ways that art and material society create each other. Thus he would have offered qualified endorsement to Stephen Greenblatt's formulation that "the work of art is the product of a negotiation between a creator or class of creators, equipped with a complex, communally shared repertoire of conventions, and the institutions and practices of society" — for such, in any event, is his understanding of the feudal inheritance.[5] This is not to say that he thought those artistic conventions or those social practices as beyond modification by criticism; to the contrary, *Democratic Vistas* is a blueprint for a kind of literary criticism designed to promote social change.

The formulations Whitman developed as a response to nineteenth-century advocates of "high culture" serve as useful correctives to some modern theoretical trends. Even though art can never be completely dissociated from the prevalent epistemological assumptions of its social context and even though it is these assumptions, as translated into narratives, that are most likely to inform the fictive material an individual uses in the process of identity formation, still, Whitman insists, the self is something far more complex than merely the local manifestation of a literary, artistic, cultural, epistemological, or ideological phenomenon. For example, he will caution that individualism is an outgrowth of such "opposite ideas" as national types. Hence "the mass or lump character" must always be "provided for. Only from it, and from its proper regulation . . . comes the chance of individualism." At the same time, he must immediately point out that "the two are contradictory, but our task is to reconcile them" (*PW* 373). This is not an easy task, for as he notes later in the essay, "[t]he quality of Being, in the object's self, according to its own central idea and purpose, . . . is the lesson of nature." Too much "cultivation," in the Victorian sense of the word, and one loses "the precious idiocrasy and special nativity and intention that he is" (*PW* 394). He would not have agreed with Louis Althusser's sweeping reduction of subjectivity to the process of ideological structuration by the "state apparatuses" of capitalism; nor would he have agreed with the notion that identity is, as Foucault says, a mere fold in language. Identity, as Whitman insisted to the nineteenth-century purveyors of "high culture," is both a cultural and a natural fact. Indeed, the natural qualities of selfhood may be the most deserving of veneration: "Shall a man lose himself in countless masses of adjustments," he asks, "and be so shaped with reference to this, that, and the other, that the simply good and healthy and brave parts of him are reduced and clipp'd away, like the bordering of a box in a garden?" (*PW* 395). The answer of *Democratic Vistas* is clearly no. But the answer only begs further questions; Whitman's elaboration of cultural democracy necessarily entails not only an understanding of how the self is born of both natural and cultural forces but also how that self must function in a democratic society.

A "Programme of Culture"

One of the primary difficulties of literature, Whitman believes, is that it does not adequately account for the natural dimension of human life; consequently, finding some language capable of doing so becomes the first order of business of his "programme" of democratic culture. "Literature, strictly consider'd," he observes, "has never recognized the People, and whatever may be said, does not to-day" (*PW* 376). Rarely does one find "a fit scientific estimate and reverent appreciation of the People — of their measureless wealth of latent power and capacity, their vast, artistic contrasts of lights and shades — with, in America, their entire reliability in emergencies, and a certain breadth of historic grandeur, of peace or war, far surpassing all the vaunted samples, of book-heroes, or any *haut ton* coteries, in all the records of the world" (*PW* 376–377). Here, Whitman wishes not only to represent but also to valorize those qualities of the "People" — both individually and collectively — that they possess existentially, independent of cultural determinants. Such a "fit scientific estimate and reverent appreciation," he is sure, will "show that popular democracy, whatever its faults and dangers, practically justifies itself beyond the proudest claims and wildest hopes of its enthusiasts" (*PW* 377). To the modern ear, this wish will seem highly problematic: even if one were to assume that selfhood could be located, even partially, outside the realm of culture, the very call for a literature — a cultural device — capable of reducing the "noncultural" aspects of self to the cultural medium of language will strike some as oxymoronic. No linguistic description of such a self, the familiar argument runs, can exist free of cultural bias. Nevertheless, we may resolve this paradox for Whitman by simply declining to describe the self in ontological terms; we may be satisfied to point to a sort of acting presence, recognizable only by its effects. In this it will be useful to return briefly to George Herbert Mead's distinction between the "I" and the "me," outlined in chapter 2. Mead understood the human sense of selfhood — self as an object of its own recognition — as a product of the relationship between two psychic functions: the subjective "I" and the objective (and social) "me." For Mead, the term "me" identifies the complex web of attitudes and values that govern social life, particularly as those cultural codes are "internalized," imagined by an individual as conditioning the interplay of daily experience. When people think of "themselves," they are conjuring up entities who are only visible to consciousness through the act of their negotiating with other objects and "selves." The "me," then, is the "cultured" aspect of the self. But there is also an uncultured aspect of the self, that which Mead calls the "I," the impulsive and immediate function of the self, whose novel responses to new situations have the effect of continuously modifying the objective "me," which is brought into consciousness. Just as the "me" is a historical entity in that it exists in time as the record of a near infinite number of human negotiations with other selves and the material forces at play in the environment, so the "I" exists outside of culture and time; it is a potentiality to act in time — a latent capacity.[6]

In this light, Whitman's focus in the above passage on the physical virtues of the people is more explicable. By honoring their "wealth of latent power" — the kind of native will to act that precedes thought, making them entirely reliable in emergencies (if perhaps less so at those times affording reflection) — he effectively marks off the impulsive "I," the natural, existential aspect of self, from critical sanction. It is the cultured self, the "me," in Mead's terms, that needs re-mediation. Whitman would appear to suggest that it is the "I" that stands as proof that the "me" is redeemable, for it is not the intellection of the people he singles out but their physicality — the many acts of personal strength and courage such as were exemplified in "the late secession war" — that "show that popular democracy, whatever its faults and dangers, practically justifies itself beyond the proudest claims and wildest hopes of its enthusiasts" (*PW* 377). This justification holds even though "general humanity," as he soon reminds us four paragraphs later, "has always, in every department, been full of perverse maleficence, and is so yet" (*PW* 379). Much later in the essay, Whitman draws on the same logic of a bifurcated self as he outlines his program for re-mediation. "Pardon us," he begs mockingly of "Culture," "if we have seem'd to speak lightly of your office." "The whole civilization of the earth, we know, is yours, with all the glory and the light thereof.

It is, indeed, in your own spirit, and seeking to tally the loftiest teachings of it, that we aim these poor utterances" (*PW* 403). Nevertheless, there is more to being human than culture: "For you, too, mighty minister! know that there is something greater than you, namely, the fresh, eternal qualities of Being. From them, and by them, as you at your best, we too evoke the last, the needed help, to vitalize our country and our days" (*PW* 403). Though Whitman seems to invest more meaning in "the eternal qualities of Being" than Mead does in the "I," it is clear that both constructs are conceived as aspects of the self that are prior to anything social or cultural; neither can fully account for the self, for the self is socially constructed as well. But since it is the social aspect of the self that is most susceptible to corruption, it is the social self that must be reconstructed through a program that makes use of those "fresh, eternal qualities of Being," the more or less physical traits for which cultural analogues (for example, moral courage and decisiveness) might be imagined. "Thus we pronounce not so much against the principles of culture," Whitman continues, "we only supervise it, and promulge along with it, as deep, perhaps a deeper, principle" (*PW* 403).

The "deeper principle" Whitman would advance is not the antithesis of culture (in either the Victorian or modern sense of the word) but a selective synthesis of cultural and natural dimensions of selfhood in a democratic model of identity. "I should demand a programme of culture," he announces in formulating the "democratic ethnology of the future" (*PW* 396); but the aim is not to create a standardized personality type congenial to prevalent economic power. Rather, Whitman's doctrine seeks to employ the cultural mechanisms necessary to "vitalize man's free play of special Personalism" in order to establish "over this continent, an idiocrasy of universalism" (*PW* 395, 396). The phrase "idiocrasy of universalism" is especially interesting because it captures the paradoxical relationship entailed in the doctrine between the self imagined as autonomous and the ubiquitous culture upon which it depends. Whitman's "Personalism" is a system of government whereby the individual self rules over itself, but this "idiocrasy" is only secured and sustained to the extent that it is ideologically informed by a universalized culture. Personalism, then, regards neither the individual nor the collective as supreme to the other in any sense, for they do not jockey for hierarchical position; they are different aspects of the same "social self," distinguished only, perhaps, by their respective functions:

For to democracy, the leveler, the unyielding principle of the average, is surely join'd another principle, equally unyielding, closely tracking the first, indispensable to it, opposite, (as the sexes are opposite,) and whose existence, confronting and ever modifying the other, often clashing, paradoxical, yet neither of highest avail without the other, plainly supplies to these grand cosmic politics of ours, and to the launch'd forth mortal dangers of republicanism, to-day or any day, the counterpart and offset whereby Nature restrains the deadly original relentlessness of all her first-class laws. This second principle is individuality, the pride and centripetal isolation of a human being in himself — identity — personalism. (*PW* 391)

As this passage suggests, such terms as "self," "society," "democracy," and "individualism" are not stable categories but mutually modifying dimensions of some larger whole. Each is implicated in the other, and all are conceived as natural as well as cultural facts — two terms that also blur and defy simple categorical separation. As we attempt to derive a schematic of the democratic self from Whitman's "programme of culture," it is with the understanding that he thought of his model of identity as less a matter of artifice (an arbitrarily designed cultural construct, superadded to natural human society) than as the cultural extrapolation of natural, existential democracy itself — an expression primarily valuable as a critical standard.

For Whitman, the ideal democratic self, the centerpiece of his "programme of culture," is based on a triadic model that stresses physical, mental, and religious development. A "towering selfhood," he calls it, "not physically perfect only — not satisfied with the mere mind's and learning's stores, but religious, possessing the idea of the infinite" (*PW* 403). Though he privileges the religious, it is clear that the other two elements, the physical and mental, are important as well — and all three dimensions are more complex than they might at first appear. Of the physical, he writes that "to our model, a clear-blooded, strong-fibred physique, is indispensable;" the mature "well-begotten self" should be "brave, perceptive, under control, neither too talkative nor too reticent, neither flippant nor sombre; of the bodily figure, the movements easy, the complexion showing the best blood, somewhat flush'd, breast expanded, an erect attitude, a voice whose sound outvies music, eyes of calm and steady gaze, yet capable also of flashing" (*PW* 397). That Whitman assumed a real correspondence between physical and moral prowess and that he further believed such powers to be inheritable are notions that modern critics often single out for their problematic implications. M. Jimmie Killingsworth, for example, is troubled that "Whitman's women — rather than developing fully as the archetypal model for creative power — become something of a cog in the eugenic machine."[7] Certainly, no thoughtful consideration of Whitman's treatment of the body in *Democratic Vistas* can pretend ignorance of his fascination with eugenics.

That said, an interpretation of the way physicality functions in Whitman's democratic theory need not be restricted by eugenicist theory. Following George Herbert Mead's construction of the "I/me" relationship, I have already argued that physicality in *Democratic Vistas* functions well as the immediate, impulsive aspect of the self, precursor and counterpoint to the cultured realm of self-consciousness. To that point I would like to add two simple but related and important points: first, that Whitman's emphasis on the physical serves to underscore the primary significance of action as a principal criterion of human value. Action is at the heart of Whitman's pragmatism, as it is at the heart of pragmatic theory generally. It is the same pragmatic impulse, for instance, that prompted Emerson to observe in "Experience" that at Brook Farm "the noblest theory of life sat on the noblest figures of young men and maidens, quite powerless and melancholy. It would not rake or pitch a ton of hay; it would not rub down a horse; and the men and maidens it left pale and hungry."[8] It is the same instinct that lay behind William James's claim in *Pragmatism* that "the possession of true thoughts means everywhere the possession of invaluable instruments of action."[9] Pragmatic thinkers have characteristically held that, fundamentally, life is an activity before it is or can be anything else. Whitman's stress on the physical, the capacity of the self to act, serves to remind us that quality in life derives in part from an ability to generate and control the activity of living.

This is the context for the second point I wish to make about Whitman's emphasis on physicality. The beauty of his "strong-fibered physique" is not at all reducible to some ideal proportionality of parts. This is no celebration of the "ideal" body. Most of the attributes Whitman celebrates are completely invisible in a motionless, resting body. They are not simply passive, inherent properties of being but qualities of action that are presumed to be indicative of essential qualities of being. These valorized qualities might thus be the recognizable features of a person who tempers or manages his or her actions — one who is "under control," able to achieve an ease of movement, or has an ability to modulate speech and mood. The same qualities might also be evinced by one liberated to act in a prudent yet decisive way in society — bravery, the expanded breast, the erect attitude, and "eyes of calm and steady gaze, yet capable also of flashing." This is neither narcissism nor the creed of a cult of athleticism: in its physicality, Whitman's model does not stand as a call to muscular symmetry and development but rather muscular achievement.

The second aspect of Whitman's model democratic self, "the mental-educational part," is one he curiously chooses to articulate in cautious, almost reluctant terms: "enlargement of intellect, stores of cephalic knowledge, &c., the concentration thitherward of all the customs of our age, especially in America, is so overweening, and provides so fully for that part, that, important necessary as it is, it really needs nothing from us here — except, indeed, a phrase of warning and restraint" (*PW* 397). Though Whitman does not detail the reason for his uneasiness with mental processes, it is still reasonably clear that it stems from his oft-stated fear of the way the too highly cultured intellect alienates a person from his or her own authentic — original — goodness. It is only when "[c]auses, original things, being attended to," he writes, that "the right manners unerringly follow" (*PW* 397). But his fear of the mind's power to distort is also a profound appreciation of its enormous power, as he suggests later in the essay when he writes that "we have again pointedly to confess that all the objective grandeurs of the world yield themselves up, and depend on mentality alone" (*PW* 404). Both the magic and the danger of mind derive from its role as mediator between the material world and the human soul.

> Here, and here only, all balances, all rests. For the mind, which alone builds the permanent edifice, haughtily builds it to itself. By it, with what follows it, are convey'd to mortal sense the culminations of the materialistic, the known, and a prophecy of the unknown. To take expression, to incarnate, to endow a literature with grand and archetypal models — to fill with pride and love the utmost capacity, and to achieve spiritual meanings, and suggest the future — these, and these only, satisfy the soul. We must not say one word against real materials; but the wise know that they do not become real till touched by emotions, the mind. (*PW* 404)

In claiming that the mind functions to make "real materials" truly real, Whitman employs two connotations of the word "real": first, the mind makes things real by vitalizing them, making them seem more immediate by investing them with a sense of emotional urgency; second, the mind *realizes* materiality by organizing it into prophetic "spiritual meanings" that "satisfy the soul." The mind both constructs the reality in which we live and directs the way we live by constructing an emotionally and spiritually satisfying vision of the future we might build. Viewed in this light, Whitman's caution is far less a call to have the workings of the mind scrupulously authenticated by the native inclinations of the primitive human than it is a keen awareness of the fact that we construct the reality in which we live.

For some, Whitman's use of the term "spiritual" to describe one of the mind's functions might suggest that he is blurring the categories of his model. After all, spirituality is often associated with the moral and the religious — and "religiousness" is the third dimension of his model. A similar concern might have been raised regarding his treatment of body and mind. In his discussion of physicality, for example, it may have appeared as though he located the moral aspect of being in the body — and hoped to preserve it from the corruptions of mind and culture. This is the source of his trepidation of European modes of culture and education. Likewise, in the context of his treatment of mentality, he discusses the importance of the conscience; in an earlier version of the essay he asserted that "the subtle antiseptic called health is not more requisite to the bodily physiology, *than Conscience is to the moral and mental physiology*" (*PW* 398, emphasis added). Taken together, these seemingly divergent trends in Whitman's thought might suggest that he was unsure about whether moral capacity was physical or mental. This is a confusion only when viewed from within the framework of a rigidly held mind/body dualism, which, as Dewey observed of all such philosophies, begins misguidedly with the "results of a reflection that has already torn in two, the subject-matter experienced and the operations and states of experiencing" (*EN* 11). Whitman's blurring of such categorical distinctions only underscores the fact that he wrote from the pragmatic perspective of an integrated self in which mind and body are understood as but conceptual tools for analysis. From this perspective, it makes perfect sense to write, on the one hand, of an individual's capacity to act on a vision of the good and, on the other, of an individual's capacity to conceptualize the good that must be acted upon.

The third component of Whitman's model democratic self, "religiousness," is also both less and more than it might seem. For instance, although he does believe that the conscience must be influenced by a powerful religious sensibility, absent which the "modern civilizee, with his all-schooling and his wondrous appliances, will still show himself but an amputation," moral instinct, for Whitman, is really more of a tangent of what he calls "religiousness" than its essential core (*PW* 398). His notion of religiousness is in line with transcendental thought. It is a highly privatized emotional state — completely antithetical to the social institutions of "churches and creeds" — characterized by "the meditation, the devout ecstasy, the soaring flight" (*PW* 398). "Only here," he writes, when one is removed from the public practices of worship, can one find "communion with the mysteries, the eternal problems, whence? whither? Alone, and identity, and the mood — and the soul emerges, and all statements, churches, sermons, melt away like vapors. Alone, and silent thought and awe and aspiration — and then the interior consciousness, like a hitherto unseen inscription, in magic ink, beams out its wondrous lines to the sense. Bibles may convey, and priests expound, but it is exclusively for the noiseless operation of one's isolated Self, to enter the pure ether of veneration, reach the divine levels, and commune with the unutterable" (*PW* 399).

Whitman's triadic model of democratic selfhood is certainly the heart of his notion of "Personalism," his "programme of culture." But it is not the whole. For Whitman, full democratic selfhood is impossible to imagine outside the context of a fully democratic society. His triadic ideal of the democratic self is inextricably connected to another triad, a three-stage developmental model of social democracy. The first stage is characterized by the "planning and putting on record the political foundation rights of immense masses of people — indeed all people" and the various political institutions dedicated to preserving those rights; the second stage is "material prosperity," by which he means the development of a broad-based industrial and consumer economy, supported by technological innovations and an educational infrastructure. Confident that in America these two stages had been achieved, Whitman now heralded the "[t]hird stage, rising out of the previous ones" — a democratic literary culture capped "by a sublime and serious Religious Democracy sternly taking command, dissolving the old, sloughing off surfaces, and from its own interior and vital principles, reconstructing, democratizing society" (*PW* 410). A democratic religious aesthetic is the ultimate achievement of individual as well as social development. The fact that he writes of this religious aesthetic as both an intensely private feature of individual consciousness and a ubiquitous cultural force capable of reconstructing all of society does not point to a contradiction in his models but underscores their reciprocity.

Whitman's conception of democratic religion is the point at which his models for democratic self and democratic society clearly intersect, and so it is important to understand what Whitman meant by "religious democracy" and particularly how he distinguished between its extremely private and its radically public functions. In order to do so it is first necessary to comment on the reciprocity of his models for self and society. The point has already been made that Whitman saw self and society as integral parts of some larger unity; it should also be remembered that "democracy" was the name he assigned to that unity and also the process by which it was achieved. And the idea of democracy as a fundamental life process — beyond the commonplace understanding of the democratic process as a political system entailing elections and the like — is central to his conception of how his models of self and society interrelate. "The purpose of democracy," he wrote early in the essay, " . . . is to illustrate, at all hazards, this doctrine or theory that man, properly train'd in sanest, highest, freedom, may and must become a law, and a series of laws, unto himself, surrounding and providing for, not only his own personal control, but all his relations to other individuals, and to the State" (*PW* 374–375). What self and society share, in other words, is a process for self-regulation; the tools, talents, and mechanics that individuals employ to govern their own lives are, in some sense, the same as those necessary for the governance of social relations. It follows that for Whitman, self and society mutually reinforce each other, for to be "properly train'd" in the process of managing one is to be schooled in the process of managing the other. Whitman's emphatic insistence that democracy validate itself "at all hazards" no doubt stems from his fear that, absent the energies of "train'd" and enlightened democratic citizens, Carlyle may well have the last word on democracy's dangers. In so fearing, we see just how far the poet has come from his faith in the notion of laissez-faire inevitability.

Whitman's caveat that self-governance is only possible once an individual has been "properly train'd in sanest, highest freedom" also requires some explanation. Read out of context, it might appear that Whitman has resolved Carlyle's complaint by constructing a deus ex machina by which democracy is stabilized by expert tutelage from without. How, and by whom, is the individual to be trained? Whitman's initial answer seems to acknowledge the need for a bureaucracy of experts: "I say the mission of government . . . is not repression alone," he writes, "and not authority alone, . . . [but] to train communities through all their grades, beginning with individuals and ending there again, to rule themselves" (*PW* 380). It soon becomes clear that Whitman does not have in mind state-sponsored instruction in the political arts; rather, he is describing the way democratic government functions as an educative experience. Since people are educated for self-governance (on both social and individual levels) only through the practice of self-governance, government's most profound mission is to maintain itself as that vehicle of training. He writes that "political democracy, as it exists and practically works in America, with all its threatening evils, supplies a training-school for making first-class men. It is life's gymnasium, not of good only, but of all" (*PW* 385). This is precisely the same point that Michael Walzer makes in his defense of multiculturalism: "[i]ndividuals are stronger, more confident, more savvy," he observes, "when they are participants in a common life, responsible to and for other people. . . . It is only in the context of associational activity that individuals learn to deliberate, argue, make decisions, and take responsibility."[10] This is exactly the dynamic expressed by Dewey's maxim that human knowledge is a function of the laboring process. "The exacting conditions imposed by nature that have to be observed in order that work be carried through to success," Dewey writes, "are the source of all noting and recording of nature's doings" (EN 102).

Whitman imagines the same basic principle except that, like Walzer, he is inclined to think of it as a fundamental of the political process in which the conditions of nature that must be learned are the social and cultural dynamics that must be successfully negotiated before collective life can move in some intelligent direction. The larger point is that, once gained, democratic knowledge — the knowledge of how to participate in cooperative, egalitarian governance — can and should be applied to the problem of building a spiritual community. Political democracy is the first stage in his social model — not its conclusion — because it provides the necessary (but not sufficient) conditions for further material and spiritual development. For this reason, Whitman regards the community, the collective practice of self-government, as more important than the notion of private individual rights: "We endow the masses with the suffrage for their own sake, no doubt; then, perhaps still more, from another point of view, for community's sake. Leaving the rest to the sentimentalists, we present freedom as sufficient in its scientific aspect, cold as ice, reasoning, deductive, clear and passionless as crystal" (PW 381). But the meaning of community is not limited to the idea of local, political organization: "Did you, too, O friend, suppose that democracy was only for elections, for politics, and for a party name? I say democracy is only of use there that it may pass on and come to its flower and fruits in manners, in the highest forms of interaction between men, and their beliefs" (PW 389).

Whitman's democratic models of self and society are connected through their interdependence: both are developmental, and each requires the energies of the other for its own development. Democracy is the process by which self and society nurture each other's growth. True to his pragmatic sensibility, in other words, democracy is for Whitman what philosophy is for William James and experience is for John Dewey — a method. As such, it must forever look to the future it wishes to make better. He writes, "I submit, therefore, that the fruition of democracy, on aught like a grand scale, resides altogether in the future" (PW 390). This is an important feature of Democratic Vistas, but it should also serve as a corrective to some modern critical appraisals. Some recent critics have interpreted Whitman's turn to the future as a measure of psychological compensation. David Reynolds, for example, writes in his cultural biography of the poet that "his evolutionary framework allowed him to deflect things to the future, and, simultaneously, to accept even the less promising facets of the present."[11] Perhaps. But if the suggestion is that the futurist orientation of *Democratic Vistas* is only significant as evidence of Whitman's desperate (and pathetic) struggle to preserve his faith in a failed democracy, then the view is misguided. *Democratic Vistas* only makes explicit a view of process and the future that had been latent, implicit, and developing from the first edition of *Leaves of Grass* (as I attempted to make clear in my discussions of "Song of Myself" and "Crossing Brooklyn Ferry"). However much this insight may have been nurtured by psychological need, it was also necessitated by the evolving logic of his own philosophy. "Thus," he concludes, "we presume to write, as it were, upon things that exist not, and travel by maps yet unmade, and a blank" (*PW* 391). In so saying, he not only describes all those who have written in the pragmatic tradition, such as Emerson, James, and Dewey, but also all who are moved to speculate on the meaning of democratic life.

Democratic Religion

We return to Whitman's interconnected democratic models of self and society — in particular, their intersecting third stage: democratic religion. For Whitman, the meaning of democracy was ultimately a religious one. Some version of religion had always been important to him, but at the divide between his earlier laissez-faire vision of democracy and his mature vision of democratic life, religion takes on a deeper significance and a more central role. Now, individual "religiousness" (and its social counterpart, "religious democracy") generally assumes an apparently mystical quality for Whitman, the emotional and spiritual core of a vital nation-building force. Along with poetry and literature, the "new Metaphysics," he writes in *Democratic Vistas*, was to be "the only sure and worthy supports and expressions of the American Democracy" (*PW* 416). In "Preface 1872 — As a Strong Bird on Pinions Free," he would put the matter more directly, asserting that religion "must enter into the Poems of the Nation. It must make the nation" (*CRE* 745). Whitman saw that to "make the nation" meant to conceptualize a national identity — not a nation of juxtaposed but dissociated souls such as he celebrated before 1860 but a public, a cohesive organization of free people motivated by an essential need to work together to build the structures of democratic life. More important, however, he recognized that this was essentially a cultural, indeed religious, project. Whitman believed that the desire to belong, to be a part of any human organization such as a nation, was a manifestation of an essential, far deeper (and far wider) human desire to feel organically connected to a power that holds together the rest of natural life. Years later, William James would make essentially the same point by arguing that religious or ecstatic experience is motivated by a deep need to sense that one's individual consciousness is actually *"conterminous and continuous with a* MORE *of the same quality, which is operative in the universe outside of him."* [12] This may very well be a fundamentally religious desire, but to the extent that the "MORE" is conceived of as social and democratic, it is also political — implying a set of social obligations.

Whitman attempts to take advantage of the bonding power of mystical experience by calling for a poetry that reimagines the connections between self and society as an analogical extension of the connections between self and the cosmos. He argues in a note to *Democratic Vistas* that however fine a literary work's aesthetic or intellectual merits, it should be dismissed if it "violates or ignores, or even does not celebrate, the central divine idea of All, suffusing universe, of eternal trains of purpose, in the development, by however slow degrees, of the physical, moral, and spiritual kosmos. I say he has studied, meditated to no profit, whatever may be his mere erudition, who has not absorb'd this simple consciousness and faith. It is not entirely new — but it is for Democracy to elaborate it, and look to build upon and expand from it, with uncompromising reliance" (*PW* 418). To celebrate "the central divine idea of All" is to use poetic expression as a vehicle for intuiting the democratic dimensions of the cosmos. This is not quite transcendental epistemology; even though he would have the individual "enter the pure ether" so as to "commune with the unutterable," as he phrased it in a passage quoted earlier, he makes no promise that hard knowledge will somehow be the result. The real gain, he believes, is a heightened awareness of and joy in the interconnectedness of life itself. He continues in the note to say that "though little or nothing can be known, perceiv'd, except from a point of view which is evanescent, yet we know at least one permanency, that Time and Space, in the will of God, furnish successive chains, completions of material births and beginnings, solve all discrepancies, fears and doubts, and eventually fulfill happiness" (*PW* 418). The awesome power of religious experience to make notions of connection seem real and immediate is also, of course, the source of its power to delude. As Whitman puts it, "even in religious fervor there is a touch of animal heat" (*PW* 415). Thus he cautions that — the emotion-induced sense of deep connection notwithstanding — the truth claims of religion are always suspect and must be subject to the critique of science; "abstract religion," he writes, "is easily led astray, ever credulous, and is capable of devouring, remorseless, like fire and flame" (*PW* 416).

Whitman's democratic religion does not offer the mystical experience as an unmediated channel to the moral universe; rather, he has coordinated an apparently innate human desire for self-transcendence — the desire to feel oneself united with a universal order — with a conception of that order that has been derived from empirical science's view of the physical universe and then cast into democratic terms. The ecstatic experience can offer a heightened appreciation of the metaphoric possibilities of the natural universe because it permits the private consciousness to project its intuition of an "All" onto a material universe already presumed to be unified by physical "laws." In moments of contemplation, when the mind is cleared of surrounding noise: "[t]hen noiseless, with flowing steps, the lord, the sun, the last ideal comes. By the names right, justice, truth, we suggest, but do not describe it. To the world of men it remains a dream, an idea as they call it. But no dream is it to the wise — but the proudest, almost only solid lasting thing of all. Its analogy in the material universe is what holds together this world, and every object upon it, and carries its dynamics on forever sure and safe" (*PW* 415). The important analogy to be drawn, then, is not so much with the sum total of disparate parts that comprise a seemingly fragmented universe; rather, Whitman is concerned with the system of relations that makes it whole. In a meditative state and through the intuitive observation of "the shows and forms presented by Nature, . . . and above all, from those developments either in Nature or human personality in which power . . . transacts itself," the poet, "by the divine magic of his genius, projects them, their analogies, by curious removes, indirections, in literature and art" (*PW* 419).

If Whitman were working within the rigid framework of some correspondence theory, he might fairly be accused of a foolish, perhaps even pernicious, naïveté. After all, the material universe is an extremely violent place, where the unifying transactions of power can just as easily seem brutal as they can loving and egalitarian. His is not a theory of correspondence, however, but a theory of poetry; the analogies for truth, right, and justice are not to be found but made. If we are to be a part of a universe far grander than ourselves and if we are predisposed by a restless imagination to understand the deepest meaning of our lives as a derivative of our place in that universe, then organizing our empirical knowledge of that universe into a spiritual argument for democracy becomes an imperative. When Whitman argues that the "Kosmos" is informed by "a moral purpose, a visible or invisible intention" that parallels the work of the "greatest literatus," he is but challenging those poets to shape the culture by reading the cosmos to warrant an "[i]ntense and loving comradeship, the personal and passionate attachment of man to man — which, hard to define, underlies the lessons and ideals of the profound saviours of every land and age, and which seems to promise, when thoroughly develop'd, cultivated and recognized in manners and literature, the most substantial hope and safety of the future of these States" (*PW* 414). In a note he adds that "democracy infers such loving comradeship, as its most inevitable twin or counterpart"; but comradeship is grounded pragmatically as well, for it "is to the development, identification, and general prevalence of that fervid comradeship, . . . that I look for the counterbalance and offset of our materialistic and vulgar American democracy, and for the spiritualization thereof" (*PW* 414–415).

Whitman's assertion that religious practice is, in words quoted earlier, "exclusively for the noiseless operation of one's isolated Self, to enter the pure ether of veneration, reach the divine levels, and commune with the unutterable," does not constitute a contradiction with his understanding of it as an essentially social, democratizing force. Religion for Whitman names a practice, a set of beliefs, an arrangement of social relationships, and a mode of feeling that, taken together, function to reconcile the private and public self. On the one hand, for example, Whitman's democracy is an individualistic, privatized way of life: throughout *Democratic Vistas* Whitman calls for an "idiocrasy," men and women whose "strong-fibered physique" and critical control over the constructions of the mind enable them to become a "law and a series of laws unto" themselves (*PW* 375). Even his endorsement of Jeffersonian political rights and Madisonian constitutional hydraulics underscores his acceptance of the notion of a bounded, autonomous self. On the other hand, the very fact that the self is bounded argues for some means of transcending those bounds, some way for the self to negotiate between its local autonomy and its place and function within a larger social — even cosmic — sphere.

The assertion that Whitman's notion of democratic transcendence is organically and appropriately linked to his avowed project of nation building is not without controversy. One especially serious challenge to the idea has come from the political philosopher George Kateb, who offers a penetrating analysis of Whitman's theory of democratic culture. For instance, in "Walt Whitman and the Culture of Democracy," Kateb is particularly concerned with what he calls Whitman's concept of "democratic individuality," which he distinguishes from the poet's "pursuit of an image of a democratic American nationality." For Kateb, Whitman's democratic individuality is based not on a celebration of the particularity of individual people — those psychologically or culturally based idiosyncrasies that set them apart from one another — but on the possibility of them coming to a deep (albeit fleeting) awareness of their fundamental sameness. All people, Kateb argues, share the same resevoir of latent potentiality; "[a]ll the personalities I encounter, I already am: that is to say, I could become or could have become something like what others are." Whitman is at his democratic best, then, when he is encouraging us to recognize this "highest truth about human beings," teaching us to live "in receptivity or responsiveness, in a connectedness different from any other. Such connectedness is not the same as nationhood or group identity." Indeed, Kateb views it as the very opposite of a heightened recognition of difference, particularity, or the "sinister project of nationalism." [13]

The difficulty in Kateb's view is not in his understanding of Whitman's "democratic individualism," for it seems that in his very subtle appreciation of Whitman's individualism he captures the essence of the poet's conception of democratic religion. The problem is Kateb's disinclination to recognize the corresponding value and necessity of group (or national) identity or to acknowledge that group identity can quite easily be reconciled with Whitman's notion of democratic individualism. Similar qualifications are raised in several (otherwise favorable) responses to Kateb. Nancy L. Rosenblum, for example, cautions that, despite Kateb's commitment to rights-based democracy, in his "faithful[ness] to Whitman, what emerges most clearly is not the institutional apparatus of democratic politics" but merely "pluralist democratic culture." [14] But democratic politics is, in large measure, a matter of seeking justice through the consolidation of particular cultural experiences, shared interests, or ideological commitments into distinct "representative" group identities. As Leo Marx observed in his response to Kateb, "[w]hat really shapes the lives of most people in the United States is their socioeconomic and cultural status: their inclusion in groups defined by class, gender, race, or ethnicity." [15] By these lights, group identity is not so odious — and neither is national identity when similarly conceived as a mechanism for harnessing political will. Even Kateb is quick to acknowledge that "it is better, however, not to pretend that receptivity can be a direct and continuous principle of public policy." [16]

When we insist that Whitman's notion of democratic religious experience be contextualized exactly as Whitman intended it to be — as one highly important ingredient in a larger, multifaceted theory of democratic culture — we can begin to see how democratic "religiousness" might not only inculcate and strengthen a sense of democratic nationality but also enlighten it by subordinating its darker possibilities. It is precisely in that context that Kateb's description of that experience becomes most powerful and poignant:

> Whitman's highest hope must be that there will be moods or moments in which an individual comes to and remembers or realizes the deep meanings of living in a rights-based democracy. These occasions of self-concentration may be rare, but they should have some more pervasive and longer-lasting effect, even if somewhat thinned out. Whitman's model for such moments is poetic inspiration, but his phrases about the mood of composition are interchangeable with those he uses in a Notebook to describe existential receptivity to the world: "the idea of a trance, yet with all the senses alert — only a state of high exalted musing — the tangible and material with all its shows — the objective world suspended or surmounted for a while and the powers in exaltation, freedom, vision," but also in democratically inspired deeds from the most casual to the most disciplined. Attentiveness and empathy, even if not continuously strong, gradually build up the overt connectedness of a democratically receptive culture: its tolerance, its hospitableness, and its appetite for movement, novelty, mixture, and impurity.[17]

Throughout this discussion I have referred to *Democratic Vistas* — particularly the theoretical framework that necessitates self-transcendence — as a theory of culture; and that it is, for something like the modern conception of culture lies beneath Whitman's recognition that "the social and the political world[s]" are not held together so much by "legislation, police, treaties, and dread of punishment, as [they are by] the latent eternal intuitional sense, in humanity, of [their] fairness, manliness, decorum, &c." (*PW* 421). But the term "culture" does not quite do justice to the importance Whitman places on ecstatic experience, particularly to his assumption that the desire for transcendence is an innate and valuable part of being human. Whitman's own interpretation of the word "religion" may come closer to describing the more apparently "mystical" aspects of his vision — yet this label, too, seems inappropriate for a vision that relies so deeply upon secular political arrangements, however corrupt, while expressing explicit hostility to the traditional religious institutions of church and creed, however sincere. Whitman's democratic vision defies categorization because democracy, as Whitman properly understood the word, can only suffer when confined to one or another corner of human life. That said, it is important to remember that *Democratic Vistas* is a democratic poetics. Near the conclusion of the essay, Whitman writes that "in the future of these States must arise poets immenser far, and make great poems of death. The poems of life are great, but there must be the poems of the purports of life, not only in itself, but beyond itself" (*PW* 421).

Much has already been said of Whitman's philosophy of death and its place in democratic ideology; here, it is important only to observe that death marks the divide between the "me" and the "not me," the private self and everything else — the beginning point of transcendence. Just as physical death is the prerequisite for material decomposition and the individual's reunion with the dusty egalitarian cosmos from which life and identity spring, so figurative death, a fictive escape from the confines of selfhood, is necessary to vividly imagine our bonds to the social world that lies beyond private subjectivity. Whitman knew that full and complete democratic life depended upon our ability to be in that world, if only occasionally and if for only a few ecstatic moments, for the shadow of such moments is enough to cast doubt on the evidence of our senses that we are each, ultimately, alone and without obligation to others. Whitman also knew that the creation of that world, and more, the dissemination of an imaginative experience of that world, lay far beyond the powers of expository discourse, for such things define the spiritual function of the democratic poet.

Conclusion
Toward an Organic Democracy

From the outset of his career, Whitman worked from the premise that his duty as the national bard was to put democratic theory, the cultural lifeblood of nineteenth-century America, to verse. The poet's "spirit," he wrote in the 1855 preface, "responds to his country's spirit," and his country's spirit was democracy (*CRE* 713). He also knew that it was only through the medium of poetry that he would be able to suggest the contours of an idea so comprehensive yet so illusive and suffused with futurity that its final and precise meaning could never be completely articulated. "Thus," he could assert in *Democratic Vistas*, "we presume to write, as it were, upon things that exist not, and travel by maps yet unmade, and a blank" (*PW* 391). But such a formulation inevitably begs the pragmatic question: Can so purposefully vague a theory of human organization — a map so "blank" as Whitman's democracy — possibly matter? More specifically, can such an abstract vision of associative life make any practical difference in the actual lives of real people? I believe it can and does. However illusive Whitman's conception of democracy is, it nevertheless does foreclose certain ways of thinking about organized public life just as it also demands thinking of it in others. To be sure, the way we conceptualize our governing ideology and its demands shapes the way we imagine a society worth building.

To understand the scope of the demands that Whitman's vision imposes on us, we should begin by recalling that democracy, for Whitman, is more than the political process: "Did you, too, O friend, suppose democracy was only for elections, for politics, and for a party name?" he asks in *Democratic Vistas*. "I say democracy is only of use there that it may pass on and come to its flower and fruits in manners, in the highest forms of interaction between men, and their beliefs" (*PW* 389). Democracy could so manifest itself in the "highest forms" of human belief and behavior because, for him, it is "organic," an ever-growing, ever-changing system of interrelated parts. The belief that democracy is an all-encompassing and dynamic ideological whole is the foundation of what Richard Rorty refers to as Whitman's "civic religion." In previous chapters, my approach has been to explicate the individual elements of Whitman's holistic vision of democracy in the order in which the poet himself encountered them — as each emerged over time within his developing poetics. Now I would like to bring these different elements together and consider how they function systemically.

Whitman's categories are never neat; nevertheless, ten democratic elements, or "departments," as he calls them, stand out: a mythology that employs its own "pragmatic" theory of truth in order to subordinate competing antidemocratic belief systems; a cosmology that argues the harmony between democratic metaphysics and natural science; a phenomenology of self that situates the individual and society in a relationship of interdependence; a psychology that dramatizes the centrality of human agency and the capacity for choice-making to democratic life; a historiography that attempts to distinguish human history from natural history; a sociopolitics that attempts to regulate the political process by ritualizing the ethic of social reconciliation; an economic creed that insists that rough material equality is a necessary condition for democratic development; a cultural theory that outlines the beliefs a society must construct in order to foster democracy; a religion that attempts to facilitate "spiritual transcendence," the ubiquitous human desire for ecstatic experience, by redefining it as the individual's quest for reconciliation with the larger (social and cosmic) democratic order; and, of course, a political philosophy that takes on faith the belief that the people are sovereign in every meaningful sense of the word and that believing so naturally means that the political process by which they speak is sacred.

It is true that Whitman's treatment of none of these subjects is complete. For example, his economics was, alternately, a critique of market capitalism and a faith in its potential for egalitarian achievements; it was not a systematic explanation of market processes. And his historiography may have conditioned the study of the human past by distinguishing it from the processes of nature, but it did not attempt to offer anything like a coherent theory of historical causation. To be sure, the value of Whitman's approach is not that it exhausts everything that can or should be said of each subject. His treatment of each discipline is narrowly focused in a way that makes democracy itself — and democracy only — a universal organizing principle. This is to say two things. First, Whitman ferrets out the democratic implications of each subject — what the knowledge and mode of thinking peculiar to each "department" further suggest about the meaning of democratic life — and then translates these implications into discipline-specific democratic imperatives.

Second, he treats each of these departments (and the democratic values that he derives from them) not as static and discrete genres of thought but as parts of a dynamic and interconnected whole. Their interconnection is particularly important: by casting into relief the democratic values implicit in each, Whitman also throws them into relation, highlighting the way each supports, compromises or modifies the democratic claims of all the others.

Whitman understood democracy as a complex of fundamental and interrelated values. More modest definitions would have undoubtedly struck him as shortsighted and even dangerous. He would have been perplexed, for example, to read one historian of democracy assert that it "is only one among many social objectives": "There are ideals of personal freedom and human justice, programs for government efficiency and economic productivity, visions of international peacekeeping and global environmentalism, along with many others, whose pursuit may well run at odds with the quest for an invigorated democracy."[1] Whitman's quest, by contrast, was for an invigorated, comprehensive version of democracy, one in which personal freedom, human justice, and collective responsibility were not at odds with the democratic political process but, in fact, organically connected to it. As two of the necessary conditions for healthy political democracy, for instance, he would have insisted that individual freedom and human justice are inextricable from any truly meaningful definition of democracy. Moreover, he would have thought it illogical to expect that an electorate, having fully internalized the democratic values of freedom and justice, could be capable of making anything other than just decisions. The ballot was the heart that pumped life to all corners of Whitman's organic democracy, but considered alone, it was not to be confused with the whole body it served.

This is not to say that organic democracy prescribes any particular policy agenda. Rightly considered, organic democracy offers no plan, no policy, no hint as to precisely how, in the context of specific historical conditions, the needs of a full and dignified democratic life should be met. This is as it must be: no conception of democracy that places such a premium on the individual citizen's capacity to deliberate and decide could in good faith proceed to foreclose the exercise of that capacity by determining in advance which decisions must be made and how. The futurity at the heart of Whitman's vision argues for a kind of democracy that is not a detailed blueprint for the final construction of human society but a framework of values by which successive societies should think about the process of making and remaking themselves. Whitman's organic democracy also should not be thought of as an ideal vision of a unified American culture. Whitman is often (and with some justification) interpreted in the communitarian mold, a poet who sought to reveal the essential connections that might bind together the diverse strands of American life. While it is true that Whitman was moved by an appreciation for the interconnectedness of life, it would nevertheless be a profound error to confuse the concept of an organic democracy with the notion of an organic American state: they are radically different, even antithetical, ideas. For Whitman, our commonality was largely a physical and material matter, and interdependence on the physical level does not entail harmonious political cooperation under the umbrella of a shared cultural identity. Interdependence does stand as an argument for the proposition that social cooperation is not only possible but deeply rewarding as well, that it is a reasonable kind of life to choose. Just as the notion of democracy as a detailed policy manual is dangerous because it effectively usurps the people's prerogative to determine their collective fate, so, too, is the idea of an organic community dangerous. When political consensus is mistakenly seen as a social norm rather than as the consequence of successful dialogue, then the heated, often rancorous clash of values and voices so essential to democratic life suddenly becomes a threat to the social order and not the deliberative process by which a free society orders and reorders itself.

Whitman's organic democracy does, nevertheless, place complex demands on the ways we attempt to fashion a meaningful associative life. To cite just one example, consider its implications for the way we approach the problem of economic privation and the distribution of wealth. Clearly, individual misery, mere subsistence living, is a profound human tragedy that troubles the heart of all conscientious persons, whether or not they believe government has any obligation to remedy it. But even if it were to be judged tolerable by the dubious logic of some other moral, economic, or political theory, organic democrats would still regard it as a virulent cancer. Poverty's threat to democracy, however, is not only in the way economic inequality subjects the individual to an inhumane level of suffering but also in the political inequality that it entails. That is, democracy can only be sustained when political power is widely disseminated; because wealth, like all other forms of power, can be converted into political currency, its concentration in the hands of a few effectively denies to the many the ability to assume an equal share of the duties — and rewards — of community governance. Universal suffrage alone cannot render democratic a citizenry that divides into beggars and middle-class benefactors. Whitman understood this point as clearly as anyone. In his vision, the belief that individual citizens are spiritually equal — and thus politically equal — is the principle that animates American democracy. But however central this ideal is to his vision of ideal America, he was under no illusions as to the political consequences of unequal wealth in real America. For example, in a brief note entitled "Who Gets the Plunder?" he rails against protectionist trade policies because the "immense revenue of annual cash" they produce does not go "to the masses of laboring-men" but rather to "a few score select persons — who, by favors of Congress, State legislatures, the banks, and other special advantages, are forming a vulgar aristocracy." Whitman, the visionary democrat, concludes by aligning himself with Swiss economist Jean Sismondi's critique of unregulated capitalism: "As Sismondi pointed out, the true prosperity of a nation is not in the great wealth of a special class, but is only to be really attain'd in having the bulk of the people provided with homes or land in fee simple. This may not be the best show, but it is the best reality."[2]

Organic democracy, then, requires us to deepen the way we define the problem of poverty. It also complicates the way we must imagine possible solutions. In effect, it extends the traditional humanist impulse to respond to privation as a personal tragedy by insisting that such suffering is a symptom of a complex social pathology. Privation, then, cannot be remedied simply by dissociating it from its full matrix of historical, cultural, sociopolitical, psychological, and spiritual conditions and consequences. To say this is merely to recognize that the minimal requirements for democratic life certainly include — but at the same time far exceed — the minimal requirements for biological life; the human as agent, the whole "Democratic Being," must be nurtured. No one aspect essential to democratic life — even subsistence — may rightfully be purchased at the price of another. Paternalistic and dehumanizing policies such as welfare are, however nobly intentioned, almost as odious as official indifference. Just as it would be absurd for a society to offer the ballot as a substitute for food, so, too, would it be unthinkable to design a policy that assists the poor by crippling their capacity for engaged democratic living — by dismantling the psychological equipment a citizen needs for self-government while simultaneously undermining the high value democratic culture places on self-reliance.

Whitman's democracy is a pragmatic democracy — a system of interrelated and mutually modifying values, ideas, and imperatives to act. Another way of putting this is to say that his vision of democracy functions as a grammar, a framework for social and cultural criticism. Electoral democracy has always been considered critical in that it requires a community to periodically render judgments on issues and people. But organic democracy takes the critical aspect of democracy several steps further by defining it as both a process and as the conditions necessary to preserve the vitality of that process — a matrix of criteria by which we evaluate our attempts to extend the meaning of human freedom. For those whose notion of freedom continues to be shaped by the Jacksonian-era faith in laissez-faire, for those who believe that a complete absence of restraint is the purest and most virtuous form of freedom imaginable, such a critical matrix may seem more like an impingement on liberty than its enhancement. And to be sure, when this laissez-faire sense of freedom is viewed not as a philosophy but as an impulse, a visceral predisposition to be wary of authority, it clearly functions as a safeguard against the tendency of power to preserve itself through institutionalization. This was Whitman's own starting point. But Whitman knew — or he came to understand — that a full appreciation for the complexities of human life meant understanding that liberty can take many different and conflicting generic forms. Identifying these forms and their various positions within a system of relations is Whitman's great achievement. His challenge to us is to identify — and reconcile — the real, historically specific content of these competing definitions of liberty. To accept that challenge is to continuously restructure the terms of associative life in ways that secure ever-newer forms of freedom.

Notes

Introduction: The Evolution of Whitman's Democratic Vision

1. See Allen, *The Solitary Singer*, 157, 173.
2. See Kaplan, *Walt Whitman*, 140–143.
3. Howells, "Editor's Study," 78.
4. Kateb, "Walt Whitman and the Culture of Democracy," 547. I discuss Kateb's view more fully in chapter 7.
5. Altieri, "Spectacular Antispectacle," 41. Altieri refers to Whitman's nationalism as "antispectacle," by which he means forms of identification not based on visable symbols, which are by nature easily appropriated by particular factions within the nation. Altieri also challenges two recent critics of Whitman's nationalism, David Simpson and Wai-Chee Dimock, who, in separate articles, argue that Whitman's inclusiveness comes at the expense of a recognition of difference and contingency. See Simpson, "Destiny Made Manifest"; and Dimock, *Residues of Justice*.
6. Rorty, *Achieving Our Country*; King, "I Have a Dream," 1959. It is worth noting that Rorty's purpose and style are more polemical in these lectures than in his other work. For a critical evaluation of Rorty's rhetoric from an otherwise sympathetic perspective, see Mark Bauerlein's review in the *Walt Whitman Quarterly Review*.
7. Rorty, *Achieving Our Country*, 14.
8. Because this is a "developmental" study in which the sequence of production is central, I have in almost every case restricted my analysis of the poems to the versions that originally appeared in print rather than to their final form in the 1892 "Deathbed" edition. In this, I am enormously grateful for the fine scholarship behind the variorum edition of Whitman's work. For the same reason, I have generally treated collections of poetry such as *Drum-Taps* as separate publications rather than as "clusters" that Whitman later incorporated into *Leaves of Grass*.
9. It is important to distinguish the notion of "organic democracy" from the idea of an "organic community" or its close cousin, "communitarianism." There are affinities and in many ways Whitman can be read as arguing for both. At the same time, however, the ideas are significantly different from one another, perhaps even mutually exclusive. The latter is based upon human connectedness, the former on a set of ideological relationships (which humans might be wise to agree on). Moreover, organic democracy, as I find it in Whitman, relies upon a certain measure of conflict, not on perpetual social harmony.
10. The notion that Whitman belongs in the pragmatic tradition is not a new one. William James seems to have made the connection explicit. See Malachuck, "Walt Whitman and the Culture of Pragmatism." One of Malachuck's especially interesting observations concerns James's reading of Whitman's poem "To You" not as an affirmation of "absolutism" or universal oneness (as critics at the time had customarily viewed it) but as a celebration of the kind of "pluralism" that informs pragmatism. For another illuminating discussion of Whit-

man's connection to William James, see Trachtenberg, "Whitman's Lesson of the City." Trachtenberg examines the poet's depictions of the excitement and chaos of city life, arguing that it is "not a place he represents but a process he enacts . . . in which self and other fuse into a new sensation of being" (164). Trachtenberg does not read Whitman as celebrating what Malachuck calls "absolutism" but makes the complementary point that Whitman's city functions as imaginative linkage among alien subjectivities.

11. In the first edition of *Leaves of Grass*, Whitman did not title his poems. He began using titles in the 1856 edition but would frequently change them in subsequent editions. For the convenience of the reader, I will refer to all of the poems by the last title Whitman assigned them, even though the texts I discuss will generally be those first published.

12. The hold of laissez-faire ideology did not always extend to the operations of state and local government or to common law practice. Several legal historians have pointed out that, below the federal level, nineteenth-century America was a highly regulated place. See, for example, Horwitz, *The Transformation of American Law*; and Novak, *The Peoples Welfare*.

13. A similar reading of Whitman's later development is advanced by Luke Mancuso in *The Strange Sad War Revolving*. Mancuso argues that in the post–Civil War period, Whitman "federalized" his poetic imagery and rhetoric, moving "away from localized 'comradship' toward the solidarity between citizens en masse" (78). In effect, Mancuso asserts, Whitman was participating in the constitutional debate at the time over the supremacy and scope of national citizenship (versus state citizenship), especially as it related to the status of former slaves. Mancuso offers an important corrective to the critical commonplace that Whitman was indifferent to the plight of former slaves and blacks generally. My own reading, however, of the postwar transformation in Whitman's poetics — while not at all inconsistent with Mancuso's — differs in both its analysis of the origins and appreciation of its scope. Whereas Mancuso quite deftly roots Whitman's rhetorical developments in Reconstruction-era political debate and sees its chief consequence as the expansion of radical democracy to African Americans, my own view is that the seeds of Whitman's poetic evolution can be found in his personal life as well as in his wartime experiences; moreover, the ultimate meaning of Whitman's development, as I shall attempt to elaborate it throughout the course of this study, reaches beyond its relevance to former slaves.

CHAPTER 1 *"My Voice Goes After What My Eyes Cannot Reach":* *Pragmatic Language and the Making of a Democratic Mythology*

1. See Bellis, "Against Representation." Bellis points out that the New Critical tendency has actually been "to separate Whitman's revolution in poetic form from its political context and contents," an inclination that still persists among some writers. Nevertheless, he insists that, for Whitman, "American speech is a 'language of [popular] resistance' rather than a discourse of authority" (72–73). My interpretation of the way Whitman joins poetry and politics differs from the way Bellis sees it, but his emphasis on the union is a point well taken.

2. Emerson, "Nature," 31.

3. Rorty, *Philosophy and the Mirror of Nature*, 6.

4. Bauerlein, *Whitman and the American Idiom*, 22, 24, 49, 52, 56.

5. Ibid., 56–57.

6. Ibid., 46–49. Bauerlein is particularly interesting on the way facial expression functioned as part of a "natural language of the flesh."

7. Ibid., 7.

8. Lakoff and Johnson, *Metaphors We Live By*.

9. Hollis, *Language and Style in Leaves of Grass*. See, especially, chapter 3, "Speech Acts and *Leaves of Grass*," and chapter 5, "Metonymy in Whitman and in *Leaves of Grass*."

10. Bauerlein, *Whitman and the American Idiom*, 5, 25, 35.

11. Emerson, "The Poet," 231.

12. Ibid., 237.

13. Poirier, *Poetry and Pragmatism*, 28.

14. Ibid., 99.

15. James, *Pragmatism*, 88.

16. Ibid., 89.

17. Dewey, *Reconstruction in Philosophy*, 122.

CHAPTER 2 *"What Is Less or More Than a Touch?":*
Sensory Experience and the Democratic Self

1. Cowley, Introduction to *Leaves of Grass*, vii–xxxvii; Miller, *A Critical Guide to "Leaves of Grass."* See, especially, chapter 1, "'Song of Myself' as Inverted Mystical Experience."

2. Mead, *The Social Psychology of George Herbert Mead*, 217.

3. Ibid., 213–214.

4. Ibid., 241.

5. Ibid., 242–243.

6. Ibid., 242.

7. Feffer, "Sociability and Social Conflict," 239.

8. Dewey, "The Reflex Arc Concept in Psychology."

9. For an elaboration of the notion of "cognitive elites," see Lasch, *The Revolt of the Elites and the Betrayal of Democracy*.

CHAPTER 3 *"The Simple, Compact Well-Join'd Scheme":*
Whitman's Democratic Cosmos

1. Buell, *Literary Transcendentalism*, 141–142.

2. Ibid., 143.

3. Abrams cites one particularly good example of this cross fertilization in the *Naturphilosophie* of Schelling and Coleridge, which essentially revived and reformulated the Renaissance idea of the "universe as a plenum of opposed yet mutually attractive, quasi-sexual forces — which was discredited and displaced by Cartesian and Newtonian mechanism." The result was, "by a peripety of intellectual history, to feed back into scientific thought some of the most productive hypotheses of nineteenth-century and modern physics." Abrams, *Natural Supernaturalism*, 171.

4. Chase, *Walt Whitman Reconsidered*, 103.

5. Ibid., 103–104.
6. Dewey, "The Development of American Pragmatism," 13.
7. Middlebrook, *Walt Whitman and Wallace Stevens*, 65. Middlebrook is less concerned with the implications of that space-time boundlessness than she is with the fact that it emerges out of and dramatizes the poet's understanding of "the extent of his powers to incorporate diverse objects" (64).
8. Beaver, *Walt Whitman*, 71–73.
9. Boslough, *Stephen Hawking's Universe*, 36.
10. Dewey, "Philosophy and Democracy," 43–44.
11. Thomas Jefferson to Samuel Kercheval, July 12, 1816. In "The Letters of Thomas Jefferson."
12. Erkkila, *Whitman the Political Poet*, 143.
13. Goudge, "Henri Bergson," 288. Allen and Davis make a similar observation in "Introduction to Walt Whitman's Poems," 330.
14. See Miller, *A Critical Guide to "Leaves of Grass,"* 82.
15. Allen, *A Reader's Guide to Walt Whitman*, 186.
16. Ibid., 190.
17. Smart, "Time," 126.
18. Larson, *Whitman's Drama of Consensus*, 10–11, 12.

CHAPTER 4 *"Not Chaos or Death . . . . It Is Form and Union and Plan":*
Laissez-faire and the Problem of Agency

1. Discussions of transcendental and Quaker influences on Whitman's work can be found in most biographies of him. For a particularly good discussion of Whitman and romantic thought, see Stovall, *The Foreground of Leaves of Grass*, especially chapter 11, "Primitivism and German Romantic Philosophy."
2. Ziff, *Literary Democracy*, 247, 249.
3. Butscher, "Whitman's Attitudes Toward Death," 16, 17.
4. Burke, *A Grammar of Motives*, 132.
5. Ibid., 134, 135.
6. Fine, *Laissez Faire and the General Welfare State*, 4.
7. Paine, "Rights of Man," 153.
8. Fine, *Laissez Faire and the General Welfare State*, 9.
9. Thomas, *The Lunar Light of Whitman's Poetry*, 56–57.
10. Spencer, *Social Statics*, 322.
11. See Miller, *Walt Whitman's 'Song of Myself,'* 90–91.

CHAPTER 5 *"The Most Perfect Pilot":*
The Problem of Desire and the Struggle for Poetic Agency

1. Notebook in Library of Congress, qtd. in Allen, *The Solitary Singer*, 216.
2. The "Calamus" poems, including the twelve "Calamus-Leaves" poems, are occasionally treated as something like a direct autobiographical account of the poet's homosexual experi-

ence. Most critics, however, seem content to note the homoerotic content in "Calamus." See, for example, Fone, *Masculine Landscapes*, especially chapter 7, "Brethren and Lovers." Although some points are a bit exaggerated, the value of Fone's work is that it places Whitman in the larger context of homoerotic literature without claiming that such interpretations are exclusive of other possible readings.

3. The twelve "Calamus-Leaves" poems have been the subject of enormous controversy. Sometimes called "Live Oak, with Moss" (or, absent the comma, "Live Oak with Moss"), the collection is an early or draft version of several of the poems that would eventually become part of the "Calamus" cluster, published in 1860. In their prepublication state, they clearly betray more of the emotional crisis Whitman experienced at the time of composition. Nevertheless, I have elected to discuss the poems in the form in which they first appeared in print in 1860, primarily because I am also discussing other "Calamus" poems, poems not a part of the twelve, and I wish to be consistent. For background on the original twelve, see Allen, *The Solitary Singer*, 221–226. For additional background as well as information on the critcal controversy, see Parker, "The Real 'Live Oak, with Moss'"; and Helms and Parker, "Commentary" (an exchange between Alan Helms and Hershel Parker).

4. M. Jimmie Killingsworth, for instance, cites Gustav Bychowski's comment to that effect but judiciously cautions against oversimplifying the issue. Killingsworth argues that passivity is more an ideological stereotype than an empirical fact; he suggests looking beyond psychology or ideology to the morality of sexual passivity and offers "that the poet wished to purge aggression from his sexual ideal." Killingsworth, *Whitman's Poetry of the Body*, 36–40.

5. Dewey, *Human Nature and Conduct*, 153.

6. Ibid., 154–155.

7. Moon, *Disseminating Whitman*, 156.

8. Miller, *Walt Whitman's Poetry*, vii.

9. Ibid., 150.

10. Black, *Whitman's Journey into Chaos*, 203. Although Black's analysis is ultimately just as reductive as most other critical applications of psychoanalysis, his approach is distinguished by his assertion that the fantasies the poems represent do not necessarily represent delusions that shape the poet's sense of reality. Drawing on Kris's notion of "regression in service of the ego," Black observes "that the most important thing in Whitman's life was the set of fantasies his poems directly and indirectly express. Yet by tenaciously clinging to a reality that jeopardized his fantasy world, Whitman avoided being seduced into autism" (211).

11. Cavitch, *My Soul and I*, xiii. Another psycho-sexual discussion of Whitman that should be mentioned here is Vivian Pollak's *The Erotic Whitman*. Pollack argues that "in proposing to heal national ills, [Whitman] was trying to heal inner tensions as well." Though she does not attempt to "reduce Whitman's achievement to the sum of his insecurities," she does try to "demonstrate that his insights into 'the problem of freedom' were always conditioned by the 'chaos' that he himself had encountered" (xv). Although I do not always agree with her conclusions, one of the virtues of Pollack's analysis is in her tendency to treat the poetry as (in part) responses to tensions that were immediate and concrete, not those imagined to be buried deep within some definitive subconscious core.

12. Kaplan, *Walt Whitman*, 239.

13. For a more fully developed and psychoanalytically oriented version of this argument, see Mack, "Ego Psychology."

14. Freud, "Mourning and Melancholia," 153.
15. Ibid., 159.
16. This is not to say that any inferences can, should, or need be made concerning the precise chronology of composition. Though it will be convenient to organize and discuss the poems in "developmental" order, that order is one I have assigned them; it is logical, not chronological. I take this liberty because I do not understand psychic development to be mechanically linear but rather full of leaps and regressions, twists and turns. Nevertheless, it would be possible to reconcile my argument with the order put forth by Parker in "The Real 'Live Oak, with Moss'" — especially since the seven "Calamus-Leaves" poems I discuss do fall on the "crisis" side of the poet's ego development and since the other "Calamus" poems I discuss, those I identify as marking the poet's ego reconstruction, were written after the "Calamus-Leaves" poems.
17. Rapaport, *The Collected Papers of David Rapaport*, 722–744.
18. Whether this process actually worked in Whitman's real life is not significant — although I'm inclined to believe that it probably did. All that is essential here is the functional integrity of the verbal model as it operates in the poetry.

CHAPTER 6 *"To Learn from the Crises of Anguish":*
Tragedy, History, and the Meaning of Democratic Mourning

1. Useful discussions of Whitman's early political activities can be found in Allen's *The Solitary Singer* and Erkkila's *Whitman the Political Poet*.
2. Thomas, "Whitman and the American Democratic Identity," 83.
3. Ibid., 84.
4. Burke, *A Rhetoric of Motives*, 20–21.
5. Ibid., 22.
6. Miller, *A Critical Guide to "Leaves of Grass,"* 219–225.
7. For a different perspective on the way *Drum-Taps* plays with the problem of history, see Mullins, "Stopping History in Walt Whitman's *Drum Taps*." Mullins argues that throughout the poems, the real historical narrative of the Civil War is frozen in order to provide an alternative "history, that of comradeship and homoerotic desire" (4).
8. *CRE* 308. See note on "Year That Trembled and Reel'd Beneath Me."
9. Thomas, "Weathering the Storm," 93.
10. Ibid., 90.
11. Hook, *Pragmatism and the Tragic Sense of Life*, 164.
12. Ibid., 10.
13. Ibid., 18.
14. Diggins, *The Promise of Pragmatism*, 50–51.
15. Hook, *Pragmatism and the Tragic Sense of Life*, 20.
16. Ibid.
17. Ibid., 19–20.
18. Adams, *The Education of Henry Adams*, 416.
19. Miller, *A Critical Guide to "Leaves of Grass,"* 111.
20. Larson, *Whitman's Drama of Consensus*, 242–243.

21. In the 1865 text, section 14 is considerably shorter; section 15 begins with the line "Then with the knowledge of death" (*LV* 535).
22. LeWinter, "Whitman's Lilacs"; Allen, *A Reader's Guide to Walt Whitman*, 201; Eiselein, *Literature and Humanitarian Reform*, 126.
23. Cavitch, "My Soul and I," 166; Larson, *Whitman's Drama of Consensus*, 240.
24. Eiselein, *Literature and Humanitarian Reform*, 126.
25. Ibid., 124, 125.
26. Ibid., 129–130.
27. Ibid., 130.

CHAPTER 7 *"The Divine Literatus Comes":*
Religion and Poetry in the Cultivation of Democratic Selfhood

1. Carlyle, "Shooting Niagara: And After?" 170.
2. Ibid., 171.
3. Carlyle, "On Heroes, Hero-Worship, and the Heroic in History."
4. Taine, "From the *Introduction to the History of English Literature*."
5. Greenblatt, "Towards a Poetics of Culture," 12.
6. Mead, *The Social Psychology of George Herbert Mead*, 212–243.
7. Killingsworth, *Whitman's Poetry of the Body*, 73.
8. Emerson, "Experience," 529.
9. James, *Pragmatism*, 89.
10. Walzer, "Multiculturalism and Individualism," 189.
11. Reynolds, *Walt Whitman's America*, 483.
12. James, "Conclusions," 774. For a related discussion of the way both Whitman and James use apparently mystical terminology to describe the process of uniting self and others, see Trachtenberg, "Whitman's Lesson of the City," on "rapture," 164–166.
13. Kateb, "Walt Whitman and the Culture of Democracy," 551.
14. Rosenblum, "Strange Attractors," 580–581.
15. Marx, "George Kateb's Ahistorical Emersonianism."
16. Kateb, "Walt Whitman and the Culture of Democracy," 563.
17. Ibid., 562–563.

Conclusion: Toward an Organic Democracy

1. Wiebe, *Self Rule*, 253. Wiebe is himself an enthusiastic celebrant of popular democracy; his larger point is that democracy as a theory suffers when it is held hostage to particular outcomes, that is, when its efficacy is judged by its ability to produce particular results.
2. Whitman, *Complete Poetry and Collected Prose*, 1067–1068.

Bibliography

Abrams, M. H. *Natural Supernaturalism: Tradition and Revolution in Romantic Literature.* New York: Norton, 1971.

Adams, Henry. *The Education of Henry Adams.* Ed. Ernest Samuels. Boston: Houghton Mifflin, 1973.

Allen, Gay Wilson. *A Reader's Guide to Walt Whitman.* New York: Farrar, Strauss & Giroux, 1970.

———. *The Solitary Singer.* New York: Macmillan, 1955.

Allen, Gay Wilson, and Charles T. Davis. "Introduction to Walt Whitman's Poems." In *A Century of Whitman Criticism,* ed. Edwin Haviland Miller. Bloomington: Indiana University Press, 1969.

Altieri, Charles. "Spectacular Antispectacle: Ecstasy and Nationality in Whitman and His Heirs." *American Literary History* 11, no. 1 (spring 1999): 34–62.

Bauerlein, Mark. Review of *Achieving Our Country: Leftist Thought in America,* by Richard Rorty. *Walt Whitman Quarterly Review* 16 (fall 1998): 104–108.

———. *Whitman and the American Idiom.* Baton Rouge: Louisiana State University Press, 1991.

Beaver, Joseph. *Walt Whitman: Poet of Science.* Morningside Heights, N.Y.: King's Crown Press, 1951.

Bellis, Peter J. "Against Representation: The 1855 Edition of *Leaves of Grass.*" *Centennial Review* 43, no. 1 (winter 1999): 71–94.

Black, Stephen A. *Whitman's Journey into Chaos: A Psychoanalytic Study of the Poetic Process.* Princeton, N.J.: Princeton University Press, 1975.

Boslough, John. *Stephen Hawking's Universe.* New York: Avon, 1985.

Buell, Lawrence. *Literary Transcendentalism: Style and Vision in the American Renaissance.* Ithaca, N.Y.: Cornell University Press, 1973.

Burke, Kenneth. *A Grammar of Motives.* Berkeley: University of California Press, 1969.

———. *A Rhetoric of Motives.* Berkeley: University of California Press, 1969.

Butscher, Edward. "Whitman's Attitudes Toward Death: The Essential Paradox." *Walt Whitman Review* 17, no. 1 (1971): 16–19.

Carlyle, Thomas. "On Heroes, Hero-Worship, and the Heroic in History." In *Prose of the Victorian Period.* Ed. William Buckler. Boston: Houghton, 1958.

———. "Shooting Niagara: And After?" In *Prose of the Victorian Period,* ed. William Buckler. Boston: Houghton, 1958.

Cavitch, David. *My Soul and I: The Inner Life of Walt Whitman.* Boston: Beacon Press, 1985.

Chase, Richard. *Walt Whitman Reconsidered.* New York: William Sloane, 1955.

Cowley, Malcolm. Introduction to *Leaves of Grass: The First (1855) Edition,* by Walt Whitman. New York: Penguin, 1986.

Dewey, John. "The Development of American Pragmatism." In *The Later Works, 1925–1953.* Vol. 2. Ed. Jo Ann Boydston. Carbondale: Southern Illinois University Press, 1981–1991.

———. *Experience and Nature.* 1929. Reprint, La Salle: Open Court, 1989.

———. *Human Nature and Conduct.* New York: Henry Holt, 1922.

———. "Philosophy and Democracy." In *Middle Works, 1899–1924*. Vol. 2. Ed. Jo Ann
   Boydston. Carbondale: Southern Illinois University Press, 1976–1983.

———. *The Quest for Certainty*. New York: Minton, Balch, 1929.

———. *Reconstructions in Philosophy*. New York: Henry Holt, 1920.

———. "The Reflex Arc Concept in Psychology." In *The Early Works, 1882–1898*. Vol. 5. Ed.
   Jo Ann Boydston. Carbondale: Southern Illinois University Press, 1972.

Diggins, John Patrick. *The Promise of Pragmatism: Modernism and the Crisis of Knowledge and
   Authority*. Chicago: University of Chicago Press, 1994.

Dimock, Wai-Chee. *Residues of Justice: Literature, Law, Philosophy*. Berkeley: University of
   California Press, 1996.

Eiselein, Gregory. *Literature and Humanitarian Reform in the Civil War Era*. Bloomington:
   Indiana University Press, 1996.

Emerson, Ralph Waldo. "Experience." In *The Norton Anthology of American Literature*.
   Shorter 4th ed. Ed. Nina Baym et al. New York: Norton, 1995.

———. "Fate." In *Selections from Ralph Waldo Emerson*. Ed. Stephen E. Whicher. Boston:
   Houghton Mifflin, 1957.

———. "Nature." In *Selections from Ralph Waldo Emerson*. Ed. Stephen E. Whicher. Boston:
   Houghton Mifflin, 1957.

———. "The Poet." In *Selections from Ralph Waldo Emerson*. Ed. Stephen E. Whicher.
   Boston: Houghton Mifflin, 1957.

Erikson, Erik H. *Childhood and Society*. 1950. Reprint. New York: W. W. Norton, 1963.

Erkkila, Betsy. *Whitman the Political Poet*. New York: Oxford University Press, 1989.

Feffer, Andrew. "Sociability and Social Conflict in George Herbert Mead's Interactionism,
   1900–1919." *Journal of the History of Ideas* 51 (1990): 233–254.

Fine, Sidney. *Laissez Faire and the General Welfare State: A Study in the Conflict in American
   Thought, 1865–1901*. Ann Arbor: University of Michigan Press, 1967.

Fone, Byrne R. S. *Masculine Landscapes: Walt Whitman and the Homoerotic Text*. Carbondale:
   Southern Illinois University Press, 1992.

Freud, Sigmund. "Mourning and Melancholia." In *Collected Works*. Vol. 4. Trans. Joan Riviere.
   London: Hogarth, 1949.

Goudge, T. A. "Henri Bergson." In *The Encyclopedia of Philosophy*. Vol. 1. Ed. Paul Edwards.
   New York: Macmillan, 1967.

Greenblatt, Stephen. "Towards a Poetics of Culture." In *The New Historicism*, ed. H. Aram
   Veeser. New York: Routledge, 1989.

Heidegger, Martin. *Being and Time*. Trans. John Macquarrie and Edward Robinson. San
   Francisco: Harper & Row, 1962.

Helms, Alan, and Hershel Parker. "Commentary." *Nineteenth Century Literature* 52, no. 3
   (December 1997): 413–416.

Hollis, C. Carroll. *Language and Style in Leaves of Grass*. Baton Rouge: Louisiana State
   University Press, 1983.

Hook, Sidney. *Pragmatism and the Tragic Sense of Life*. New York: Basic Books, 1974.

Horwitz, Morton J. *The Transformation of American Law: 1780–1860*. Cambridge: Harvard
   University Press, 1977.

Howells, William Dean. "Editor's Study." *Harper's Monthly* 78 (February 1889): 488–492.

James, William. "Conclusions [to *The Varieties of Religious Experience*]." In *The Writings of*

William James: A Comprehensive Edition. Ed. John J. McDermott. Chicago: University of Chicago Press, 1977.

———. *The Meaning of Truth: A Sequel to "Pragmatism."* New York: Longmans, 1909.

———. *Pragmatism.* 1907. Reprint, New York: Prometheus, 1991.

Jefferson, Thomas. "The Letters of Thomas Jefferson: 1743–1826." http://odur.let.rug.nl/~usa/P/tj3/writings/brf/jef1246.htm.

Kaplan, Justin. *Walt Whitman: A Life.* New York: Touchstone, 1980.

Kateb, George. "Walt Whitman and the Culture of Democracy." *Political Theory* 18, no. 4 (November 1990): 545–600.

Kennedy, Robert F. *To Seek a Newer World.* New York: Bantam, 1967.

Killingsworth, M. Jimmie. *Whitman's Poetry of the Body: Sexuality, Politics, and the Text.* Chapel Hill: University of North Carolina Press, 1989.

King, Martin Luther, Jr. "I Have a Dream." In *The Heath Anthology of American Literature*, ed. Paul Lauter et al. Lexington, Ky.: D. C. Heath, 1990.

Lakoff, George, and Mark Johnson. *Metaphors We Live By.* Chicago: University of Chicago Press, 1983.

Larson, Kerry C. *Whitman's Drama of Consensus.* Chicago: University of Chicago Press, 1988.

Lasch, Christopher. *The Revolt of the Elites and the Betrayal of Democracy.* New York: Norton, 1995.

LeWinter, Oswald. "Whitman's Lilacs." *Walt Whitman Review* 10, no. 1 (March 1964): 10–14.

Mack, Stephen. "Ego Psychology and the Interpretation of Walt Whitman's Struggle." *PSYART: A Hyperlink Journal for the Psychological Study of the Arts* (1999) http://www.clas.ufl.edu/ipsa/journal/articles/psyart1999/macko.

Malachuck, Daniel S. "Walt Whitman and the Culture of Pragmatism." *Walt Whitman Quarterly Review* 17 (summer/fall 1999): 60–68.

Mancuso, Luke. *The Strange Sad War Revolving.* Columbia, S.C.: Camden House, 1997.

Marx, Leo. "George Kateb's Ahistorical Emersonianism." *Political Theory* 18, no. 4 (November 1990): 595–600.

Mead, George Herbert. *The Social Psychology of George Herbert Mead.* Ed. Anselm Strauss. Chicago: University of Chicago Press, 1956.

Middlebrook, Diane Wood. *Walt Whitman and Wallace Stevens.* Ithaca, N.Y.: Cornell University Press, 1974.

Miller, Edwin Haviland. *Walt Whitman's Poetry: A Psychological Journey.* Boston: Houghton Mifflin, 1968.

———. *Walt Whitman's 'Song of Myself': A Mosaic of Interpretations.* Iowa City: University of Iowa Press, 1989.

Miller, James E., Jr. *A Critical Guide to "Leaves of Grass."* Chicago: University of Chicago Press, 1957.

Moon, Michael. *Disseminating Whitman: Revision and Corporality in "Leaves of Grass."* Cambridge: Harvard University Press, 1991.

Mullins, Maire. "Stopping History in Walt Whitman's *Drum Taps.*" *Walt Whitman Quarterly Review* 17 (summer/fall 1999): 4–14.

Novak, William J. *The Peoples Welfare: Law & Regulation in Nineteenth-Century America.* Chapel Hill: University of North Carolina Press, 1996.

Paine, Thomas. "Rights of Man." In *Basic Writings of Thomas Paine.* New York: Willey, 1942.

Parker, Hershel. "The Real 'Live Oak, with Moss': Straight Talk about Whitman's Gay Manifesto." *Nineteenth Century Literature* 51, no. 2 (September 1996): 145–160.

Poirier, Richard. *Poetry and Pragmatism*. Cambridge: Harvard University Press, 1992.

Pollak, Vivian R. *The Erotic Whitman*. Berkeley: University of California Press, 2000.

Rapaport, David. *The Collected Papers of David Rapaport*. Ed. Merton Gill. New York: Basic Books, 1967.

Reynolds, David. *Walt Whitman's America: A Cultural Biography*. New York: Knopf, 1995.

Rorty, Richard. *Achieving Our Country: Leftist Thought in America*. Cambridge: Harvard University Press, 1997.

———. *Philosophy and the Mirror of Nature*. Princeton, N.J.: Princeton University Press, 1979.

Rosenblum, Nancy L. "Strange Attractors: How Individuals Connect to Form Democratic Unity." *Political Theory* 18, no. 4 (November 1990): 576–585.

Simpson, David. "Destiny Made Manifest: The Styles of Whitman's Poetry." In *Nation and Narration,* ed. Homi K. Bhabha. London: Routledge, 1990.

Smart, J. J. C. "Time." In *The Encyclopedia of Philosophy*. Vol. 8. Ed. Paul Edwards. New York: Macmillan, 1967.

Spencer, Herbert. *Social Statics*. New York, 1872.

Stovall, Floyd. *The Foreground of Leaves of Grass*. Charlottesville: University Press of Virginia, 1974.

Taine, Hippolyte-Adolphe. "From the *Introduction to the History of English Literature*." In *Criticism: The Major Texts*. Ed. Walter Jackson Bate. New York: Harcourt, 1970.

Thomas, M. Wynn. *The Lunar Light of Whitman's Poetry*. Cambridge: Harvard University Press, 1987.

———. "Weathering the Storm: Whitman and the Civil War." *Walt Whitman Quarterly Review* 93 (fall 1997/winter 1998): 87–109.

———. "Whitman and the American Democratic Identity before and during the Civil War." *Journal of American Studies* 15, no. 1 (April 1981): 73–93.

Trachtenberg, Alan. "Whitman's Lesson of the City." *Breaking Bounds: Whitman and American Cultural Studies*. Ed. Betsy Erkkila and Jay Grossman. New York: Oxford University Press, 1996.

Walzer, Michael. "Multiculturalism and Individualism." *Dissent* (spring 1994): 185–191.

Whitman, Walt. *Complete Poetry and Collected Prose*. Ed. Justin Kaplan. New York: Library of America, 1982.

———. "Democratic Vistas." In *Prose Works, 1892*. Vol. 2. Ed. Floyd Stoval. New York: New York University Press, 1964.

———. *Leaves of Grass: A Textual Variorum of the Printed Poems*. 3 vols. Ed. Scully Bradley, Harold W. Blodgett, Arthur Golden, and William White. New York: New York University Press, 1980.

———. *Leaves of Grass: Comprehensive Readers Edition*. Ed. Harold W. Blodgett and Scully Bradley. New York: Norton, 1965.

Wiebe, Robert H. *Self Rule: A Cultural History of American Democracy*. Chicago: University of Chicago Press, 1995.

Ziff, Larzer. *Literary Democracy: The Declaration of Cultural Independence in America*. New York: Viking, 1981.

Zweig, Paul. *Walt Whitman*. New York: Basic Books, 1984.

Index

The Iowa Whitman Series

Intimate with Walt:
   Selections from Whitman's Conversations with Horace Traubel,
   1888–1892,
   edited by Gary Schmidgall

The Pragmatic Whitman:
   Reimagining American Democracy,
   by Stephen John Mack

Whitman East and West:
   New Contexts for Reading Walt Whitman,
   edited by Ed Folsom